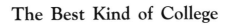

The Best Kind of College

The Best Kind of College

An Insiders' Guide to America's Small Liberal Arts Colleges

Edited by

SUSAN McWILLIAMS
AND JOHN E. SEERY

SUNY
PRESS

Published by
STATE UNIVERSITY OF NEW YORK PRESS
Albany

© 2015 State University of New York

All rights reserved

Printed in the United States of America

For information, contact
State University of New York Press
www.sunypress.edu

Production, Laurie D. Searl
Marketing, Michael Campochiaro

Library of Congress Cataloging-in-Publication Data

The best kind of college : an insiders' guide to America's small liberal arts
   colleges / edited by Susan McWilliams and John E. Seery.
      pages cm
   Includes bibliographical references and index.
   ISBN 978-1-4384-5771-0 (hardcover : alk. paper)
   ISBN 978-1-4384-5773-4 (e-book)
   1. Small colleges—United States.   2. Education, Humanistic—United
States.   3. Universities and colleges—United States—Guidebooks.
I. McWilliams, Susan Jane, 1977–   II. Seery, John Evan.
   LB2328.32.U6B47 2015
   378.73—dc23   2014040698

10 9 8 7 6 5 4 3 2 1

Contents

Acknowledgments

We are grateful for the many ways in which our colleagues and students at Pomona College have supported this book. In particular, we are indebted to Shayna Citrenbaum, who trained her expert editorial eyes on these pages and improved them immeasurably.

We also thank acquiring editor Michael Rinella, the staff at the State University of New York Press, and the anonymous reviewers of the manuscript for their thoughtful suggestions and hard work in helping this book come to be.

Introduction

SUSAN McWILLIAMS AND JOHN E. SEERY

Higher education is, these days, in the news. Much of that news is grim. The price of tuition is increasing at a phenomenal rate. Student loan debt is at an all-time high. Many universities are overfilled, and students cannot enroll in the courses they need to graduate. The fast pace of technological change makes many degrees seem almost immediately obsolete. Graduates have trouble finding jobs.

In response, all sorts of debates have been raging about the future of higher education in America, in particular the future of the liberal arts in the country's colleges and universities. Virtually everyone in the chattering classes has had his or her say on the matter; those who have proposed sweeping reforms to higher education include government officials, CEOs, politicians, think-tank researchers, journalists, media pundits, and university administrators, as well as parents and students and some prominent professors.

But drowned out in all this noisy punditry are the people we may need to hear most: those persons who actually teach the liberal arts exclusively to undergraduates—namely, the faculty who teach in the nation's small liberal arts colleges. As the voices of those who teach in such colleges are left out of public debate, so, too, are America's small liberal arts colleges themselves discounted, or essentially forgotten, in the clamor over the nation's educational future.

We think it is hard to overstate the massive error of this neglect. Small liberal arts colleges should be at the heart of any discussion about American higher education rather than relegated to the sidelines or overlooked altogether. Small liberal arts colleges deserve such pointed consideration, we propose, because they are the best things going in American higher education and probably the best things going in higher education around the globe. No small claim, that.

Drawing attention to these small liberal arts colleges is what this book is all about. We know that having a discussion about American higher education that doesn't include small college classroom teachers is like having a discussion about the future of American agriculture without consulting family farmers (or even making any reference to family farms). It is also similar to having a discussion about the future of American health care without engaging the doctors who see patients daily or having a discussion about the future of baseball without talking to anyone who has ever stepped on a pitcher's mound. In other words, the current conversation about American higher education leaves out the perspectives of the people who might be best positioned to think broadly, thoughtfully, and critically about the subject, the people who have the wisdom of hands-on and hard-won experience.

This book brings those insiders into the discussion. Only professors at small liberal arts colleges have been included in this volume. We are undergraduate teachers, first and foremost and full-time. There are no professional administrators—deans, chancellors, presidents[1]—among us, though many of us at some time or another, as part of our institutional duties, have attended to administrative tasks, such as chairing departments or supervising programs. And while our academic activities are not limited to the classroom—we also all conduct scholarly research and publish our findings in professional venues—teaching is our main focus and top priority. Most of us have won awards and honors for our teaching, and because the teaching of undergraduates is the focus of our careers and our colleges, we have each given intense and serious thought to what it means to teach and to learn well.

By no means do we claim that *The Best Kind of College* has all the answers to the many woes afflicting American higher education today—in fact, we asked our contributors merely to reflect on their particular experiences at these schools, without necessarily expanding those experiences into policy proposals or general lessons—although we do think that this book offers more than simply a collection of provincial narratives. All told, by insisting on the importance of individual voices and particular perspectives, we think the book adds up to more than the sum of its parts, put here as an overall proposition: The best approach to education requires face-to-face discussions, quirky explorations, classroom and laboratory risk-taking, relational learning, and singular rather than standardized approaches to pedagogy. In short, the best approach to education is the small liberal arts college approach to education, and this is a truth that our nation's movers and shakers, and citizens at large, would do well to heed. We know what works. We are speaking on behalf of a kind of institution that has a long and abiding history, a time-tested record of success. We think it is important for the rest of the country to hear us sing the virtues and offbeat ways of the SLAC (Small Liberal Arts College) model of teaching, learning, and living.

What's the Big Deal about Small Liberal Arts Colleges?

Few Americans seem to know much about small liberal arts colleges, probably in large part because, at present, such colleges educate only about 1 percent (if that)[2] of the nation's undergraduates.

But even if you've never set foot on the campus of a small liberal arts college, doing just a little research reveals why they should be recognized, and regarded widely, as the gold standard in American higher education.

Against the impersonal, lecture-hall, multiple-choice-exam, and teaching-assistant-aided system that dominates our nation's most famous universities, small liberal arts colleges are places where professors teach undergraduates directly and exclusively. Taking undergraduate teaching—and taking undergraduates themselves—so seriously tends to affect students, so that they begin to take their own learning seriously. Small liberal arts colleges are places where the kind of close teacher-student relationships that you see portrayed in films like *Dead Poets Society* or *Good Will Hunting* actually exist—and are the rule rather than the exception.[3] These are schools with small classes, usually face-to-face seminar discussions, where students are known by name and not by ID number, where students are missed if they miss class, where students are encouraged and advised and counseled to develop their individual abilities and to think about how those abilities might be used in service to others.

At small liberal arts colleges, professors and students get to know one another outside official class meetings—doing research together in labs, engaging in artistic and creative production, and going to each other's sports games and concerts and lectures and debates. Where we teach, at Pomona College, we (and our colleagues) regularly see and spend time with our students at local coffee shops, on the campus quads, at the city farmer's market, and even in our homes.

This romantic-sounding educational experience can be the daily reality at liberal arts colleges because of their smallness. Not only are classes small, but also the schools and campuses as a whole are small—smaller, in many cases, than the high schools our students attended before matriculating. That intimate size almost demands that professors and students get to know each other, both inside and outside the classroom, as real persons, that is, as living, breathing, thinking, feeling, fully rounded, undigitized human beings.

This proximity means that our students are learning even when they don't fully realize that they are learning; education at a small liberal arts college exceeds the formal classroom, and everyone at these schools eventually figures out that the true idea—the spirit or ethos—of the liberal arts goes beyond book learning. Small liberal arts colleges are places where we try to live the truth that each person matters, every day, and thus such students learn, by implication and example, what it means to matter to and within a community of people.

The residential nature of small liberal arts college reinforces that lesson. At most small liberal arts colleges, students are expected to live on campus, with each other, for at least part of the term of their formal education—an experience that provides its own education in individual and social responsibility. The notion of a classroom extends to the sports field, where students pursue intervarsity, intramural, and recreational competition; to stages and auditoria, where students perform in plays and musical concerts; to dorms and dining halls, where academic and nonacademic discussions dovetail into one another; to biological field stations, and organic farms, and green spaces, and the outdoor skies, where geologists and astronomers and other student-scientists conduct their critical lab work and experiments; to surrounding towns and cities, where students do internships, field trips, community service, work, and outreach. And these campuses typically feature beautiful landscaping and dedicated architecture, creating some overall feel of otherworldly oases, if short of paradise. ("College is our American pastoral," writes Andrew Delbanco.)[4] They thus provide three-dimensional spaces and three-dimensional experiences, which cannot be and will never be replaced by two-dimensional, on-screen, campus-less surrogates. These spaces house various temporal communities, which eventually become generational communities: a member of the first-year class becomes a fellow pilgrim on a four-year journey with other classmates, and she and her classmates start to realize, in those close confines, that they are and have been experiencing life under similar terms and under similar circumstances, unique to their age cohort. They come to share friendships, loves, memories, all bound to a place where thinking and learning matter.

What outsiders may not realize is that a SLAC provides and initiates one into not just a curriculum, certainly not just an "educational outcome," but rather a distinctive community and even an entire way of life. Call it a liberal arts way of life, a way of life so encompassing that you might not want to leave, as depicted in the arrested development that informed the plot of the 2012 movie *Liberal Arts*. Even if, after graduation, one never again performs in a band, one still has that music, from that period, in the back of one's head. Campus architecture, installed as a backdrop in one's mental apparatus, continues to inform one's future construction projects. Conversations continue to reverberate from past seminar and dining hall discussions. Formative memories from extracurricular activities continue, years later, to inspire. As a devoted alum, you look back fondly on your small college days (these colleges tend to induce fondness, as opposed to pride) not because of the college "brand," or the college reputation, but because of the particular people you encountered, and encountered so intensely, in those classrooms, sports fields, laboratories, and dining halls.

Small liberal arts colleges were designed with the expansive purpose of teaching individuals how to live lives that are strong, thoughtful, responsible, and free. In fact, the "liberal arts" were so described, starting in the Middle Ages, to distinguish that form of education by which a freeman might learn the arts of liberty from that which would train him merely for a life of servitude. One learns at a small liberal arts college not simply how to write or calculate well, not just how to demonstrate a disciplinary expertise. One learns at a small liberal arts college not only how to face difficulties and think rigorously and prepare for a challenging career. One learns all those things. But more: One learns how to move through the world.

That particular combination of worldliness and idealism is, perhaps, a big part of the reason why the small liberal arts college has been called a "distinctively American" educational institution by Steven Koblik, the former president of Reed College.[5] The small liberal arts college has a history and mission tied up with that of our republic, which has not always depended solely on having skilled workers but also on having inventive, independent, and intelligent people as its members—people who not only know a set of facts but also know how to function well as participants in diverse and often rancorous communities.

At Pomona College, one of our recent seniors summed up the experience of going to a small liberal arts college by saying that by the time you leave, you can look around at any campus gathering and think: "I know something about everyone in this room that they do not know that I know." Of course, that also means that the converse is true. The graduating senior could also look around any campus gathering and realize: "Everyone in this room knows something about me that I do not know that they know." That realization is discomfiting, in some senses, but it's also the mark of being in a functioning community where each individual counts.

Simply by placing our students in small and close-knit communities where they do matter, not just as seat-fillers but as in-the-flesh persons, small liberal arts colleges encourage individuals to learn how to live well in a world where their lives are intertwined with those of so many other people. We who teach in such small residential colleges think this broad missionary purview helps students develop habits of acting with dignity, integrity, faith, and purpose, both in and out of class. The hopeful idea, then, is that when our students go out into the big and often bad world, they will likely refuse to relinquish the kind of resolve and engagement they have already experienced in college, that sense of mattering. Once you have up-front and firsthand experience of mattering to other persons, beyond your kith and kin, it's not something you easily relinquish.

If you think about college as a holistic, residential, 3-D, full-Technicolor, full-analogue experience conducted in real-time, an introduction into an entire way of life and of a liberal arts curriculum consistent with that receptive, broad-minded, idea-seeking outlook, then you might not find it surprising that, although small liberal arts college graduates account for only 2 percent (over time) of all the college graduates in this country, small liberal arts college graduates account for 20 percent of all US presidents, 20 percent of Pulitzer Prize winners, and 20 percent of the scientists elected in recent years to the National Academy of Scientists. Liberal arts colleges produce disproportionate numbers of Peace Corps volunteers, Fulbright scholars, Mellon fellows, and PhDs. Moreover, about one in twelve of the nation's wealthiest CEOs is a small liberal arts college graduate.[6]

If you think about it that way, it's also no wonder that the people who choose to teach at small liberal arts colleges have to care about teaching in a deep, rigorous, and thoroughgoing way. Barry O'Connell, a longtime professor of English at Amherst College, summed up the liberal arts college teaching ethos this way: "Teachers teach subjects, but they also teach people." The professors who are drawn to work at small liberal arts colleges are professors who want to put the education of young people—as people—first.

As mentioned, small liberal arts colleges are themselves devoted to undergraduate education and undergraduate teaching. At a small liberal arts college, there are no teaching assistants standing in for professors, and there are no graduate students competing for time and attention. But there is yet another crucial reason why the smallness of the SLAC provides cover for another kind of educational experience altogether, as compared especially with our nation's research universities.

When a student enrolls at a SLAC, he or she is stepping out of time, just a bit, and stepping off the great treadmill of the modern economy, just a bit—and knows it. That is part of the bargain. When you choose to come to a SLAC, you've chosen not to attend a big glitzy university with instant national name recognition, a prominent school that courts corporations for stadium-naming rights and enjoys an expensive television contract for broadcasting its Division I football games. You've chosen instead to fly under the radar, to enter what our own students call existence in a "bubble." That kind of self-selection tends to assemble students who are more likely to attend to their books and discussions and educational pursuits for, as it were, the intrinsic, rather than extrinsic or ulterior, benefits of such activities. You tend to attract students who are more willing to suspend, for a four-year stretch, their pressing utilitarian concerns about why, exactly, they are poring over the pages of long novels, debating abstruse ideas around a table, throwing clay on a wheel, or studying the geology of the ground beneath them. Perhaps overt economic incentives, as a way of structuring curricula and careers, motivate some salutary forms of learning. But instrumentalizing education thus, or too much, also tends to curtail undergraduate bouts of brooding, talking, reading, fellowship, and unscripted solitude. SLACs are national sanctuaries wherein a good number of students can still find an educational environment in which they are allowed the luxury, the freedom, to learn according to their not-necessarily-for-profit aspirations toward truth, beauty, justice, friendship, and personal reverie. (The untold story, by the way, is that more often than not, those students who de-instrumentalize their undergraduate years of education, pursuing truth for the sake of truth, attending faithfully to their curiosities, exploring vigorously their intellectual passions and commitments, find later on that such dedication is eventually rewarded handsomely in the hard-to-predict modern economy.)

Small Liberal Arts Colleges versus the "Competition"

Contrast the aforementioned SLAC vision with the R-1 (research university) model, and you'll probably come to the conclusion that the way the country's research universities treat undergraduates constitutes nothing less than a national scandal. Such schools receive all the attention when it comes to public discussions about undergraduate education. But at those institutions, Ivy League and state school alike, few participants, if any, believe that teaching undergraduates is the first priority. At best it is a secondary concern, ranked at some distance behind either graduate education or specialized research. (Actually, our own experience at research universities has convinced us that at most of these schools, undergraduate education comes in a distant third to both graduate teaching and research. As one of our colleagues was told when he took a job at a prestigious university, professors are expected to do excellent research, but, for teaching, they are held to a mere standard of "well, don't suck.") True, research universities do have their abundant virtues and decided advantages. But as far as the education of undergraduates goes, the R-1 organizational plan depends on channeling a large number of students through large lecture-hall experiences, with hundreds and sometimes thousands of students enrolled in a single course. Students have breakout sessions with underpaid teaching assistants who proctor the exams, read all the papers, and do all the grading. Often, these teaching assistants are themselves loaded down with hundreds of students a semester, even as they are trying to finish their own graduate degrees. At American research universities, undergraduate students are often paying exorbitant sums of money to be treated, in the halls of their own institution, as second- or third-class citizens. Businesses in the commercial marketplace usually treat their customers with greater attention and respect.

To be fair, some research universities have made strides at prioritizing some measure of undergraduate education within their behemoth structures. A number of big universities now feature demarcated "honors college" programs in the liberal arts, embedded and largely segregated from the rest of the undergraduate curriculum, and some try to offer their students the chance to take occasional small-seminar classes. Having those programs is better than not having them, to be sure. But they are gestures at the true liberal arts experience rather than a full embrace of that experience—not to mention that the existence of such programs is tacit acknowledgment of the superiority of the small liberal arts college way of doing things.

It is worth noticing that many of the loudest complaints heard regularly about higher education—professors who don't teach, crowded lecture-hall classrooms, and academic hyper-specialization—apply only to the research university model. It is also worth noticing that many of the things that lately have been proposed to "improve" American higher education would be improvements only on the current research university experience. They wouldn't, though, constitute educational improvements on the small liberal arts college experience.

Take, for instance, Massive Open Online Courses (MOOCs). The idea of MOOCs, open-access courses offered on the Internet, took off around the year 2010, with the bright promise that such courses would be a less expensive and more accessible way of offering college-level learning on scales never before imagined. Although they began as little more than collections of videotaped lectures, MOOCs have evolved to include features such as online discussion sections and "crowd-sourced" interaction. It's not hard to imagine how MOOCs, especially as the technology behind them improves, might offer certain advantages over the large canned-lecture delivery system that characterizes the research-university classroom. But it *is* hard to imagine how MOOCs can have any kind of pedagogical advantage over the small liberal arts college experience, where the standard class session is based on dialogue rather than monologue, and each student gets extensive and scrupulous attention across multiple courses and outside of the classroom as well, and all are embedded in the thick relational ties of a distinct, intentional, flesh-and-blood place.[7]

A curiosity surrounding many of the recent initiatives for improving higher education is that such proposals are often billed as trying to bring certain qualities and features to the American academy that are already in existence, in spades, at small liberal arts colleges. Yale University claims to be able to provide visionary guidance and experience in founding a new small liberal arts college in Singapore. The start-up for-profit Minerva Project is trying to bring MOOCs into small (albeit online) classroom venues. Abroad, numerous countries have been turning to the US SLAC model, even founding self-standing, American-style SLACs, as a way of reforming their own higher educational systems. But note: All of these initiatives are attempts to emulate and import the SLACs. Intuitively, reformers seem to know that the SLAC model is the gold standard on which their approximations are parasitic. But most of these reformers fail to give full credit where credit is due and often end up compromising the SLAC model rather than living up to it.[8]

The Money Issue

Some will cry at the foregoing: Yes, of course, small classes with dedicated professors on beautiful campuses would be great, but it all comes down to cost. The SLAC model may be ideal, but at what price, and who's going to pay that price? Small classes for undergraduates, with attentive professors, are costly undertakings because they are so labor-intensive and inefficiently scaled. The research university model, and now the MOOC model, offer greater access at lower prices. Those models may not be ideal, but they're more affordable (usually). Besides, many SLACs are struggling financially. Those now flourishing, and those that will survive, are (and will be) the wealthy ones. SLAC education will abide in America, but the remaining colleges will increasingly become precious enclaves, reserved for an elite or lucky few.

We don't deny that in the short term, educating people costs money. Despite the claims that various entrepreneurial types regularly offer up to venture capitalists, you definitely can't *make* money by educating people well; no one has ever made profits merely by offering quality education to students. As Robert McChesney observes, for-profit education companies "seize public funds and make their money by *not* teaching."[9] Education is a public good, and like most public goods, it requires long-term financial investment that doesn't lead to immediate monetary returns. Any form of education is going to involve some expense. There's no way around that.

And small liberal arts colleges do remain expensive propositions, especially given the alternatives that are and will soon be out there. It *is* more expensive to educate a student with a top-notch, tenured faculty, as part of a distinct and dedicated community, in a real brick-and-mortar place than it is to offer prefab classes taught by a short-term contracted employee to a student over the Internet. That's why we worry that the MOOCs (or some latter-day successor to them) will turn American higher education into a truly two-tiered system: Rich SLACs and rich universities, populated by rich students and funded by rich alumni, will survive; everyone else will be taking out big loans or else going to "college" by watching video after video on Khan Academy, or the like. Although lots of people will have college degrees on paper, few people will have the benefit of a really serious, engaged, and embedded college education. Even Andrew Delbanco, the author of *College: What It Was, Is, and Should Be*, seems to accede to the inevitability of such a two-track educational system: "It is a pipe dream," he writes, "to imagine that every student can have the sort of experience that our richest colleges, at their best, provide."[10]

But we want to question whether this two-tiering of American education must necessarily take place, whether we must shrug our shoulders and give in to the idea that truly great education can be the purview of only a lucky few (which is also giving in to the idea that we should aspire to educational mediocrity for the masses). For one thing, small liberal arts college education does not have to be so expensive as to be out of reach of all but the elite. Colleges, if they get their number-one priority straight—classroom teaching—can cut a lot of fat. That fat is usually administrative overload and bureaucratic bloat. In most schools, you could cut back significantly on employees with fancy titles who don't teach, plain and simple. They are usually dispensable and merely ancillary, not essential, to the mission of teaching. It's also nice to have well-appointed campuses, but some colleges are flourishing under modest or spare conditions. (One of our own colleagues is fond of reminding us that Pomona was a good school before it was a rich school; the goodness of the college does not depend on the fanciest accoutrements of our present existence.) Berea College, for example, is a model of the kind of frugality that other schools could embrace: Berea does not have a football team or fancy dorms, and all students are required to hold part-time jobs on campus, but in exchange for eschewing certain luxuries, Berea students receive full-tuition scholarships and a stellar education.

We also think it's worth putting the expense of SLACs into perspective, more generally speaking. So let's crunch some numbers and consider some possibilities. Pomona College is currently ranked as the second richest college (or university) in the country in terms of endowment per pupil. Pomona trustees, alums, administrators, and faculty have steered that material advantage decidedly toward certain values: a broad-based liberal arts education available to those qualified, regardless of need. Pomona has held firm to a "need-blind" admissions process, with the understanding that sufficient financial aid will be forthcoming to all those admitted, with the financial aid package including no loans. In theory, and largely in practice, no one who is graduated from Pomona College should be in debt. We don't see our entering students as "elites"—for example, about 20 percent of them are the first in their families to attend college; we see them as do-gooders and underdogs. Indeed, we wish our good fortune could be extended to others, the educational model democratized and somehow, someday made available to many throughout the country, and beyond. But how could that happen?

Perhaps needless to say, we don't believe Pomona itself could get much bigger without compromising the smallness that, as we have argued, is constitutive of the true liberal arts education. To bring a Pomona-quality experience to more students, we have to imagine how we could fund the creation of more small liberal arts colleges like it.

We could first consider private funding. Bill Gates's personal worth is reportedly $72 billion; the Gates Foundation's endowment is around $36 billion. Warren Buffett's net worth is around $54 billion (and he will be bequeathing a good portion of that to the Gates Foundation). Right there, two philanthropic-minded individuals who care about education command $162 billion. That sum could found and endow—overnight—108 Pomona Colleges (for present purposes we are modestly estimating Pomona's endowment at $1.5 billion for 1,500 students), providing a top-of-the-line, debt-free liberal arts education to forty thousand graduates year after year after year, if only Gates could get his educational priorities straight (learning from Buffett's investments in Grinnell College) and move away from whiz-bang technological gimmicks.

There are public resources that could be brought to bear on this project as well. You ask about the public sector with its depleted coffers? The public cost of the Iraq and Afghanistan wars is estimated to have been around $4 trillion. Had that one-time discretionary expenditure been allocated instead into founding new Pomona Colleges with $1.5 billion dollar endowments each, we in this country would now be able to provide four million of our eighteen million undergraduates with a Rolls-Royce caliber liberal arts education, completely debt-free for those on financial aid, year after year after year, an investment that would keep on providing individual and national dividends well into the future. Such a program would also have the advantage of keeping federal student aid funds out of the grip of those for-profit universities that have proven so good at failing to do their job yet take federal funds and leave a huge percentage of their one-time students in debt—and without a degree.

Simplistic, you say? Surely, but this is one of those cases where a simple analysis helps us to think about a more important, and very realistic, point: that this is a society—one of the wealthiest societies in the history of human civilization—that can afford to spend money in the pursuit of what it deems to be long-term public goods, or call it long-term R & D, an investment in ourselves, our future. All we have to do, to enable high-quality higher education to flourish rather than flounder in this country, is recognize that education is a true public good.

We submit that calling a vision like this a "pipe dream" is an alibi, a cover for grossly misplaced priorities, a failure of vision and will. We believe that the "distinctively American" approach to higher education should be and could be made available to many more Americans. Once we identify the best and clarify our priorities, we the people can indeed decide to do what can and ought to be done.

This Book

One of the reasons, perhaps, that there hasn't been a cultural declamation of the sort outlined here, or more recognition that a democratization of this gold-standard form of higher education is possible, is because those of us at small liberal arts colleges have not gathered together to sing the praises of the places where we teach.

That's where this book comes in, and that's why we think concerned readers should encounter a group of essays penned by SLAC professors. We do think this book has much to contribute to the national debate on higher education, and yet, as a group, we largely have been ignored. One reason we haven't been heard from, limned earlier, is that SLACs are small and out of the way and thus overlooked.

But another reason for this silence is that, since SLAC professors are so involved with teaching students, we haven't prioritized high-profile advocacy initiatives and PR campaigns on our own behalf. Small liberal arts college professors are not, as a rule, seeking celebrity or "star" status. We are first and foremost teachers who tend to relish and safeguard the space of the classroom, to treat that space with a kind of sanctity. We tend to keep it away from cameras and reporters and advertisers. We don't aim to be pundits or celebrities or profiteers. We didn't go into teaching for fame or fortune. (If we wanted to be performers on a large stage, we would have gone to places with large stages.) We don't tend to seek the attention of public fame, probably because the classroom is so intense and so rewarding on its own.

Moreover, in comparison with our colleagues at research universities, we spend a lot more of our time in the classroom. Those aware of the academy know that SLAC professors teach more classes than do research university professors. But even the moderately informed may be shocked to know that at many high-profile research universities, professors are expected to teach only one undergraduate course a year—and it is understood that "teaching," in this context, means delivering a set of lectures to a hall of nameless undergrads. (It is not unusual to hear of the research university professor who "teaches" in, say, Cambridge but lives in New York, flying out and back once a week to read his prepared lecture notes.) By contrast, at small liberal arts colleges, professors usually are expected to teach at least two courses (and as many as four or five) a semester, focusing the bulk of their energies during the academic year on the enterprise of teaching. And in the SLAC context, teaching means teaching. It means leading discussions. It means grading. It means meeting with students outside of class. It means being readily available to those students, in person and by phone and over email, throughout each week. It means writing numerous letters of recommendation. It means spending hours and hours advising, about the present and the future. The upshot is that even if we wanted to do so, SLAC professors don't have a lot of leisure time to cultivate relationships with reporters or appear on talk shows or cultivate personal "brands."

Thus this book, encompassing our coordinated acts of stepping forward and outward, is unusual. We are compiling it because we believe strongly in the SLAC form of education. And although many of us teach at institutions that are likely to weather whatever the next trend in educational reform is (as such colleges have weathered such trends in the past), we are worried that much of the current talk of transformation is misguided, and American higher education risks deteriorating in the name of innovating.

These are testimonials, and they present various points of view and don't all square with one another. We editors solicited and invited essays from various persons from assorted disciplines across many small liberal arts colleges, but we weren't seeking complete disciplinary or geographical coverage. The essays that follow are thus illustrative rather than exhaustive.

We also want to emphasize that each institution represented here is unique, as to some degree each small liberal arts college is unique. There is no cookie-cutter, one-size-fits-all SLAC model, a Platonic ideal that animates all of the on-the-ground instances. But we think these testimonials matter, nevertheless, on general grounds. We want to recover and dwell upon the importance of *this* professor's particular approach to a subject, and the importance of *this* particular group of students in *this* particular seminar in *this* particular year, at *this* particular institution, with *these* particular priorities and traditions.

Those particularities—and the extrapolated importance of such particularity, personality, and localism—cannot be aggregated into measurable "data" and commensurable outcomes. These essays have to be read and pondered, not flattened and tallied on spreadsheets. If some generalizable notion of "best practices" emerges from this volume, it will be one that goes very much against the national tendency to assume that numerical data provide the best empirical information on which to base policy judgments. We assert, instead, that qualitative norms and exceptional experiences, not merely quantified and quantifiable mass behavior, should be given their due in guiding our future. Just because the kind of evidence we offer is localized, anecdotal, and personal does not mean that it is not evidence. It is, rather, evidence of the importance of taking the local, the anecdotal, and the personal seriously.

When it comes down to it, education, especially at its highest levels, is not about feeding standardized data into the brains of an undifferentiated mass. Taken beyond a fairly basic level, standardization precludes rather than paves the way for high-quality education, which is why standardizing approaches to higher education totally miss the point.

High-quality education is about acknowledging and respecting the differences among particular people, cultivating the kind of careful relationships that allow for serious dialogue, creative inspiration, and independent thought. Just as Helen Keller's genius couldn't emerge until a particular teacher took her particular challenges and strengths seriously and worked with her over a long period of time, no student can achieve his or her full potential if treated like another cog in the wheel or another avatar in the intersphere or another dollar in the pocket. Education is relational, and human relationships are particular. They are also small scale, which is a truth that the nation's small liberal arts colleges, in so many different ways, embody.

Without presuming to interpret the essays for our readers before they read them, or preempting the actual reading of them, we have divided *The Best Kind of College* into five sections: The Classroom, The Career, The Curriculum, The Community, and The College. As editors, we think these categories might be helpful in a very preliminary way as guideposts to readers when they crack the book for the first time. A reader might be drawn to one cluster and then read a few pieces within that cluster. But quickly we want to concede that these are loose and porous categories, and we're not pretending that the essays build upon one another into a cumulatively coherent narrative structure. Several essays could fit into one or more of the categories, and finally these organizational rubrics may be prove to be more Procrustean than illuminating. We understand the usual conventions of editing academic collections, and yet we are hesitant at this point in this introduction of ours to offer the typical thumbnail encapsulations of each essay, which are supposed to explain why each essay belongs in the book squarely where it has been put and how it contributes to the whole. By admitting this design failing, we are trying to call attention to what we think is unusual, and distinctive, about this book, a genre-bender of sorts, and are inviting readers to pop in and pop out of the book, reading selectively, as they see fit. We could have arranged these essays according to geography, or discipline, or contributor age, or college SAT scores, or perhaps *U.S. News and World Report* rankings. Instead, we've proposed these very general categories; yet within them, we've conspicuously included each author's extended biography at the outset of each essay. That editorial innovation is meant to underscore the particularity of each teacher's approach, perspective, and priorities in teaching. We often advise students to choose classes, first and foremost, if they can, on the basis of the particular professors involved (as opposed to considerations about subject matter, requirements, grades, the major, educational outcome, skills, or jobs). For our readers, in the pages that follow, we want to re-create something of that "person-centric" approach to negotiating college.

A final note: The late David Foster Wallace, who was our friend and colleague, haunts and inspires many of these pages to come. Several of our contributors explicitly mention his influence. We want to openly confront his liberal arts legacy here. He was, it could be argued, the latter-day, cross-country exemplar and iconic spokesperson for American SLAC-ness, from Amherst College undergraduate to Pomona College professor to Kenyon College commencement speaker. Indeed, the movie *Liberal Arts* portrays the careful reading of his books, for better and for worse, as the quintessence of small college liberal artsy-ness in the present day. In that movie the character Jesse, in lonely fits of postgraduate nostalgia for his small liberal arts college days, entertains a compensatory fantasy in which attentive, brainy, and soul-searching readers might populate the world outside the ivory tower, a David Foster Wallace Republic. On his return to his alma mater, Jesse identifies with a fellow DFW reader, an "aggressively unhappy" and over-intellectualizing undergraduate named Dean; and the two of them seem to bond over the proposition that reading long DFW-like books both combats and exacerbates social isolation and loneliness. Later in the movie, after Dean attempts suicide, Jesse recommends that Dean stop reading DFW's books—because DFW himself committed suicide. Maybe such liberal artsy-ness is, after all, misbegotten and debilitating, even dangerous. And yet Jesse answers Dean's question about why Jesse would care at all about Dean by saying that he, Jesse, appreciates good readers; in fact, then, their common appreciation of DFW is what saves Dean's very life.

The movie on the whole presents an insider's critique of the liberal arts way of life, now depicted, in shorthand, as DFW bookishness. Such a life provides (the movie's setup goes) an intense and capacious orientation to the world that seems to promise some kind of salubrious recuperation for the world at large, if only we pay greater attention to everything around us, as if we were perpetually in college, ever curious and alert. Yet such raised hopes and intensified expectations (as Jesse says in the movie, "One of the things I loved the most about being here was the feeling that anything was possible") can lead, it seems, to depression. Zibby, Jesse's love interest in the movie, asks him whether things in the world outside of college "suck" and whether she should prepare herself "for suckiness." Jesse smirks as he replies, "No, a liberal arts education solves all your problems."

Taking that sarcasm as our cue, we in *The Best Kind of College* don't want to overpromise what the following essays can deliver. The small liberal arts colleges won't solve all of our country's educational problems (not to mention that intellectual inquiry is risky, holds no guarantees, and can incite its own vexations), but these colleges are, we think, the best places in which to ask the best questions and to seek the best answers, all the while offering the best self-critique, too. ("Why does everyone here always speak in superlatives?" asks Dean.)

Notes

1. College presidents know a lot about administrative matters but not necessarily much about classroom teaching, even on their own campuses. Of the top one hundred SLACs (Small Liberal Arts Colleges), as ranked by *U.S. News & World Report*, only 30 percent of current small liberal arts college presidents had prior teaching experience in a SLAC before heading one up. Fifty-two percent of SLAC presidents today—a majority—never stepped in a SLAC classroom, either as a student or a professor, before heading one up.

2. It's hard to say with any precision what percentage of students attend or have attended SLACs, if only because the term "liberal arts"—already a contestable signifier—keeps evolving, and colleges nominally operating under that rubric also evolve and/or alter their missions. Moreover, there's never been a definitive list of *small* liberal arts colleges. Ranking services today, such as *U.S. News & World Report* or *Washington Monthly*, typically list around 250 colleges as "Liberal Arts Colleges," but these ranking services make few distinctions based on size. Several of the institutions on those lists have undergraduate student enrollments of over four thousand students, up to a few with seven thousand plus students. http://www.washingtonmonthly.com/college_guide/rankings_2013/liberal_arts_rank.php. David Breneman, in a 1990–1991 study based on the Carnegie Foundation Classification of Institutions of Higher Education, named 212 colleges that met his criteria for designating an institution as a liberal arts institution, and most of those institutions were quite small, but a few had enrollments reaching four thousand students. See David W. Breneman, "Are We Losing Our Liberal Arts Colleges?" *AAHE Bulletin* 43.2 (1990): 3–6; David W. Breneman, *Liberal Arts Colleges: Thriving, Surviving, or Endangered?* (Washington, DC: Brookings Institution, 1994). Vicki L. Baker and her coauthors published a study in 2012, based on 2009–2010 IPEDS data (http://nces.ed.gov/ipeds/) that re-tallied the number of institutions that met Breneman's earlier criteria for designating an institution as a liberal arts college; and Baker et al. concluded that only 130 institutions had, in 2010, met those 1990 criteria (but Baker didn't publish the names of those 130 colleges). See Vicki L. Baker, Roger G. Baldwin, and Sumedha Makker, "Where Are They Now? Revisiting Breneman's Study of

Liberal Arts Colleges," *Liberal Education* 98.3 (Summer 2012): 48–53. In 2000 the Carnegie Foundation dropped its distinction between "Liberal Arts I" and "Liberal Arts II" institutions and started distinguishing between "Baccalaureate Colleges—Liberal Arts" and "Baccalaureate Colleges—General" (http://classifications.carnegie-foundation.org/downloads/2000_edition_data_printable.pdf). The current Carnegie classification system makes no attempt to designate liberal arts institutions as such, contending thus: "A high concentration of majors in the arts and sciences is not the same as a liberal arts education, and we do not view any particular location on this continuum as the special province of liberal education. Examples of high-quality liberal education exist across the spectrum" (http://classifications.carnegiefoundation. org/descriptions/ugrad_program.php). Never have these classificatory listings included tribal colleges (http://www.aihec.org/colleges/), nor have they included "honors colleges" embedded within large universities. Bruce Kimball now counts four hundred such embedded honors colleges. See Bruce A. Kimball, "Revising the Declension Narrative: Liberal Arts Colleges, Universities, and Honors Programs, 1870s–2010s," *Harvard Educational Review* 84.2 (Summer 2014): 243–264. (For our part, we editors of *The Best Kind of College* have deliberately refrained in this volume from defining a one-size-fits-all template for all SLACs across the country, thinking it best to keep that designation self-identified, localized, and aspirational.)

3. We are aware that the close teacher-student relationships portrayed in these two films take place in institutions other than a small liberal arts college, namely, a prep school in *Dead Poets Society*, and MIT and a community college in *Good Will Hunting*. Also, we mention *Dead Poets Society* as an example of teacher-student closeness but not as an example of good humanities teaching. See Kevin Dettmar, "*Dead Poets Society* Is a Terrible Defense of the Humanities," *The Atlantic* online, February 19, 2014, http://www.theatlantic.com/education/archive/2014/02/-em-dead-poets-society-em-is-a-terrible-defense-of-the-humanities/283853/.

4. Andrew Delbanco, *College: What It Was, Is, and Should Be* (Princeton and Oxford: Princeton University Press, 2012), 11.

5. Steven Koblik and Stephen R. Graubard, eds., *Distinctively American: The Residential Liberal Arts Colleges* (New Brunswick: Transaction, 2000).

6. See also: "The Value and Impact of the College Experience: A Comparative Study," Research by Hardwick Day, Commissioned by the Annapolis Group, November 2011, http://collegenews.org/_wp/wp-content/uploads/Annapolis-Group-study-results.pdf

7. Alexander W. Astin, "To MOOC or Not to MOOC the Liberal Arts: Why Not Consult the Evidence," 2014 paper, http://www.westmont.edu/institute/conversations/2014_program/documents/AstinFullPaper.pdf

8. See Janet D. Stemwedel, "Why I Can No Longer Donate to Wellesley College," http://scientopia.org/blogs/ethicsandscience/2014/06/01/why-i-can-no-longer-donate-to-wellesley-college/.

9. Robert McChesney, *Digital Disconnect: How Capitalism Is Turning the Internet against Democracy* (New York: The New Press, 2013), 194.

10. Delbanco, *College*, 7.

PART ONE

The Classroom

What's Love Got to Do with It?

.•———•.

Shakespeare: A Liberal Art

MARTHA ANDRESEN

Martha Andresen, University of Minnesota, BA, BS, summa cum laude, Phi Beta Kappa, Yale University, Woodrow Wilson Fellow, MA, PhD, is Professor of English Emerita at Pomona College, hired in 1972, and appointed as the Phebe Estelle Spalding Professor of English Literature from 1989 until 2006. She is a specialist in Shakespearean scholarship and teaching and the recipient of numerous teaching awards, including seven Wig Distinguished Teaching Awards at Pomona College, the Council for Advancement and Support of Education (CASE) California Professor of the Year (1992), and the Robert Foster Cherry Award for Great Teaching, an international award sponsored by Baylor University (1992). In May 2006, Pomona College granted her a Lifetime Teaching Award. Outside the academy she has engaged professional, corporate, university, and theater audiences through her publications, lectures, workshops, seminars, public television presentations, and dramaturgy. She has been affiliated with the Ashland, Oregon, Shakespeare Festival and a longtime friend of the Shakespeare Center Los Angeles, an endeavor that fosters innovative performance, education, and broad community outreach. She was elected a Fellow of the Radcliffe Institute for Intellectual Renewal in 2000 and has served as Visiting Director of the Arden Summer Seminars, Theatre and Thought, affiliated with Shakespeare & Company in Lenox, Massachusetts, an ongoing opportunity for outreach, intellectual enrichment, and leadership

development. At this venue and many others, she has created semi-
nars designed to connect Shakespeare's art to present-day issues
and audiences. Her publications include essays on Shakespeare,
creative teaching, and the liberal arts. She is completing a book, To
Bring Forth a Wonder: Shakespearean Awakenings, *a teach-*
ing memoir and analysis of her transformative encounters with
the plays. Most recently, the Shakespeare Center Los Angeles
named her a recipient of the 2012 Crystal Quill Award, given
to "scholars, patrons, and artists whose work and philanthropy
advances appreciation of the immediacy of Shakespeare's plays."

ॐ

As long as men can breathe or eyes can see,
So long lives this, and this gives life to thee.

—Sonnet 119

Many years ago, I smiled to read a note hastily scribbled on the back of a class evaluation. "Thanks to this class," my student wrote, "Shakespeare has not been a terminal experience."

What she meant to say (I hoped) was that Shakespeare had a future in her life, a presence not terminated at the term's end. Something in our shared experience, and in the learning environment that fostered it, had brought his art alive and might endure. I smiled at her way of saying this, for she implied that Shakespeare had not killed her. That, possibly, like a mortal disease, he could be deadly to anyone exposed to him. I was intrigued by her surprise at his liveliness and her own. How had he come to life for her? How was she enlivened in return?

For many years, as a scholar and teacher in the English Department at Pomona College, a small, private liberal arts institution, I have sought to foster such reciprocal enlivening and to fathom its mystery. Shakespeare leaps from the page, I have learned, when his art becomes something personal, when we inhabit as well as study it, when imagination and identification are wedded to textual scrutiny and contextual scholarship. His plays surely speak as complex artifacts of the Early Modern period, answerable to historical analysis and literary theory. But so too, if we find a way in, are his plays mysteriously animate, catching our lives in the moment and beyond, speaking to what matters to us. They change as we change, ever responsive to our lives now, and to what the years may bring. An intimate encounter in art and education—as in life—transforms everything. Such an encounter, says actor and director Louis Fantasia, happens "where we meet as strangers and hope to be understood."[1] Long ago, in my classroom at Pomona College, I wondered: How can we meet Shakespeare as a stranger—of another time and place—and yet find ways to understand and to be understood?

What follows is a story of an encounter I had with Shakespeare long ago that transformed my understanding and pedagogy. It is also—crucially— a story of how Pomona College fostered such intimacy of knowledge and experience. At home in a small, residential institution steeped in the values and practices of the liberal arts, I found a liberty to experiment and innovate, and my students did too. Our shared creativity was grounded in academic rigor and enriched by breadth of study. We were met with institutional generosity of spirit and support for many years. As a scholar and teacher within this vibrant community of liberal learning, I was free (as the old song goes) to do it my way.

A Story of Origins: Shakespeare on Stage

"You have to love your character," he said. How strange, I remember thinking at the time. *What's love got to do with it?* I wanted to ask, but didn't. Now I wish to reply, nearly a lifetime later, at the close of my career.

He was an actor and a poet, beyond my ken. I was an academic, newly minted and recently hired. He was some older than I, but we were both young Shakespeareans. He dreamed of stardom on stage and had a passion for language and an ear for its music. I sought acclaim as a scholar and teacher, trained well by English Departments in elite institutions who (in those days) taught that Shakespeare was best served by the "theater of the mind." Theater Departments were separate domains, another country. And the rough and tumble of working theaters was a world apart from what literary scholars like me thought and did. Passion? No—we were cool experts, not heated actors or poets. We competed for a place in the vast field of Shakespeare studies by staking claim to specialized territory or theory, say, Shakespeare as history, philosophy, politics, or rhetoric. We had our own way of thinking about Shakespeare, and our own way of writing and speaking about him, a specialty style. Love was not a word we used.

But here I was among actors, indulging a curiosity and seeking adventure in a foreign land: the Ashland, Oregon, Shakespeare Festival, 1978. A call had come from Professor Homer "Murph" Swander, a Shakespearean in the English Department at UC Santa Barbara. Famed for his mane of white hair and manic energy, Murph was legendary too for his innovative "cross-over" endeavors that fused scholarship, teaching, and theater in the classroom and beyond. A full-time faculty member, he was also director of Actors-in-Residence, an international Shakespeare program enlisting the Royal Shakespeare Company in London and selected American theaters, and Theatre in England, a travel-study program for students of all ages. Ebullient and generous, he was notorious too for his proselytizing and recruiting talents. No doubt he had detected in my timorous, bookish ways a convert to be made. And so he targeted me as a candidate for his new summer program in Ashland, grandly called The Shakespearean Renaissance Academy, cosponsored by UC Santa Barbara and Southern Oregon State College.

As enticement, Murph sent along a brochure entitled: "A Festive Campus: Playgoing and Studying at the Institute of Renaissance Studies." The cover photo featured a hunched actor garbed in a period costume of an inky velvet cap and cloak, his neck adorned with a massive gold chain. Caught in an aside to an audience, he emerges from the shadows, his pale face a smirk of malice. He leans on a leg ominously clad in thigh-high, brass-studded, black leather boots. His left hand gestures casually: dark deeds are easy. Sinister and seductive, he invites conspiratorial intimacy. Richard III!

Opening the brochure, I found a pitch for Murph's academy. It was his voice, enthused and unedited.

> A Renaissance retreat in which the way of life and of study will take everyone more completely inside Shakespeare's plays. Taking the plays of the Festivals as the primary subject matter, students will live and dine together in a small dormitory where the atmosphere will move thoughts, conversations, and activities toward Shakespeare's world: the dancing, the games, the music, the paintings, the entertainment, a Renaissance ball and feast, will suggest that world.
>
> Meetings and activities of various kinds, lectures and class discussions; sessions with Festival actors, directors, and designers; sessions of Renaissance music and dance; visits backstage to study the Elizabethan stage; and projects created by individual students in order to pursue special interests.

Here was a new kind of prose—and a new kind of program. Richard III beckoned too. How could I refuse? I had time that summer, and Pomona College offered to support such faculty development. But this opportunity was unique. *Institute* and *academy* had prestige. But a *festive* campus? A Renaissance *retreat*? I had to check it out. I was a snob who secretly yearned to play.

We did play that summer, we happy few, a brave band of scholars and teachers who gathered for Murph's four-week academy in Ashland. In a dorm at Oregon State University, we lived, dined, and talked together.

Our festive "atmosphere" did indeed "move thoughts, conversations, and activities toward Shakespeare's world." That world was manifest in four plays of the season, *The Tempest*, *The Life of Timon of Athens*, *The Taming of the Shrew*, and *The Tragedy of Richard III*, all performed on the Ashland festival's outdoor stage, a looming, half-timbered approximation of an Elizabethan playhouse. It was not a precise historical replica of Shakespeare's Globe, achieved in recent years by the spectacular New Globe Theatre on London's South Bank. But never mind: all those years ago, that rambling festival outdoor stage worked its wonders for me, once so proudly wedded to the "theater of the mind."

A first wonder: *The Taming of the Shrew*. A sparkling production emblazoned an obvious truth: Shakespearean comedy was written to be performed—and performance is revelatory. I had a front-row seat to a show that was visceral and cerebral, a bawdy mélange of the silly and sophisticated, sexy and witty. The play's nod to prevailing convention was undercut by the actors' sly comic irony—a gesture or tone or pause on stage that mocked the powers or prejudices that be. In so doing, this show provoked giddy laughter as well as sober recognition. I had once dismissed *The Taming of the Shrew* as mere slapstick and misogynist rant. On the festival stage, it was something more.

A brilliant husband-and-wife duo, actors Rick Hamilton (Petruchio) and Fredi Olster (Kate), carried the show. They played warring and witty partners who were animated, it seemed, by the savvy of a real-life marriage as well as seasoned theatricality. Their romp on stage was a fast dance of competing power plays, fired by simmering erotic energy. But all that funny business morphed into a closing spectacle of ironic reversal and tender bonding. They began as "players" who perversely overplayed their gender roles, mirroring each other as outrageous caricatures: the Shrieking Shrew, the Bully Tamer. But then, by the fourth act, they got it—and so did the audience, deliciously more clued into the changing game than the characters who watched it on stage.

What Kate and Petruchio got is that the old game served only to isolate and defeat them both. Each saw in the other a cartoon of pride and prejudice. Battle weary, shrew and shrew-tamer alike hungered for something more. Stunned by the dullards around them, awed by the brio of each other's wit and will, suddenly they were smitten by equalizing admiration and desire. Soon this spirited twosome *joined* as partners in a new game. In the end, they performed a stealth action. True to the script, Petruchio—in response to a wager by men on stage—commands Kate to place her hand under his foot, a public display of male dominance and female submission. But this pair subverted the ritual by signaling their private recognition and new bonding. Kate locked eyes with Petruchio while she slowly knelt before him, proffering her hand to his boot. But he bowed down, gently taking her hand. Then he knelt too. Now they were face to face, hand in hand, holding each other in a show-stopping gaze of electrifying intimacy. Only then Petruchio said: "Come on, and kiss me, Kate"—and "Come, Kate, we'll to bed." He didn't crow in mastery; he crooned an entreaty, uttering her name (once a taunt) as a term of endearment. He beckoned her to shared marital bliss, and she happily accepted what was promised: the joy of sex—and the abiding pleasures of mutual valuing and accord, well earned.

The audience roared.

Not everyone would agree with such choices then or now. No one would deny that patriarchy rules in this play, a system oppressive and dangerous to women, even when exceptional individuals (men and women alike) find a way to thrive within it. But this show taught me that provocative choices *could* be made—and made to work as dazzling theater. But how and why (I wondered) had this gifted pair made these choices? What was their interpretive and creative *process*, their progression from "page to stage" (Murph's mantra for the path to enlightenment)?

An answer came from Richard III.

"You have to love your character," he said.

Richard III was Michael Santo, a resident actor in Ashland that summer who offered a workshop for Renaissance Academy scholars and teachers. He promised to reveal how he prepared for his first role as Shakespeare's infamous villain. It was Michael, in full costume and makeup, whose photo adorned the brochure; on stage too he was a menacing, mocking presence, lurching between dark shadows and white light. But on this sunny morning, off stage and unmasked, he chatted genially with academics like me, strangers to his world.

"The tradition is daunting," he began, "mostly terrifying. How to follow Olivier? The bravura style of his deformed and sardonic villain who exults in self-pity to justify evil-doing?" He mimicked Olivier's crooked back and deformed arm, his halting gait, his nasal sneer: *But I, that am rudely stamp'd, and want love's majesty* . . .

"How to find the part and make it your own?" he asked. "You have to find the pulse. And a quickening."

Quickening? A word as strange as love.

"Shakespeare's language is alive," he said. "You begin by reading and rereading aloud, listening for the iambic pentameter, seeking the pulse. You learn to breathe its rhythms, to feel its sound and sense. You make a strange idiom familiar—and revealing: Why does he talk this way? How does he think and feel? Then you'll find your character. And you have to love your character. Not mindlessly. You don't dote. You imagine and inhabit, incorporate and enact. What's hard is not how Shakespeare says it but where he takes us, to places known and unknown within us. Richard's charm, for example. How does ugly get sexy and sly? How does villainy get flaunted, justified—and *fun*? For warped perpetrator and complicit witness alike? And how do we, as actors, perform these dark pleasures? So that an audience, in the mirror we hold up, finds the part too? Seduced and shocked into seeing a reflection there—of who they could be too, of all that is humanly possible? Actors and audiences partner in the quickening. Shakespeare always asks for this, an exchange of imagination that *amends*."

Amend. I was struck by this word too, familiar to me from *A Midsummer Night's Dream*. It is Shakespeare's word for the power of imagination to enhance, improve, or repair. I recalled it in a key exchange in act 5 between Duke Theseus and his bride Hippolyta at their wedding feast. They are watching bumbling amateur actors perform an unwittingly hilarious travesty of the tragic tale of Pyramus and Thisbe. She says, "This is the silliest stuff that ever I heard." But he says: "The best in this kind are but shadows; and the worst are no worse, if imagination amend them." He adds: "If we imagine no worse of them than they of themselves, they may pass for excellent men."

I remembered too that Puck echoes Theseus in his epilogue to the audience. Alone on stage, he speaks in character as Robin, a "shadow" (or immortal spirit) within the play—but he also speaks as the actor playing Robin, also a "shadow" (a trade word for an actor) who gives substance to a playwright's dreams. In both roles, he implores mutual amending, a generosity of exchange between both sides of the stage. *If we shadows have offended, / Think but this, and all is mended. . . . Gentles, do not reprehend. / If you pardon, we will mend. . . . Now to scape the serpent's tongue / We will make amends ere long; . . . Give me your hands, if we be friends, / And Robin shall restore amends*. We seek only to please, he says. Don't hiss in offense (*the serpent's tongue*), but do applaud in approval (*give me your hands*). Here's a handshake too: let's meet as friends, not strangers. We will amend ourselves if you amend us too. We create harmless illusions. You forgive and improve us, granting us reality and excellence, imperfect "shadows" that we may be.

That charged encounter between actor and audience was now happening in a workshop in Ashland. An actor (Michael) and his shadow (Richard) rendered it palpable and intelligible. I was rapt—and soon to be amended.

"Who is my Richard?" Michael asked. Searching the text, he had found a clue. It was hidden in a passage he had read many times, Richard's closing soliloquy in act 1, always played as an aside to the audience. He reminded us that Richard, in every aside, is darkly funny, a wicked tease. Earlier he had gloated, "Plots have I laid, inductions dangerous." But now he gleefully targets his victims, first his brother Clarence, whose death (he hopes) will be mortal to his ailing father, the rightful king. Michael now paused on the last line of the soliloquy, relishing a single phrase: "'Which done, God take King Edward to his mercy, / And *leave the world for me to bustle in.*'"

"There it is," Michael said. "An action verb, a way in." He repeated the lines, slowing the pace, accenting the iambic rhythm of single syllable words, then rolling out the two-syllable verb, the punch line: And *leave the world* for *me*—[pause] [now triumphantly] to **bustle** in.

"Can you hear it?" he asked. "How the beat and pitch capture Richard? His heated ego, his cool malice? The way he evenly paces himself, blithely dismissing God, making his moves, marking his victims—without losing a beat? And the verb 'bustle' has an offhand note of perfect poetry. It rings with a sinister hiss *and* comical fussiness. *So many murders, so little time.* The hassle of endless domestic chores. House-cleaning. In a royal house littered with guilty dupes and fools, a villain's work is never done! That's what I want to capture on stage. A heartless, cheerful evil that operates like a busy housewife, not a limping monster. She clucks as she tidies up a cluttered room, pleased with her industry, never mind her aching back. Richard clucks and kills and preens too, clearing his world of rivals in order to rule it. That's what is horrid about him, and funny, and pathetic too. Evil can be ordinary in its workings, big and small. So can reparation, human and divine. If Richard is heaven's scourge, God sometimes works in banal ways. Richard cleans house, then the House of York falls on him and around him. He dies in battle, crying out not for glory or revenge, but for—a horse. Any old nag will do."

Oh. That's when I got it. I *felt* it: the quickening. His Richard III, and possibly mine too, whether akin to his or not. What mattered was a process of canny discovery and embodiment, informed by shrewd analysis of language, extravagant empathy for a character, and fresh insights into a play's significance. It mattered too that for an actor, this was an urgent, high-stakes endeavor. He took it on as if his life depended on it, and the life of the play. What if mine did too? What if studying and teaching Shakespeare were no longer "academic" exercises? Rather, so to speak, a matter of life and death? An act of do-or-die revival—not only on stage but also in the classroom?

That encounter changed everything for me. *The Tragedy of Richard III* was no longer only an "inferior early work," or mistaken Tudor mythology, or *that* old chestnut again. The play was something else, something wonderful. Language had come to life, piercing in its particulars, ringing with new possibilities. Character had freshly arisen, as from the grave, a visceral, vocal presence. Poetic text, now a playscript, had morphed into a miraculous co-creation, potent for reader, actor, and audience alike. I had a role in this process; my imagination was activated too. It was a paradigm shift, and more—a *coup de foudre.* I fell in love.

Thus was prompted my passion for Shakespeare's living art—and with it, my conviction that such enlivening can happen in a classroom. In a workshop next to a faux Elizabethan playhouse, an actor searching for his part helped me find my part too. It would be to practice what Murph had always preached: *From page to stage*. It begins with "close reading," an exercise I enjoyed as a literary scholar. But an actor's practice, I discovered, has Value Added—the value of an intimate encounter. Such intimacy calls for a special quality of knowledge, awareness, and openness. History and theory have their place; it is crucial to know matters of fact and context. But crucial too is fluency in Shakespeare's poetic idiom, a teeming, supple language (sometimes strange to us) that was written to be spoken and inhabited—and speaking it makes a difference. Equally important is scope of apprehension, a nimble but considered leap from details of language to comprehension of character and play as a whole. Another essential: theater as an *ensemble* art—it is never just about you. But something personal can be found: subjectivity matters too. *Your* imagination can be activated and liberated by the fluidity of a script to be performed. But a home must be found for such co-creative endeavors.

That summer in Ashland, I did learn to play. And, like Hamlet, I learned that *the play's the thing*. I returned to Pomona College, seeking a home for my new vision and mission.

Shakespeare in the Classroom and Beyond

But I had my doubts. There were issues and obstacles.

I resided in the English Department, not the Theater Department. And at that time, our curriculum and major were organized by historical periods—and our classes were often historical surveys. We lectured, led discussions, assigned papers, and required midterm and final exams. My Shakespeare courses followed suit, listed in the catalogue as "Shakespeare's Comedies and Histories" (fall term) and "Shakespeare's Tragedies and Romances" (spring term.) Students had already enrolled, expecting to read many plays, to write many papers, and to take a final exam. Could I incorporate "from page to stage"? I was not formally trained in theater arts, nor did I presume to offer pre-professional training. Students of all majors enrolled in my classes, many of them looking ahead to postgraduate studies and professions in fields spanning the sciences, social sciences, and humanities. I relished their breadth of learning and welcomed their varied interests and aspirations. But would students expecting a general Shakespeare survey to fulfill a graduation requirement in the humanities respond to a new way of experiencing his art—and value it? Would my department and the college approve? Would such a venture "count" in my own advancement? Could I maintain a spirit of play?

The short answer is—yes: I created a new template, and my player-inspired Shakespeare courses were welcomed and accepted. Over the years, they took on a life of their own. They were far from perfect, but they were always a pleasure—and they offered, I believe, new pathways to learning. A highly selective college provided stellar talent: my exceptionally gifted and motivated students made my classes work. And a small, residential college allowed for close association among students, as well as ready access to gatherings at every hour and frequent attendance at arts events on campus, including music, dance, film, and studio arts as well as theater. It was always a treat (and a component of our course that term) when the Theater Department mounted a Shakespeare play. And so we found a home at Pomona College, an institution that has always valued and supported the performing arts—and now encourages college-wide curricular efforts to integrate the arts into every field of study.[2]

My course template was a hybrid of old and new. I respected traditional ways of studying Shakespeare in an academic milieu, in that we paid careful attention to historical and critical contexts, we engaged in informed class discussions, and I assigned and graded essays that called for critical acumen and writing excellence. But I made two significant changes: the course was no longer a survey, and I jettisoned the final exam—substituting for it a class "performance exercise." Assessment was based on student self-evaluations, student evaluations of one another's work, and my own evaluations.

First, we took on fewer plays each term, so as to master the technique of "page to stage" analysis, reading closely for thematic significance, linguistic and psychological detail, and emotional resonance—and always open to many possibilities for interpretation and performance. We were aided in class by British director and actor John Barton's brilliant television series (then on video, now on DVD) and his companion book, *Playing Shakespeare*.[3] Barton offered scintillating workshops with his most promising young Royal Shakespeare Company actors, many of whom have become major stars, including Judi Dench, Ian McKellen, Patrick Stewart, and David Suchet. Such grand talent offered my students the vibrant encounters with Shakespeare I had experienced in Ashland.

Second, in addition to the Barton series, the term's major writing project served to prepare students for their end-of-term performances. I required a lengthy, detailed "page to stage" analysis of a passage each student had chosen to memorize and perform. Every word had to be annotated, aided by commentary in major editions and by Shakespeare dictionaries that spell out archaic and multiple meanings, literary allusions, and metaphorical content. And every detail of verse and style had to be noted and interpreted as clues to enactment. This project, all told, created for each student an individualized promptbook. I sought to facilitate acutely personal investment in a final outcome, the "do or die" endeavor of public performance that revealed all.

Third, my template for the final exercise called for collaboration and competition as keys to success. My classes were often large, enrolling fifty students or more. The first week I passed out a syllabus, indicating six plays to be studied in class, as well as required scholarly readings and suggested resources. And then I announced my choice for their final exercise, say, *Hamlet* or *The Tempest* or *Richard III*, a play we did not discuss in class. It belonged solely to my students. They were required to work independently in small groups in order to perform their play, act by act, at various locations on campus, on a Saturday or Sunday at the end of the term. (The mildness of our Southern California climate permitted outdoor locations all year.)

The rules were these. Each group was randomly chosen: I counted off my students into five groups, each group assigned to an act. Random selection meant luck of the draw; students had to use the talent at hand. They were asked to collaborate on their meeting time and place, their "concept" for their act, their location on campus for performance, and their casting for roles. No "central casting" was allowed; gender, race, appearance, or any other markers of identity were not to count. What counted was each student's willingness to "take another's part," to understand and inhabit the Other, always a leap of empathic, theatrical, and moral imagination. Ensemble work counted too: no solo effort or starring role could carry the show. As a group, they were permitted to cut the script but not to alter Shakespeare's language. And they were not to raid the Theater Department for costumes or props. They had to create their own. Simpler is better, I would say, and ingenuity is best.

Collaboration was the rule within each group, but competition among the five groups sparked excellence. I asked that each group, all term, guard the secret of their creative ideas and campus location from other groups—and from me. At term's end, on our Day of Revels, we gathered in our classroom, eager to be surprised. Each group had worked all term to be the best! Now five groups appeared *en costume* with their props. Each group provided a program signaling the location and casting of their act. Often, visiting parents would join us, along with my colleagues and community friends. With our itinerary in hand, we departed *en masse* to various locales on campus where we were treated to five totally different acts of a single play. That day, every student was a player and an audience. And what they achieved, singly and collectively, was revelatory of Shakespeare and themselves. They had once met as strangers, hoping to understand and to be understood. Now they were joyful celebrants of theatrical encounters, strangers no more.

There were problems with this format, of course. Students found most difficult the problem of time. Untold hours for meeting and rehearsing were called for in the lives of high achievers always struggling to balance academics and extracurricular activities. And collaboration within groups was never easy; students often complained that "getting along" was harder than mastering Shakespeare! Their greatest challenge (and their greatest reward, they said) was to move beyond solo braininess to shared cultivation of theatrical, musical, artistic, and leadership gifts, all of which vastly enriched their performances—and their learning.

I found most difficult the problem of assessment. I labored uneasily to assign individual and group grades. During the performance, I watched closely and took notes, and students did too, when they were the audience. We all filled out standard evaluation forms for individuals and groups, noting the quality of location, concept, and realization—and singling out exceptional work. Most important, I asked each student to write a self-evaluation in narrative form.[4] In it they charted their group process, noting their own contributions and expressing what they had learned. And so I had abundant data for assessment. But the quality of student performances was often so remarkable, and student narratives so original and compelling, that grading them in any conventional way seemed irrelevant, though necessary.

I never got right the "assessment" part of the class, and I never did justice to all that I wished to cover during the term. What I did get right, though, was an exercise that allowed my students to play. In mastering "from page to stage," in performing as well as studying Shakespeare, they learned, grew, and dazzled. To this day, I cherish their pleasure and pride in achievement. And I believe that such knowledge, creativity, and mastery are transferrable powers that will serve my students well in their every life endeavor.

But our revels now are ended—after almost thirty years. As I roam our beautiful Pomona College campus these days, some years after my retirement, every locale holds a memory of the intelligence, heart, and hilarity my students enacted there. A massive sycamore tree on the quad, where Puck once sprawled; the balcony of a dorm, where Juliet answered Romeo's call; a great fountain outside a dining hall, where a ship from Milan sank near Prospero's island; the parapet of the observatory, where Hamlet cried out to his father's ghost; the service entrance behind another dining hall, where among the garbage bins, Isabella visited Claudio in Vienna's prison; the formal conference room in our student center, where students as corporate executives with dueling laptops or as Mafioso thugs in fine suits played out bitter rivalries in Verona or Elsinore or on battlefields of England's War of the Roses.

One term, in our historic hall of music, a spectacularly talented group of students (many in Glee Club or Orchestra) created a musical version of *The Tempest*, act 3. Each character sang, danced, and played a musical instrument. On stage, Prospero (who had composed the score) ruled at his piano, fitfully at work, playing thundering threats and gentle harmonies. Caliban stole the show as she sang her gorgeous aria, *The isle is full of noises, / Sounds, and sweet airs, that give delight and hurt not . . .*

Another term, in a sun-dappled campus courtyard, a student in a motorized wheelchair played his part. Severely disabled in body but not in mind, he gleefully hissed his lines, amplified by his wheelchair's microphone: *But I that am rudely stamped, and want love's majesty . . .* Richard III! Before the performance (he later told me), he wheeled into a circle of his fellow students, joining their customary ritual of summoning collective creative energy. He said, "I felt the pulse."

Postscript: Richard III Again—in the Graveyard and Beyond

On February 4, 2013, I watched online, enthralled, as scientists at the University of Leicester officially announced a wonder. A skeleton unearthed in a Leicester car park, amid the ruins of the Church of Grey Friars, was positively identified as that crook-backed English king, the last of the Plantagenet monarchs, who had been killed by Edmund Tudor at the Battle of Bosworth Field in 1485: Richard III!

A team of archeologists and geneticists, using radio-carbon dating of his bones as well as DNA extracted from his teeth, confirmed the identity of the remains—an identity that was surmised when the skeleton, with its slender stature, pronounced spinal curvature, and weapon-scarred skull and pelvis, first emerged from the earth. Startling photographs of these skeletal remains were followed by genealogical tables of Richard's family descendants over many generations, still bearing his telltale DNA markers. Historians of fifteenth-century England also spoke out, citing laudatory accounts of King Richard by his contemporaries—and highlighting yet again the demonizing bias of Tudor historians (Shakespeare's sources). Richard III, they said, was no monster.

But where, on this occasion, were the Shakespeareans? This unfolding drama was equal to Hamlet in the graveyard! He too watches, enthralled, as gravediggers unearth scattered bones and then a skull. Cradling the skull, he croons his wry and melancholy musings: *Alas, poor Yorick! I knew him, Horatio.* It was my turn to ask a question, provoked by the Leicester find and historical evidence. Poor Richard: Did we, as scholars and actors of Shakespeare, truly *know* him?

To my mind, the discovery of King Richard's remains provides a great teaching moment at a small, residential liberal arts college. If I were still in my classroom at Pomona College, I would seize the opportunity to probe with my students a distinction between the "facts" of science and history and the "truths" of art. I would welcome a visit from my nearby colleagues in science, history, and theater. Together we would talk about the wonder at Leicester, and then we would explore what knowledge means in each of our fields and how it changes over time. Then my students and I would return to Shakespeare's play, newly alert to its historical distortions and fantastical fictions, but still finding in them an artist's dramatic rendering of human realities and timeless insights. We would honor Richard in the script, ever seeking ways to "find the part." Enriched by liberal learning, we might—once again—feel the pulse.

Notes

1. "A book, like a workshop, an accident on the street, or a theatrical performance, is an example of an encounter, where we meet as strangers and hope to be understood." Louis Fantasia, *Instant Shakespeare: A Proven Technique for Actors, Directors, and Teachers* (Chicago: Ivan R. Dee, 2002), 13.

2. For an eloquent essay by the current president of Pomona College, detailing the college's commitment to the arts and a rationale, see David W. Oxtoby, "The Place of the Arts in a Liberal Education," *Publications: Association of American Colleges and Universities*, http://www.aacu.org/publications-research/periodicals/place-arts-liberal-education.

3. John Barton, *Playing Shakespeare* (London and New York: Methuen, 1984).

4. Here is a sampling of portions of student narratives (self and group evaluations) following their performance of *The Tempest*, act 3. I will identify them only by their stage names.

(My notes): Prospero, the composer and pianist, wrote a complex analysis of his musical concepts and included with it a copy of the score and an audio tape. (He began to work on the score before he enrolled in my class.)

Miranda:

I have to say that this experience is one of the most memorable of my college career. Who would have believed that anything close to what we produced was possible. We knew we had the talent and potential to do a musical version of an act and to perform well, but none of us envisioned the special magic of our creation. Words cannot express how much this experience has meant to me. I was a part of something that was special and transcended time. My memories of the performance are all in soft focus, as if Vaseline were smeared on my mind. Time had stopped and removed me from myself. This is the magical part of the project that will remain with me forever.

Caliban (who also served as director of the act):

When we saw a draft of the score, we were blown away! Then we brainstormed to capture the deeper, subtler sides of the text. Then we hit on it, our theme of *artist at work*. Our composer/Prospero was already in control at the piano, so why not extend the metaphor? The music would unify our act better than any imposed theme. The composer as visionary also simplified other technical questions that were bogging us down. Costuming, objects on stage, and set design would be minimal and functional. The music would tell all.

Caliban then assessed her fellow students, her own role, and the project.

Prospero, the composer:

A genius, truly amazing, yet never a sign of ego or temperament.

Ferdinand:

He had more experience in musical theatre than any of us. Once things 'got serious,' his professionalism and sheer acting talent were a model for us all.

Miranda:

She performed beautifully, learning to keep a straight face and to play the sap and schmaltz so that it would be believable. Her interpretation was true to the text, and she worked extremely hard to capture her isolation from 'real world' feminine roles.

Stephano:

She felt out of place from the beginning. She sings, but is not a member of Glee Club. She was very insecure about her part and had to practice three times as much, but once she felt secure, she became a leader. It meant a lot to us all that when we stood in a circle and held hands just before we went on stage, she told us she *knew* she could do it, and do it well. Her artistic growth was the greatest of all.

Trinculo:

She has always been behind her piano. She is a brilliant pianist. But we took away her security blanket and told her to use her other talents. At first she was scared to death, but in the end she was fabulous. It was a big step for her to admit to herself something that the rest of us have known for years, that she is an amazing artist and a natural talent, not just a pianist.

Ariel:

"Bravely" he performed, "A grace it had, devouring!" I couldn't say it better. It was amazing that he kept popping up with talents we hadn't counted on, like playing the recorder.

It is difficult to sum up my own contributions. I kept things organized and was a liaison to the Music Department. I still don't understand Caliban, and I think that was a great weakness. The problem is my song—it is a strange moment of beauty and pathos that doesn't fit the comic or evil portrayals we saw in other groups. I never saw Caliban as naturally evil—capable of evil, but also capable of hearing, seeing, feeling, and expressing a dimension of reality that no one else guessed at.

How can you sum up a moment, a performance? We all made mistakes. Some of us were better in performance than rehearsal; others showed real vocal fatigue. I was on a huge natural high for the next forty-eight hours after performing. My impressions are still as sharp as they were on stage, while our Miranda tells me that hers are in soft focus. It's strange how we respond differently to the special moment in our lives. In spite of the long hours and close contact with people we never seemed to escape, it came off well. The one thing I do know for certain is that this will be one of those magical moments I will remember for the rest of my life.

In Defense of Small

.•——•.

Some Personal Reflections on Teaching Chemistry at a Primarily Undergraduate Institution

Dasan M. Thamattoor

Dasan M. Thamattoor, Professor of Chemistry at Colby College, received a Bachelor of Science (BSc) degree in chemistry from the Government Arts and Science College, Karwar, India, and a Master of Science (MSc) degree in organic chemistry from Karnatak University, Dharwad, India. After beginning his graduate work at Vanderbilt University, he transferred to Princeton University, where he obtained his PhD. He then spent a year at Oberlin College as a Visiting Assistant Professor, followed by another year as a postdoctoral research associate at the University of Notre Dame before joining the Colby Chemistry Department in 1999. At Colby, Thamattoor has taught the first half of the general chemistry sequence, both halves of introductory organic chemistry, advanced courses in reaction mechanisms, and a course for nonmajors. His research interests include reaction mechanisms, reactive intermediates, organic synthesis, photochemistry, and computational chemistry. As a graduate student, Thamattoor received a Teaching Assistant of the Year Award at Vanderbilt University and the Miles Pickering Distinguished Teaching Award at Princeton University. At Colby, he has won the Charles Bassett Teaching Award, which is determined by the vote of graduating seniors. He was recently included in The Princeton Review's list of Best 300 Professors. Thamattoor's research program, which is driven by undergraduates, has been externally funded by agencies such as Research Corporation for Science Advancement, the Petroleum

*Research Fund administered by the American Chemical Society,
and the National Science Foundation. His work with undergraduate co-authors appears regularly as publications in peer-reviewed
journals and presentations at national and international meetings.*

About fifteen years ago, while finishing up graduate work, I was confronted
with the usual predicament. Where do I go from here? What do I do now?
Oddly, these were questions that I had anticipated, and thought answered,
even before I entered graduate school. After stints in a bulk chemical
company and then a pharmaceutical firm in India prior to coming to the
United States to pursue a PhD, it was pretty clear in my mind that I would
return to the chemical industry, hopefully with better prospects secured by
the advanced degree. I could not have been more wrong. Graduate school
grabbed me by the shoulder and turned me toward my true calling: *Teaching.*
As a graduate teaching assistant for the organic chemistry courses, I realized
that not only was I enjoying working with undergraduates, but they were
responding to me in a way that made the effort I put into my work worthwhile and fulfilling. So when the time came to choose from a postdoctoral
position at a major research university, a visiting assistant professor position
at another PhD-granting institution, and a one-year sabbatical replacement
faculty position at Oberlin College in Ohio, I decided to do an experiment.
I chose Oberlin. Having lived most of my life outside the United States,
I had very little idea about what a liberal arts college was, but I knew it
focused on undergraduate education. I figured, based entirely on the positive
experience I had had as a graduate teaching assistant, that I would invest
one year of my life in the Oberlin job if only to see whether teaching at a
small liberal arts college would be a viable career option for me. That was
easily among the better decisions I have made in my life.

I will forever remain grateful to Oberlin for showing me what a thrill
it is to work with undergraduates and clarifying for me that teaching at a
small liberal arts college was a vocation I could gladly pursue for the rest
of my career. Even though I was a temporary hire, Oberlin offered me an
opportunity to conduct research with undergraduates. That worked out very
well as I directed the thesis of my first undergraduate student, Josh Ellison,
and also publish my first independent paper with an undergraduate coauthor,
Abigail Person. I also had terrific colleagues who were outstanding teacher-
scholars, wonderful human beings, and perfect role models. The combined
experiences of classroom teaching and laboratory research at Oberlin were

heady to say the least, and by the time I was near the end of my term, my mind was made up. I wanted a career at a primarily undergraduate institution. Eventually, in 1999, a position opened up at Colby College for a physical organic chemist. I applied, interviewed for the position, and was subsequently hired as an assistant professor of chemistry on a tenure track. I have been there ever since.

When I first started at Colby, I was teaching both semesters of the traditional introductory organic chemistry course (including a laboratory section each semester) and an advanced course that was titled Mechanistic Organic Chemistry. I also taught other courses in subsequent years, such as Chemistry for Citizens, a course directed at students not intending to be science majors, and introductory general chemistry (lecture and laboratory session(s) each term). My classes were typically quite small compared to what one might see at larger universities. For example, my organic chemistry class would usually have about thirty to forty students and the advanced course often enrolled about five to ten students. To me, these small numbers highlight the unique advantage of teaching and learning at a college such as Colby. It is very easy for me to get to know my students quickly and establish a rapport with them, something that would be considerably daunting in a class that has several hundred students enrolled. This aspect of education at a small liberal arts college cannot be overemphasized. Even when I lecture to my larger classes, I have noticed that I am able to incorporate a style and tone that is decidedly conversational and interactive. I can and do, for instance, walk up to a student and address her or him by name, solicit an opinion about a mechanistic issue, invite a volunteer to come forward and write on the blackboard, poll the class by a show of hands to get a sense of its understanding of a concept, and generally create a learning atmosphere that is friendly, nurturing, and yet rigorous. I try to teach chemistry as a true liberal arts discipline, a respectable and worthwhile intellectual pursuit that fosters lifelong learning skills. At every opportunity I try to get my students to see a beautiful experiment with the same admiration and awe that they might accord an exquisite work of art. As I grade my own exams, quizzes, and tests, I am also in a position to easily identify students who might be struggling and formulate, with them, a plan to help them get more out of my courses (e.g., assign tutors, arrange small group meetings, help with problem sets, offer extra office hours, etc.). Students are not allowed to simply "fall through the cracks." Perhaps the most rewarding aspect of such an atmosphere is that it allows the students to enter into a conversation with me about what I am trying to teach them. They are free to ask, reason, and, if need be, argue with me as they try to grasp the material. The ultimate result is the establishment of an environment that is particularly favorable to student inquiry and learning. It is hard for me to imagine creating an equivalent atmosphere in the massive lecture sections that often characterize introductory/service courses at larger research universities. I have seen a colleague from a large school shake his head wistfully when I told him about my teaching experiences many years ago. He said he has to collect identification from his students before handing out their exams to make sure they were really in his class. His classes are so big that he would not be able to even recognize many of his students if he were to run into them outside of class. One might ask, as I am sure he has, "How can this be a model for a good educational system?" Quite simply, it is not. As most introductory chemistry courses also include laboratory components, the enrollment pressures add another dimension. When laboratory sections get overcrowded, all kinds of problems arise. First, there is the issue of safety. With large numbers of inexperienced students trying to learn experimental chemistry in a teaching laboratory comes the issue of designing and implementing experiments that are safe, cost effective, pedagogically valuable, and manageable for graduate students and/or postdocs who often serve as laboratory teaching assistants at larger institutions. Another issue is one of access to instrumentation. If one of the goals of the teaching laboratory is to provide students with hands-on experience with sophisticated, research-grade equipment used by practicing chemists (e.g., a nuclear magnetic resonance spectrometer and gas or liquid chromatograph/mass spectrometer), it is virtually impossible to achieve that objective when several hundred students have to wait their turn to use the instrument. In practice, these limitations frequently lead to cookbook-type exercises that are "guaranteed" to work and do little to capture the true essence of chemistry. Worse, it leaves the students ill prepared to undertake future research and can also turn them off to the science. I submit that small liberal arts colleges, with their much lower course enrollments, are in a vastly better position to afford students a laboratory experience that captures the joy of doing science and, at the same time, effectively prepares them for a professional career in the field. It is often the case that a faculty member (or specifically trained staff) is in charge of laboratory instruction and has firsthand knowledge of the experimental assignments. With the smaller section size comes more personalized instruction, closer supervision, better access to instrumentation, and the ability to implement pedagogical experiments with a research flavor.

Acknowledging the importance of active and cooperative learning, we have involved undergraduates in research-like activities in the introductory organic chemistry course. Indeed, there is ample testimony in the chemical education literature attesting to the success of such an approach in sustaining student excitement and improving learning.[1] In the present model at Colby, students are offered three loosely defined research projects, chosen by the course instructor, at the beginning of the second semester of the two-semester organic chemistry sequence. They then work in self-selected groups of two or three and identify the project they want to undertake. Students may also choose projects of their own as long as they consult with the instructor and obtain preapproval. The criteria for preapproval of student-initiated projects are the same as the ones applied by the instructor to his or her own choices, namely, the proposed activity must be safe, have appropriate academic rigor, have a realistic chance of providing meaningful results in the four weeks allotted to the project, use available equipment, and be reasonably cost effective. Occasionally, some students do propose their own projects and obtain preapproval.

The next step for students is to learn as much as possible about the project by doing a thorough literature search. To facilitate this process, the instructor involves the science librarian for support on literature searching with the search engine SciFinder Scholar.[2] After perusing the literature, each group is expected to devise a reasonable research plan and articulate it in the form of a written research proposal. The proposal consists of a brief introduction, an experimental approach including safety considerations, a list of required equipment and chemicals (with CAS registry numbers, prices, and vendors), a section of proposed computational studies to complement the wet chemistry, and a complete bibliography. These proposals, which are usually due about four weeks following the project announcement, are collected, graded, and returned to the students with comments and suggestions. Each group is expected to respond to the instructor's remarks before undertaking the project.

Finally, the groups carry out the project toward the end of the semester over a period of four weeks. In the fifth week, they submit a comprehensive written report that includes a complete description of their experimental observations, results, and discussions. Surely the students have "good days" and "bad days" in the course of carrying out the project, but they consistently give this research-like experience rave reviews in the evaluations.

As a bonus, these projects have led the students and myself in other interesting and productive directions. For example, in the spring of 2000 a few students undertook the synthesis of the epoxide of ethyl *trans*-ß-methylcinnamate, a strawberry flavoring agent, by two different routes. The project was so successful that it was adapted as a pedagogical experiment the following year to illustrate epoxidation in the organic chemistry laboratory. Subsequently, the experiment was written up with undergraduate coauthors and published.[3]

All of this, of course, was made possible by having laboratory sections with fewer students as is often the case with small liberal arts colleges. Such an approach would be simply too unwieldy, and prohibitively expensive, in courses with large enrollments.

In my advanced organic course the enrollment is even smaller and the students who are in it are often those who have performed strongly in the introductory classes. It is a joy to teach this class because with the small number of students many different pedagogical approaches become possible. Although I have often taught this course in a lecture-discussion hybrid format, I have been able to include such advanced topics as laser flash photolysis, atomic carbon chemistry, and x-ray crystal structure solution. The course has no formal text. Instead, I assign original research articles from the primary literature and expect the students to read them and come prepared to discuss the material in class. I often choose topics that are controversial in the field. In his 2007 George C. Pimentel Award address, Professor A. Truman Schwartz makes the following observation: "We do our students a great disservice by protecting them from the controversies in our discipline. If chemistry were as bereft of ambiguity as it is sometimes taught to be, no one with more than half a wit would ever become a chemist."[4]

Too often our students are hesitant to question what they read, especially if it is something published in a reputable scientific journal. By picking groups of articles that offer conflicting views, and showing how sometimes even good scientists make mistakes, I have learned that it is possible to persuade students to reflect more critically on their reading assignments.

Another important aspect of chemistry at a small liberal arts college is undergraduate research. What is it? Why should we do it? How should we do it? Is it important? The American Chemical Society's Committee on Professional Training has formulated formal answers to these questions,[5] but here I provide some personal observations.

Although teaching is the primary mission of a liberal arts college such as Colby, I believe that having an active research program that engages undergraduates is absolutely essential to its intellectual life and success. I fully subscribe to the premise that it is possible to do first-rate research entirely with undergraduates. Such activities develop critical thinking and provide students with the necessary skill sets to be successful in their post-college careers. It is also my sense that achieving excellence in teaching and research are not mutually exclusive goals, and research can play a powerful role as a pedagogical tool. By grappling with real problems framed as research projects, and personally experiencing the frustrations and triumphs of such an activity, a student will likely learn more about the field than by any other means. There are also unique teaching and learning opportunities that stem directly out of faculty-student interactions in the course of carrying out research projects. Professor Jerry Mohrig captures the essence of these interactions in his review of the Research Corporation publication *Academic Excellence*: "In my opinion, there is nothing nearly so powerful in teaching organic chemistry as the conversations that can occur between teachers and students when neither know the answers to the question being addressed, but both care deeply about seeking them out."[6]

Well said! It is often the case that undergraduates seem to think that I, as a professor, already know the answers to questions that they are starting to address. While there might be an element of truth to that in a classroom lecture setting, it is simply not the case while conducting original research. I suspect that it sometimes startles my students a little when I say, for example, "Gee! I am not so sure I understand this reaction" or "I don't really know what this spectrum is telling us." I can almost hear the wheels in their head turning as they wonder internally, "But you are the professor. You should know." In the long run, though, they recognize that I too am learning with them, and once they get comfortable with that idea they often tend to drop their inhibitions and engage with me as full partners in the research enterprise. Indeed, some of my proudest moments as a faculty have come when students walk into my office, excited about a new idea that they want to try and argue with me the merits of their case. They usually get to try out their plan, and the thrill that they (and I) experience when it works is what makes this undertaking worthwhile. Even when things don't work as anticipated, the students appreciate the opportunity to try something of their own and inevitably learn important lessons from the process.

To be sure, there are challenges in conducting undergraduate research. By the very nature of where they are in their careers, the students are short on experience. This, to me, precludes research projects that involve especially dangerous chemicals and reactions. Furthermore, the students also have a fragmented time schedule during the school year as they try to squeeze in research with classes, athletics, music recitals, student organization commitments, and various other extracurricular activities. At Colby, the only times of the year that students can devote to full-time research is during the summer months (when classes are not in session) and during the one-month winter term known as JanPlan. Yet I understand the wisdom of Professor Michael Doyle, a well-known champion for undergraduate research, who had the following sage observation in an email that he sent me recently: "The guiding principles that directed me were to always remember that research is a full-time engagement, not just something for the summer, and I always trusted in the observations made by my students."

Given these particular constraints, it is clear that undergraduate research projects ought to be designed with special care. They should address important scientific issues but also be safe, have a high "education content," and match the skill levels of the students. Developing meaningful research projects that meet these feasibility criteria is no small task. In our research laboratory, we try to develop research projects that specifically teach students to design and set up experiments; synthesize, purify, and analyze compounds; use research-grade instrumentation; become proficient in modern computational methods; retrieve information from the chemical literature; interpret results; work both independently and collaboratively with other scientists; write reports; give oral presentations; and publish their work in peer-reviewed journals. An especially important aspect of my research program is to help students realize their maximum potential in a friendly, supportive, and nurturing atmosphere.

Another significant challenge to creating and sustaining a vibrant and productive undergraduate program is the ever-present issue of funding, be it for personal research projects or for acquiring essential research-grade instrumentation. Mercifully, funding agencies such as the National Science Foundation (NSF), Research Corporation, and the Petroleum Research Fund administered by the American Chemical Society, among others, have been staunch supporters of undergraduate research, and I would be remiss if I did not gratefully acknowledge the fact that our laboratory has benefited from their generosity since the time I joined the Colby faculty. Over the past fifteen years, sixty bright and capable undergraduates have benefited from these external funds and participated in a variety of research projects. It truly has been a privilege to work with these students, and I have come to greatly appreciate the value of their enthusiasm, talent, and insights in the course of carrying out research work. More than a third of the students went on to complete thesis work to earn honors in chemistry. Many of the students have gone on to some of the top graduate and professional schools in the country. Others have found employment in private- and public-sector organizations.

The productivity of a research program, as measured by peer-reviewed publications and conference presentations, is an important indicator of its effectiveness. Although chemistry faculty at a place such as Colby cannot, and probably should not, seek to match the quantitative output of those working at larger research-oriented universities, it is entirely reasonable to expect a steady rate of publications and presentations from them. According to data gathered by the Research Corporation for Science Advancement, the average publication rate for faculty at liberal arts colleges is 0.6 publications per faculty per year. A newer survey of fifty-five liberal arts colleges shows the average rate for the most recently surveyed decade, 1996 to 2005, as 0.56 per faculty per year. These numbers may seem rather modest to those unfamiliar with the special circumstances of working with undergraduates, but in reality the pedagogical value of training students to do research is priceless.

We have been also fortunate to find other ways of integrating research and education. For instance, one summer a Colby undergraduate, Traci Speed '03, and I, were engaged in a research project aimed at the synthesis of two naturally occurring marine metabolites, Montiporynes A and B, that were reported to possess in vitro anticancer activity against human tumor cells.[7] The final step in the synthetic protocol, which we published together as a research paper, was a well-known reaction (the Wittig reaction) that students encounter in the second-semester organic chemistry course.[8] It was soon realized that the procedure might actually serve as a useful experiment to illustrate the Wittig reaction in the organic teaching laboratory. A survey of the chemical education literature revealed that the key ingredients, despite their ready commercial availability, low cost, and reasonable stability, have not been used in a teaching context. Accordingly, a new in-house Wittig reaction for the teaching laboratory was developed based on Traci's work and implemented with great success. A paper describing this experiment, with Traci as the lead author, has been published in the *Journal of Chemical Education*.[9] As a more recent example, another undergraduate, Jessica Levasseur '09, and I, recently published the synthesis of cassiferaldehyde, a biologically active material found in the twigs of certain cinnamon species,[10] and six of its analogs.[11] Again, some of the synthetic steps had considerable pedagogical value and were incorporated into the organic chemistry teaching laboratory.

Other outreach initiatives that serve the local community have become possible thanks to NSF funding. For example, I realized that a positive pre-college experience in mathematics and science, along with timely counseling about careers and opportunities in these areas, can play an important role in persuading high school students to consider becoming majors in STEM disciplines when they enroll in college. One effective way of promoting interest in science among high school students is to provide them with opportunities to participate in the scientific enterprise. Recognizing the importance of high school science education, our laboratory has hosted thirty-five high school students so far over the summer months and involved them in paid collaborative research activities. My students and I have served as mentors to the high schoolers, shared with them the excitement of conducting scientific research, and assisted them through their journey of learning and discovery. The hope was that the students would become excited about STEM disciplines and higher education and go on to productive careers beyond high school. This program has been an unqualified success and, thanks to NSF support, is now entering its twelfth year. Indeed, on two separate occasions in the past, the overwhelmingly positive student response prompted me to request, and obtain, supplemental funds from the NSF to expand these research opportunities to additional students. On occasion, I have also entered into a partnership with the Maine Research Internships for Teachers and Students (MERITS) program to identify talented high school students in the area and share some of the costs. The high school students, who came

from rural Maine and economically disadvantaged backgrounds, participated
in research over the summer months. They worked side by side with Colby
undergraduates and were full partners in the scientific enterprise. They were
somewhat tentative at the beginning but quickly learned the rudimenta-
ry techniques of running reactions, applying chromatographic techniques
to purifying compounds, and using instruments. They also learned to use
sophisticated computer programs for modeling, drawing chemical structures,
and searching the literature. Importantly, the excitement and enthusiasm
that the participants showed highlighted the value of such summer activities in cultivating an interest in science among high school students. In
my experience, the undergraduate students who mentor their high school
wards are conscientious about their responsibilities and also seem to benefit
from their role as teachers. I should also mention that through NSF funding
we have been able to support educational activities at the elementary and
middle school levels as well, in partnership with the teachers.

In closing, I suggest that the word "small" preceding liberal arts colleges is perhaps the most critical ingredient to the unique and high-quality
undergraduate education provided by such institutions. One of the major
reasons why students choose to go to a place such as Colby or Oberlin is the
close personal attention they expect to receive from their professors. Thus
the relationships that faculty cultivate with their students can enrich the
lives of both and are an important part of the overall educational experience offered by the institution. I have therefore made it a point to get to
know my students well and also to let them get to know me. I actively seek
out or create opportunities where such relationships can be fostered in a
friendly yet professional way. These include hosting students for dinners at
my home; taking trips with them to the museum, bowling alley, restaurants,
and ball games; and attending student events such as concerts, plays, and
recitals. As it turned out, during my first five years at Colby, I served as a
faculty-in-residence, which meant that my family and I lived among students in dormitory apartments. In that capacity, we worked closely with the
residence hall staff and the Dean of Students Office to provide educational,
cultural, and social activities for students. I also got to learn more about
student life outside of the classroom, and what I learned helped me forge
closer ties with the students.

I am well aware of the fact that many families make enormous sacri-
fices so that their kids can go to college. Thus, it is very important to me that
the students who end up in my classrooms and laboratories get the absolute
best instruction that I can offer them. I believe that if I have been able to
achieve that, even in some small measure (excuse the pun), it is because of
the personal relationships and rapport I have built with my students over the

years. These close relationships not only continue to facilitate the teaching/ learning process but also forge lifelong friendships. Watching my students develop intellectually continues to be the most rewarding aspect of my work as an educator. The small number of students I typically work with in my classrooms and laboratories is precisely what affords such a deeply personal and fulfilling experience—call that the chemistry of a small college.

Notes

1. See, for example, M. R. Dintzner, J. J. Maresh, C. R. Kinzie, A. F. Arena, and T. Speltz, *Journal of Chemical Education* 89 (2012): 265; C. B. Russell, A. K. Bentley, D. J. Wink, G. C. Weaver, *Chemical Educator* 14 (2009): 55; N. E. Carpenter and T. M. Pappenfus, *Journal of Chemical Education* 86 (2009): 940; G. Horowitz, *Journal of Chemical Education* 84 (2007): 346; T. A. Newton, H. J. Tracy, and C. Prudente, *Journal of Chemical Education* 83 (2006): 1844; K. J. Graham, C. P. Schaller, B. J. Johnson, and J. B. Klassen, *Chemical Educator* 7 (2002): 376; and D. S. Davis, R. J. Hargrove, and J. D. Hugdahl, *Journal of Chemical Education* 76 (1999): 1127.

2. See, for example, I. J. Rosenstein, *Journal of Chemical Education* 82 (2005): 652; S. A. O.Reilly, A. M. Wilson, and B. Howes, *Journal of Chemical Education* 79 (2002): 524; and D. D. Ridley, *Journal of Chemical Education* 78 (2001): 557and 559.

3. G. J. Pageau, R. Mabaera, K. M. Kosuda, T. A. Sebelius, A. H. Ghaffari, K. A. Kearns, J. P. McIntyre, T. M. Beachy, and D. M. Thamattoor, *Journal of Chemical Education* 79 (2002): 96.

4. A. T. Schwartz, *Journal of Chemical Education* 84 (2007): 1750.

5. See T. J. Wenzel, C. K. Larive, and K. A. Frederick, *Journal of Chemical Education* 89 (2012): 7.

6. J. Mohrig, *Journal of Chemical Education* 79 (2002): 165.

7. B. H. Bae, K. S. Im, W. C. Choi, J. Hong, C.-O. Lee, J. S. Choi, B. W. Son, J.-I. Song, and J. H. Jung, *Journal of Natural Products* 63 (2000): 1511.

8. T. J. Speed and D. M. Thamattoor, *Tetrahedron Letters* 43 (2002): 367.

9. T. J. Speed, J. P. McIntyre and D. M. Thamattoor, *Journal of Chemical Education* 81 (2004): 1355.

10. T. M. Ngoc, I. S. Lee, D. T. Ha, H. J. Kim, B. S. Min, K. H. Bae, *Journal of Natural Products* 72 (2009): 1205.

11. J. L. Levasseur and D. M. Thamattoor, *Synthetic Communications* 42 (2012): 292.

An Invitation to Get Lost

The Right Kind of Place for Liberal Learning

Nicholas Buccola

Nicholas Buccola is Associate Professor of Political Science and the Founding Director of the Frederick Douglass Forum on Law, Rights, and Justice at Linfield College. He is the recipient of Samuel H. Graf Faculty Achievement Award and Allen and Pat Kelley Faculty Scholar Award at Linfield as well as numerous teaching awards at the University of Southern California. He is the author of The Political Thought of Frederick Douglass, *and his essays have been published in scholarly journals including* The Review of Politics *and* The Journal of Social Philosophy, *as well as popular outlets including* Salon, Dissent, *and* The Claremont Review of Books.

ঌ

Introduction

It's finals week. In colleges and universities across the country, students are arriving in classrooms with bluebooks in hand and sitting in desks aligned in neat rows (in the smaller classes) or desks fixed in the ground in a large auditorium (in the larger classes). In the moments before the final exam begins, the scene will be familiar. We will see students taking swigs of energy drinks and looking through their notes one last time. We will hear students sighing and chatting nervously. We will feel a sense of anxiety permeating the room. Soon the professor and/or a small brigade of teaching assistants will arrive with the exams. Once the exams are distributed, two hours of vigorous writing will commence.

If you were to wander into the space reserved for the "final exam" of the Great Political Thinkers course I teach every semester at Linfield College, you would find a different scene. You will not see any desks or bluebooks or hear much sighing, but there will be some chatting and, of course, there will be energy drinks. What you will see is a large open space—I never use a conventional classroom for my "final exam" session—with fifteen to twenty chairs arranged in a circle. There may be one table in the room, but on it you will not see any exams; just some donuts and coffee. For the next two hours, the students of Great Political Thinkers will be engaging in a conversation about fundamental questions of political philosophy. I call this conversation the Lost Scenario. The Lost Scenario is difficult to "assess"—and to a passerby it may appear that the students are having too much fun to be learning anything—but semester after semester it provides me with a strong sense that my students and I are participating in a wonderful thing called liberal education.

Many folks wiser than me have articulated profound explanations of the meaning and value of liberal education. Rather than offering another abstract defense of the liberal arts, my aim in this essay is to describe one thing I do that I believe constitutes a contribution to the liberal education of my students. In order to do so, I rely on the philosopher Michael Oakeshott's definition of liberal learning as "learning to respond to the invitations of the great intellectual adventures in which human beings have come to display their various understandings—of the world and of themselves."[1] After describing the Lost Scenario and showing how it is related to what Oakeshott calls liberal learning, I conclude with some arguments about why I think the small, residential liberal arts college is the best kind of place for this sort of learning to occur.

An Invitation to Get Lost

The Lost Scenario is the culminating event in a course I teach called Great Political Thinkers (GPT). GPT is an introductory course in political theory. The fifteen to twenty students typically enrolled in the course tend to be there for one of three major reasons: some are enrolled to fulfill a requirement in the Political Science major, others are enrolled to fulfill the "Ultimate Questions" distributional requirement in our general education program (the Linfield Curriculum), and some are there because they are intrigued enough by the topic that they have registered to take the course for elective credit. GPT is a fairly typical "great books" in the Western political tradition sort of course. We are a small department (three tenure-track lines), so we offer introduction to political theory in a semester instead of a year-long sequence. As a result, it is nowhere near comprehensive. In a usual GPT course, I teach Plato's *Republic*, Machiavelli's *Prince*, excerpts from Hobbes's *Leviathan*, Locke's "Letter Concerning Toleration" and the *Second Treatise*, Rousseau's *Discourse on Inequality* and *Social Contract*, Mill's *On Liberty*, and we conclude with excerpts from Marx's *Economic and Philosophic Manuscripts* and *Communist Manifesto*. It is an insane whirlwind tour through some important voices in the Western political tradition. Due to the fact that we must move at a steady clip (Plato usually gets about eight hundred minutes; Machiavelli gets about three hundred minutes; Hobbes gets about three hundred minutes; Locke gets about four hundred minutes; Rousseau gets about four hundred minutes; Mill gets about three hundred minutes; and Marx gets about three hundred minutes), my goals in the course are, in a sense, fairly modest. I hope my students get a sense of the ultimate questions that occupied the mind of each great political thinker we read, how each thinker answered those questions, and what we (as readers) think of both the questions asked and the answers given.

The typical class session is devoted to conversation; there is very little formal lecturing beyond a few introductory remarks on each thinker. Our conversations take place both in small group (three or four students) and large group (the whole class) formats. I see my role as a facilitator and (when necessary) a provocateur in these conversations. Our topics of conversation are generated in part by me (because there are a few topics we must, in good conscience, discuss with each of these thinkers) and in part by the students (a small group will arrive each session with discussion questions they have prepared based on the reading). Occasionally, the conversation will be more structured. Several times throughout the semester, for example, students participate in debates in which they argue for or against a position held by a thinker we have read. At the conclusion of the formal debate, a class-wide conversation begins about what has been said. In other words, the debate continues and the debaters are called to account for undefended claims and hyperbolic statements. My primary "agenda" in all of these conversations is to encourage students to take each great political thinker seriously and to attempt—to the greatest extent possible—to understand why each thinker was preoccupied with a *particular* set of questions and why he gave the *particular* answers he gave. As we work our way through these "particulars," I also try to encourage students to keep an eye out for *universals*. Is there something "ultimate" or "universal" about these questions and answers? In sum, the aim of Great Political Thinkers is to invite students to enter into a conversation with each author we read and to contribute to a conversation about the major questions and answers at the core of each text. This last point is worthy of extra emphasis. Each and every one of my students is encouraged to engage with the major questions and answers at the core of every text, and each of my students has the opportunity to contribute to our conversations about the texts.

With all of these wonderful conversations during our class sessions, it just would not seem right to end the semester with a written final exam. In place of an exam, I host the *Lost* Scenario. You will not be surprised to learn that the name—and the initial inspiration for this activity—came from the hit ABC television series that aired from 2004 to 2010. The show, for the uninitiated, is about the adventures of passengers on a plane that crash lands on a mysterious island. In the GPT version of *Lost*, a plane crashes on an isolated island and Plato, Machiavelli, Hobbes, Locke, Rousseau, Mill, and Marx are among the surviving passengers. Prior to the scenario, students sign up to teams of three or four. Each team has the task of "embodying" the ideas of a particular great political thinker during the scenario. According to the basic ground rules of the scenario, the students are asked to imagine that the survivors of the crash realize they are unlikely to be saved and decide to assemble to discuss how they should organize themselves politically. Each great political thinker group has five to seven minutes to make a pitch on behalf of the principles of political morality that ought to guide the community. How will the members of the community make decisions? By what principles will resources be allocated? How should individuals treat one another? How will conflicts be resolved? By only giving each group five to seven minutes, I am hoping to encourage the groups to get to the core of what really matters to the thinker in question. The only major rule I establish is that each group must make arguments rather than proposing to, say, whittle bamboo into spears and force the others on the island to accept certain principles of political morality.

The real fun begins after the short speeches from each group. At that point, the groups are invited to "mingle" to discuss how they might be able to forge alliances based on the principles they have defended. Whose comments caught Plato's ear? Do Locke and Mill really have that much in common? Can Rousseau and Marx agree upon how collective decisions should be made in the future? Without exception, the mingling period is pure joy. The students proceed to persuade one another, argue with one another, challenge one another, and intervene in conversations they find unreasonable—in sum, they engage in a serious, but playful, conversation about big ideas. Picture the scene: to your left, you will see students from the Rousseau group talking with students from the Plato group about how future generations should be educated on the island. Straight ahead, you will see students from the Locke group chatting with students from the Mill group about the relationship between private ownership and freedom. To your right, you will see students from the Machiavelli group scheming with students from the Hobbes group to come up with ways a leader can consolidate power.

Every time I have hosted the *Lost* Scenario, the conversations have flowed remarkably well and *every* student has been engaged in the activity. Things usually go so well, in fact, I have to intervene (I hang back during the scenario, watching my students argue about ultimate questions) to stop the conversations so we can move to the next phase of the activity. It almost always seems that if I did not intervene, the conversations would carry on for another few hours (or at least until we ran out of donuts and coffee)!

When we are down to about twenty minutes left in the "final exam" period, we reconvene as a large group to discuss (and argue about) the alliances that have been formed. A group of students might have to explain, for example, how each of their teams had to compromise some of their beliefs to join with others. Members of an alliance might offer an explanation of what a society governed by a mix of Platonic and Hobbesian principles might look like. Students on the Rousseau team might offer an explanation of why they just couldn't in good conscience join the Locke-Mill alliance. All the while, students defending these views face questions and challenges from their classmates.

On some occasions, these discussions move in a different direction: some students question the assumptions built into the entire scenario. By pretending that our political arrangements are the product of rational argument (instead of brute force), I might be establishing a scenario that is too far removed from politics as it is really practiced. Political arrangements, a student might say, are often based on who has the most might and not who has the right arguments. With that idea on the table, the entire class can engage in a discussion of this question—a question that strikes at the very foundation of political philosophy—and, on some happy occasions, a student will recall our conversations from the second meeting of the semester when Socrates had his conversation with Thrasymachus in book 1 of *The Republic*.

On other occasions, students challenge the assumption that we would want to be guided by the ideas of *any* of the great political thinkers if we found ourselves in the position of the passengers on the plane. If we are going to have a really meaningful discussion of political morality, a student asked last year, should we not try to liberate ourselves from the ideas of the great political thinkers (and not bind ourselves to their ideas in these teams)? This challenge can lead to a great discussion of the value of "great books" as resources to guide our political lives. Might we be better off if we did not feel so wedded to the ideas contained in those books? Would not the conversations during the scenario be even more interesting if students were representing their own views rather than interpretations of some long-dead philosopher?

Another interesting discussion we have had on a number of occasions has to do with the nature of compromise and what constitutes "success" in the scenario. "I am confused about the point of this exercise," a student has said at the conclusion of the mingling. "Who did the 'right' thing—my Locke team, which reached a rational, coherent alliance with the Mill team, or that weird Hobbes-Rousseau-Marx alliance over there? I mean, come on, didn't each of them 'give up' way too much to form that alliance?" This question leads to an interesting discussion about the tensions between principles we hold in the abstract and the concrete realities of political life.

Students occasionally offer questions and comments that interrogate other assumptions built into the foundations of this exercise. What does the "starting over" premise of the scenario veil about real political decision making? Are the passengers operating in circumstances of relative material abundance? Are the passengers under any real threat from anyone or anything already on the island? How will the absence of advanced technology change the way the passengers deliberate about politics?

I absolutely adore these sorts of meta-discussions that often occur at the conclusion of the mingling period of the *Lost* Scenario. It is wonderful to see students—mostly freshmen and sophomores—asking and answering ultimate questions about politics and—love them or hate them—drawing on the ideas of great political thinkers to do so. My students have joined a great conversation about matters of fundamental importance. At the conclusion of the *Lost* Scenario, there are no winners or losers and we may not have gotten any closer to ultimate answers to the ultimate questions we have been asking, but semester after semester, I conclude (and I am convinced most of my students do as well) that the scenario was a profound success.

The *Lost* Scenario as an Occasion for Liberal Learning

The *Lost* Scenario is, in my estimation, what Oakeshott would call an "occasion" for "liberal learning."[2] Liberal learning is, to again borrow his wonderful definition, "learning to respond to the invitations of the great intellectual adventures in which human beings have come to display their various understandings—of the world and of themselves."[3] In Great Political Thinkers, my students and I devote several weeks to engaging with the "great intellectual adventures" of Plato, Machiavelli, Hobbes, Locke, Rousseau, Mill, and Marx. Like Oakeshott, I believe these particular intellectual adventures are worthy of our attention not because, taken together, they amount to "a doctrine or a set of consistent teachings about human life," but rather because they provide the students with several "languages of understanding"—several "voices"—that are often in profound disagreement with one another.[4] When my students are engaged with these voices throughout the semester and when they attempt to give life to these voices in the *Lost* Scenario, they are participating in a conversation. In Oakeshott's words, a conversation is "an endless unrehearsed intellectual adventure in which, in imagination, we enter into a variety of modes of understanding the world and ourselves and are not disconcerted by the differences or dismayed by the inconclusiveness of it all."[5] There is little question that by the end of the *Lost* Scenario there is a sense of inconclusiveness. Rather than lamenting this fact, I hope my students draw lessons from it. After all, as Oakeshott reminds us, the "pursuit of learning is not a race in which competitors jockey for the best place . . . it is a conversation," and conversation "is not an enterprise designed to yield an extrinsic profit" and it is not "a contest where the winner gets a prize."[6] During the *Lost* Scenario, my students are engaged in a conversation about several important intellectual adventures in the realm of political philosophy. They are engaged in liberal learning.

Why is this sort of conversation worthwhile? Again, rather than reinvent the wheel, I rely on Oakeshott to help me answer that question. Liberal education—the reflective engagement with fundamental questions about ourselves and the world—is worthwhile because it is essential to our dignity as human beings. The forms of liberation aimed at by liberal education—from "the distracting business of satisfying contingent wants," from "the here and now of current engagements," and from "the tyrannical course of irreparable events"—have the potential to provide us with the freedom to lead more dignified lives.[7] Although Oakeshott was careful to distance himself from overly moralistic declarations, he did make clear that the more "intelligent form of consciousness" made possible by a liberal education is related to the sense of freedom and responsibility that makes a more meaningful human life possible.[8] "Education," he wrote, "is not learning to do *this* or *that* more proficiently; it is acquiring in some measure an understanding of the human condition in which the 'fact of life' is continuously illuminated by a 'quality of life.' It is learning how to be at once an autonomous and a civilized subscriber to human life."[9] Liberal education is rooted in the proposition that "there is something more important" than technical or vocational training. While these things may provide us with the knowledge and skills to make and acquire what we want, a life concerned with only such matters would be an impoverished one.[10] Liberal education reminds us that it "is never enough to say of a human want: 'I know how to satisfy it and I have the power to do so.' There is always something else to consider."[11] When my students are conversing about the great books of the Western political tradition, they are participating in something that is non-vocational and non-utilitarian. While we are lost in conversation in that room, we are all learning something significant because we are free from our usual preoccupation with our contingent wants and our immediate desires. We are participating in a meaningful conversation about what it means to be a human being in community with others.

The Best Kind of College for Liberal Learning

What kind of place is most conducive to the sort of liberal learning I believe manifests itself in Great Political Thinkers and culminates in the *Lost* Scenario? First, such learning is only possible in a place that protects and promotes opportunities for students to take courses in the liberal arts. This protection and promotion can take a variety of forms ranging from a prescribed curriculum in the liberal arts to a set of distributional requirements that will track students into a number of liberal arts courses. At institutions (like mine) where there are large pre-professional programs, the strength of the liberal arts depends upon going beyond just maintaining a loose system of distributional requirements. In addition, there must be a firm commitment on the part of faculty, students, administrators, trustees, and alumni to protect and promote the liberal arts. This support must go beyond mere rhetoric to real institutional support. In other words, while we must constantly remind anyone who will listen why the liberal arts core matters, we must also institutionalize mechanisms to protect and promote a strong liberal arts culture on campus.[12]

Second, an occasion for liberal learning like that presented by the *Lost* Scenario is best offered at a small, residential college. The conversations that occur during the *Lost* Scenario would only be successful after a semester of conversations like them. These conversations occur because Great Political Thinkers is a class of fifteen to twenty students and, as noted earlier, it is taught in a manner that is conversational in nature. "A conversation," Oakeshott reminds us, "does not need a chairman," and in a small, discussion-based classroom, no chairman is needed.[13] In addition, on a residential campus the conversations that take place in the classroom are continued on other parts of campus, and my students often meet outside of class to discuss the readings and prepare for in-class activities like debates and the *Lost* Scenario. Furthermore, because I am only teaching thirty to forty students a semester, I have time to provide one-on-one and small group attention to students as they think through the ultimate questions at the heart of the course. Finally, I think there is something very valuable about engaging these ultimate questions in a setting where students can speak to one another and listen to one another face-to-face. We live in a world in which our interactions with one another are increasingly mediated by screens. The academic realm has not been spared this fate and there are more than a few administrators and even instructors celebrating this phenomenon. While it is beyond my scope to discuss these phenomena in any detail, I will say that I do not believe something like what happens in a course like Great Political Thinkers (and its culmination in the *Lost* Scenario) can be recreated on a "massive" scale and/or in an online setting. A *Lost* "chat room," blog, or video conference might have certain virtues, but none would capture the dynamism and joy of what happens in that room when fifteen or twenty of us are gathered to have a meaningful conversation. When we communicate through a screen, something human is lost.

Conclusion

There are so many things about the *Lost* Scenario that are out of step with our educational times. It is not graded. It is difficult to assess. It is not "experiential" in the sense favored in most academic circles. It is not "relevant" to the work world in the obvious ways favored by the prophets of vocationalism. It is not massive. It is not online. When I reflect on the fact that the *Lost* Scenario is the activity that makes me feel most like I am a practitioner of liberal education at the best kind of college, it is tempting to feel a sense of pessimism about the future. If the best thing I do is so deeply out of step with the spirit of our educational times, is there much reason for me to feel hopeful? I think there is. What continues to amaze me is that in an academic culture where the vast majority of those with power—within and outside of the academy—chase the hottest trail of efficiency, students continue to express an interest in engaging in the sorts of conversations that are at the core of liberal education. We must continue to talk and write about why the liberal arts matter and take action in order be sure liberal education is protected. In addition, we can promote liberal education by continuing to do what we do. Every time we create a space—inside or outside of the classroom—for serious conversations about ideas that matter and we treat the voices of our students with the dignity and respect they deserve, we model our commitment to liberal learning. Liberal education may be countercultural, but those who have felt its power feel it deeply and will not easily give up on its perpetuation for future generations. It is for this reason that I remain hopeful that the liberal arts and the best kind of college will persevere.

Notes

1. Michael Oakeshott, "A Place of Learning," in *The Voice of Liberal Learning* (New Haven: Yale University Press, 1989), 32.
2. Ibid., 27.
3. Ibid., 32.
4. Ibid., 32, 38, 39.

5. Ibid., 39.

6. Ibid.; Michael Oakeshott, "The Idea of a University," in *The Voice of Liberal Learning* (New Haven: Yale University Press, 1989), 98.

7. Oakeshott, "A Place of Learning," 28, 30; Oakeshott, "The Idea of a University," 98.

8. Oakeshott, "A Place of Learning," 19.

9. Michael Oakeshott, "Education: Its Engagement and Its Frustration," in *The Voice of Liberal Learning* (New Haven: Yale University Press, 1989), 71.

10. Oakeshott, "A Place of Learning," 26.

11. Ibid.

12. The idea of pursuing projects to institutionalize commitments to the liberal arts may sound a bit vague, so allow me to provide a couple of examples. At Linfield, there have been two recent successes on this front. First, over the past several years a group of faculty developed a campus-wide initiative called the Program for the Liberal Arts and Civic Engagement (PLACE). The basic idea behind this initiative is to "highlight" different parts of our liberal arts core (the Linfield Curriculum) through lectures, student activities, course transformation grants, faculty development programs, and student fellowships all focused on a particular theme. During our first two pilot years of the program, the theme has been Legacies of War. The faculty, students, and staff involved in PLACE have invigorated the liberal arts core on my campus. In the Department of Political Science, we established the Frederick Douglass Forum on Law, Rights, and Justice in order to promote serious discussion of ultimate questions in politics. During our first year, we hosted several scholarly lectures and debates as well as undergraduate speaking competitions. Both PLACE and the Douglass Forum have the potential to institutionalize our commitment to liberal arts beyond the classroom.

13. Oakeshott, "The Idea of a University," 98.

From Observation to Engagement to Collaboration

·•——————•·

The Liberal Arts Journey

JERUSHA B. DETWEILER-BEDELL

Jerusha B. Detweiler-Bedell is Professor of Psychology at Lewis & Clark College in Portland, Oregon. She received her BA and MA in psychology from Stanford University and her PhD in clinical psychology from Yale University. In 2008 Detweiler-Bedell was named the United States Professor of the Year for Baccalaureate Colleges by the Council for Advancement and Support of Education (CASE) and the Carnegie Foundation for the Advancement of Teaching. She holds an appointment as the Distinguished Teaching Consultant for the College of Arts and Sciences at Lewis & Clark, where she teaches Introduction to Psychology, Health Psychology, Psychology of Gender, Clinical Psychology, Psychology Internship, and Community Psychology. She also co-directs the Behavioral Health and Social Psychology laboratory, where she conducts research with undergraduate student collaborators. Detweiler-Bedell was awarded a National Science Foundation grant in 2008 to further develop and disseminate her methods of mentoring undergraduates in research, and she has published extensively on the scholarship of mentoring. She has co-authored two books: Doing Collaborative Research in Psychology: A Team-Based Guide *(2013) and* Treatment Planning in Psychotherapy: Taking the Guesswork Out of Clinical Care *(2003). Her broader program of research brings together investigations of human decision-making, health psychol-*

ogy, and clinical psychology, with the goal of promoting health behaviors by understanding why people fail to do "what's best" for their physical and mental well-being.

≥o.

Life at a liberal arts institution is transformative for both professor and student. In this spirit of transformation, I sit in my office on a drizzly Tuesday afternoon and listen to my supervisee describe his struggles with a patient whose panic disorder is so severe that she has become house-bound. That day, I work with supervisees on therapeutic interventions for problems ranging from the frightening (uncontrollable anger, self-injury) to the heart-breaking (severe depression, social isolation) to the bizarre (irresistible compulsions to stand on manhole covers). These are extraordinary cases, not only because of the symptoms described, but also because they are based on carefully researched role-plays, not on real patients. My supervisees are not graduate students. Instead, they are undergraduates in my Clinical Psychology course who, prior to starting my class, study an autobiography of a person with a psychological disorder in order to be able to portray that person as a patient. Throughout the semester they meet weekly with another student from the class, taking turns acting out the roles of patient and therapist. As therapists to their simulated patients, my students apply the empirically supported techniques I teach them each week. This experience requires each student to work closely with another person throughout the term, and accountability to one another is an essential ingredient for their success. Further, students are organized into peer mentoring groups, where "therapists" treating similar disorders regularly meet with one another as well as with me. My work as a professor at a small liberal arts college is grounded in a fundamental understanding that collaboration is an essential yet highly challenging task, and to become skilled collaborators, students must practice working closely with their peers and professors throughout their college career.

The process of becoming an effective collaborator is not easy, in part because a group can serve to undermine the good intentions of an individual. Let me share one such example here: Imagine that you are sitting in your doctor's waiting room along with other patients. After a few minutes, you begin to notice smoke wafting from the vent in an adjacent door. After another few minutes, the smoke is not just wafting, it is pouring out from the vent into the waiting room. How quickly will you alert the receptionist that something might be wrong? And is the receptionist likely to be alerted more quickly, given that you are not alone? After all, there are other people in the waiting room with you. A scientific study similar to this scenario was carried out in the late 1960s by social psychologists Bibb Latane and John Darley, who found that most people report the smoke if they are alone, but very few do so if they share the room with other people.[1] The moral here is disturbing: when we are part of a group, most us will passively remain in that doctor's waiting room, coughing, waving the smoke away, and rubbing our eyes. Perhaps we feel inhibited by the presence of others, or we regard others' inaction as information and we want to follow their example, or we assume responsibility to act must lie not with ourselves but with other people. In any case, we fail to respond.

The typical university classroom is remarkably similar to the smoke-in-the-room situation. When students sit in a classroom surrounded by others, it becomes all too easy, all too natural, for them to fall into the role of the unresponsive bystander. My first goal as a liberal arts college professor is to transform each of my students from *bystander* to *participant*, leading them not just to observe but to engage: to better understand human physiology, they eat a spoonful of sugar after drinking a tea that knocks out taste receptors (making the sugar taste like a mouthful of sand); to better understand the power of social labels, they discuss what to do if their child were born intersexed; and to better understand the interaction between psychological and physical health, they monitor their stress levels and bodily symptoms and identify effective coping strategies. This form of participation moves my students from simply observing to actively engaging in the pursuit of knowledge.

In the smoke-in-the-room experiment, active engagement would mean taking responsibility for identifying and responding to a potential fire. And, to be sure, some research participants did act, and some of those who failed to act asked the experimenter what they should do differently in the future to be more engaged. *But this isn't enough.* The challenge is for participants to think beyond their own individual experiences in order to ask much bigger questions: "How can I better understand how the situation works, why are people this way, and what can prevent this from happening to others? I want to help find the answers by joining the research team, as a collaborator."

In university classrooms, professors often engage students by assigning small group work, where students participate in cooperative learning. Yet the traditional (and, arguably, more typical) path to cooperative learning is one that emphasizes individual accountability with little or no attention to how to organize students into effective project teams or how to supervise the group's efforts. Unfortunately, "many faculty who believe they are using cooperative learning are, in fact, missing its essence."[2] Practical constraints such as large class sizes make it difficult for professors to attend to team dynamics and to teach teamwork skills. Instead, individual efforts are rewarded, and group work is "group-based" in name rather than in practice. This not only undermines the students' experiences in the group but also sets them up for difficulty after graduation. A demonstrated ability to collaborate with others and work effectively in teams is critical for success in the workplace. For example, in a survey of over three hundred business executives, teamwork was rated as the most sought-after skill of potential new hires.[3] And in a more recent survey, 67 percent of employers said that colleges should place *more* emphasis on teamwork skills and the ability to collaborate with others in diverse settings.[4] But how do students go about mastering teamwork skills in the classroom?

Fortunately, the "essence" of cooperative learning *is* within the reach of the liberal arts college professor. Small faculty-to-student ratios allow for frequent interactions with my own students, and when students meet one-on-one with me, I can ask them questions and find inroads to their passions. But as the survey of business leaders suggests, the world outside of academia is not necessarily one in which knowing how to talk to a mentor is enough. Knowing how to work effectively as a member of a group is essential, and most employers will not have the time or energies to carefully mentor employees in teamwork skills. This learning must take place earlier, and I believe there is no better place for it than in the small liberal arts college classroom.

In each of my courses, I help my students move from bystanders to participants to *collaborators* by working closely with their peers to understand course concepts more fully, by participating in small group debates, and by designing and conducting experiments together. The idea that college life is not "real life" is a misconception, and I regularly remind my students that the work they do in their courses has applications well beyond the classroom. For example, in my Community Psychology course, students work throughout the semester in teams, carrying out a systematic investigation of a problem they identify on our own college campus. I accompany my students to a regional Community Psychology conference, where they hone their professional skills and learn from experts in the field. Armed with theoretical and practical knowledge, my students formally survey their peers, interview relevant professionals, write literature reviews, and then design an intervention incorporating what they have learned. The semester-long, team-based project culminates with presentations to campus administrators, faculty, staff, and students. Most notably, the skills students learn in collaboration with their peers are not put to rest at the end of the term. One of the many benefits of a small liberal arts college is that the students know and are known by campus deans, program directors, and even the college president (who is a guest speaker in my class). In recent years, my students have continued to meet and collaborate with college administrators and have seen elements of their coursework incorporated into campus projects as diverse as a redesign of the student center, the launch of an on-campus cafe, and a reorganization of the career development office.

Beyond the classroom, students learn to collaborate with their peers and their professors in research teams. Especially at a small liberal arts college, the distinction between teaching and research is blurred, and the manner in which undergraduates are incorporated into the research process becomes an essential part of their education. Upon arriving at Lewis & Clark College, I co-created the Behavioral Health and Social (BHS) psychology research lab, which is made up of a number of student-run teams, each consisting of three members—a team leader (an advanced student with experience in research), a team associate (a midlevel student), and a team assistant (a student new to psychology). Students engage in every aspect of the research process and evolve from novices into accomplished graduate-level researchers. A large number of these students continue on to doctoral- and masters-level programs after graduation, but equally important, others apply their experiences in the workplace as practitioners, statisticians, administrators, and educators.

Employers underscore the value of collaborative research skills (e.g., 74 percent of over three hundred employers surveyed believe such skills help students succeed beyond graduation), and so do the students.[5] In a recent BHS lab alumni survey, students who participated in team-based research communicate their appreciation for learning how to be a collaborator in a small college setting such as ours: "One of the things I appreciated most about my involvement [with the lab] was the opportunity to really work with and get to know two of my professors. I enjoyed the professional aspect of it as well as the personal." Students learn how to be skilled collaborators, not because of the threat of a bad grade, but because they have taken owner-ship of their education and appreciate the depth of learning that occurs as a result of group-based work. According to another recent alum:

> On a purely official level, [lab work] looks great on my resume. But the value of my experience [in the lab] goes way beyond that. . . . As my comfort and knowledge grew, I began to feel more confident in the lab and more able to take on difficult tasks and responsibilities. And as I began to feel I knew the logistics of conducting research, I felt confident enough to lead other [lab] members. In addition, other [student] researchers became some of the best friends I ever had, and I know that our passion for research and the collaborative environment helped to bring us together. So beyond looking good on a resume, [the lab] has served to enrich my life on many levels.

One of the greatest privileges I have as a professor at a small liberal arts college is the opportunity to offer students enriching life experiences through fostering close collaborations with peers and mentors. This is the type of education I champion: It's the passion for asking *how* and *why*, and it's the courage to seek out answers together. Students at small liberal arts colleges are taught to ask good questions, design an approach to answering these questions, implement the approach in collaborative groups, and openly share their knowledge with others. I see this process as an iterative one, and I teach my students that the best way to improve upon one's work is to seek feedback from others. At a liberal arts college, the stage is set to push students' cooperative learning beyond mere repetition of lessons typically "fit" for young people. Students are pressed to discover new knowledge in the classroom and the laboratory through joint effort and with close mentoring.

I am deeply rewarded in watching my students do the extraordinary, ranging from treating simulated patients to sharing research findings. My students do not just *observe*—they *engage*. And they do not just engage— they *collaborate*. I encourage and provide extensive support to group projects and presentations, because this is how students leave my classroom knowing what it means to be a collaborator. I expect to be challenged *by* my students as well—an expectation I communicate to each class early on. I regularly encounter the limits of my knowledge in one-on-one meetings, the classroom, and the research lab, and it is my students who help me to hone my skills as a professor, thus enriching my own life through this process. Each day of my professional life is filled with new challenges, new knowledge, and ongoing opportunities to inspire my students to tackle complex problems by working together in the process of learning. At a small liberal arts college, students become motivated, insightful, and enthusiastic thinkers through collaborative work, and it is a joy to watch their knowledge and skills as collaborators translate well beyond the walls of the classroom.

Notes

1. Bibb Latane and John M. Darley, "Group Inhibition of Bystander Intervention and Emergencies," *Journal of Personality and Social Psychology* 19 (1968): 215–221.

2. Karla A. Smith, Sheri D. Sheppard, David W. Johnson, and Roger T. Johnson, "Pedagogies of Engagement: Classroom-Based Practices," *Journal of Engineering Education* 94 (2005): 9.

3. Peter D. Hart, *How Should Colleges Prepare Students to Succeed in Today's Global Economy?* a report conducted on behalf of the Association of American Colleges and Universities, www.aacu.org/leap/documents/Re8097abcombined.pdf (retrieved July 30, 2013).

4. Peter D. Hart, *It Takes More than a Major: Employer Priorities for College Learning and Student Success*, report conducted on behalf of the Association of American Colleges and Universities, http://www.aacu.org/leap/documents/2013_Employer-Survey.pdf (retrieved July 30, 2013), 4.

5. Ibid., 5.

Magic in the Classroom

.•·————·•·

Arthur T. Benjamin

Arthur T. Benjamin earned his BS in applied mathematics from Carnegie Mellon and his PhD in mathematical sciences from Johns Hopkins University. Since 1989, he has taught at Harvey Mudd College, where he is Professor of Mathematics and past Chair. In 2000, he received the Haimo Award for Distinguished Teaching by the Mathematical Association of America and served as the MAA's Polya Lecturer from 2006 to 2008. Benjamin is a past editor of Math Horizons Magazine *for the MAA. He has created four DVD courses for* The Great Courses on The Joy of Mathematics, Discrete Mathematics, The Secrets of Mental Math, *and* The Mathematics of Games and Puzzles. *He is a past winner of the American Backgammon Tour. He was selected as one of America's 300 Best Professors by* The Princeton Review *in 2012. Benjamin is also a magician who performs his mixture of math and magic to audiences all over the world, including the Magic Castle in Hollywood. He has demonstrated and explained his calculating talents in his book* Secrets of Mental Math *and on numerous television and radio programs, including* The Today Show, CNN, *and National Public Radio. He has been featured in* Scientific American, Omni, Discover, People, Esquire, *the* New York Times, *the* Los Angeles Times, *and* Reader's Digest. *In 2005, Reader's Digest called him "America's Best Math Whiz."*

ঌ

When I was a high school student, I performed magic at many children's birthday parties. It was through this experience that I learned most of what I know about teaching today, even at the college level.

Ask any children's entertainer for the most important ingredient to a successful show and they will tell you it is *audience participation*. In my shows, this would sometimes involve having people "on stage" with me and frequently asking the audience for assistance by yelling out magic words or helping me find the missing ghost. In the classroom, I am constantly asking questions of my classroom, sometimes to the class at large but often to a specific student. Not only does this technique keep the students on their toes, it also makes the class easier to follow, just like it is usually more interesting to hear a conversation than a monologue.

When you ask for a volunteer to assist, it's polite to ask them their name. In the classroom, I find that it's helpful to learn their names before the first class even begins. Once I find out who is registered for my courses, I locate their photos. (At my school, we have "Mudd Shots" that make this process automatic, but in the "old days" I would cut out photos from the first-year student picture book.) Using the photos as flash cards, I would memorize students' names with the associated face. With a completely new set of students, this process could take an hour or two. (My typical class has fewer than thirty-five students, but sometimes classes are larger.) On the first day of classes, as I go through the roll call list (and ask students for preferred nicknames or corrections to my pronunciation), I look closely at students' faces, especially those students who don't resemble their photo too much. After that, I try to go through the class, student by student, and try to give their names. I usually get at least 75 percent on the first try, and I will know all of their names solidly within the first two or three weeks. This has many positive benefits. Aside from allowing me to call on students by name, even when they don't raise their hands, it tells the students that I care about them. (And if I manage to get 100 percent, I'll get applause from the students, which, I confess, still feels good!)

My goal as a magician, especially when performing for children, is to entertain them. I do not try to fool them, since they already believe in magic. I am simply putting my magic powers to entertaining use. In the classroom, my goal is not to show students how smart I am but rather how smart they can be. Whether you are performing or teaching, a little bit of humor goes a long way, as does spontaneity. When performing, some of the most memorable moments are those that seem unplanned, where you come up with a great ad-lib to a surprising event. Of course, if you've performed many times, then you can start to expect some unexpected things to happen, and it's a good idea to be prepared for them. Likewise, in the classroom, it's great if you can present material in such a way that a student naturally asks a question that leads to the next topic.

Of course, to be successful as a performer or teacher, you need to have complete mastery of the material, and the more practice and guidance you can find, the better you will be. But don't expect a standing ovation the first time. Putting together the perfect lecture or performance piece is an evolving process that may take many iterations before it all comes together. Incidentally, as a professor of mathematics, my intended reaction from the audience is very similar to my goal as a magician. I want my students to say, "That's really cool! Why does that work?" If you can get them to actively wonder, "How did you do that?" then you are halfway home.

By the way, for as much as I've learned from magic, I seldom perform tricks in the classroom, unless it somehow motivates the lecture material. Although, I still recall my first day of teaching, when I taught with a deck of cards in my pocket. I brought the cards with me so that if the lecture bombed, I could still show them something fun at the end. As it happened, the lecture went well, and I showed the card trick to them anyway.

PART TWO

The Career

Learning to Live a Life of Learnable Moments

JUSTIN CROWE

Justin Crowe is Associate Professor of Political Science at Williams College, where he teaches courses on American politics and public law. His book, Building the Judiciary: Law, Courts, and the Politics of Institutional Development *(2012), examines the causes and consequences of the institutional development of the federal judiciary—especially, but not exclusively, the Supreme Court—from the Founding to the present. In addition to the book, he has published articles on the Supreme Court and American political development in the* Journal of Politics, Perspectives on Politics, *and* Studies in American Political Development. *He is currently at work on projects about the development of federal police powers surrounding vice regulation in the Progressive Era and constitutional amendments as agents of political change. He received his BA from Williams in 2003 and his PhD from Princeton in 2007. Prior to teaching at Williams, he taught for two years at Pomona College.*

৯৪

I once had the occasion to counsel a student—let's call him Ephraim—upset about how his Williams career had unfolded. The substance was, by Ephraim's own admission, nothing tragic, but that didn't mean the disappointment and regret and guilt he felt—for not meeting his own academic

standards, for not distinguishing himself on campus, for having spent so
much of his time doing things he no longer felt were worthwhile, for failing
to make the connections he wished he had—wasn't acute or painful. At
the end of a long email to him, one of several emails he and I exchanged
over the course of a week or two, I wrote the following:

> This is, perhaps, an unorthodox statement for a faculty mem-
> ber—especially one who emphasizes academic rigor as much as
> I do, especially one who is so demanding in terms of attendance
> and deadlines and grades—but I'll make it anyway: your time
> here isn't solely—or even mostly—about becoming a better
> *student*; it's about starting to become a better *person*. A smarter,
> stronger, funnier, more passionate, more compassionate, more
> involved, more aware, more forgiving, more responsible, more
> determined, more focused, more productive person. I, for one,
> think the academic experience is part and parcel of that process,
> but it's far from the only part—and, for some people, it isn't
> even a main part. I think it has been a big part for you, but so
> have other things. And you should be proud of that and proud
> of yourself; I know I am.

I wrote this willingly and genuinely in the context of Ephraim, but, almost
immediately after sending it, it occurred to me that I wasn't sure I actually
believed it as a general matter.

Then, only a few days later, I went to orientation night for parents
of kids heading into kindergarten, and I was absolutely floored. Not simply
by the fact that my once-little boy was suddenly old enough to attend kindergarten but by the totality of the goal—the scope of the aspiration—of
primary (and especially early primary) education more generally. Here I
was, simultaneously questioning, on the one hand, whether college could or
should really seek to *transform* the person and realizing, on the other, that
the central—unacknowledged but undeniable—task of elementary school
was to *create* a person. Parents do the biological work, of course, and (in
the best of circumstances) are deeply enmeshed in the psychosocial work
as well, but the school is where so much of what we see as our children is
made and shaped, where their mess of urges and passions are disciplined and
encouraged, where they first become participants in something larger than
themselves and first learn to think and speak and act beyond our watch-
ful eyes and helping hands. We drop them off as creatures and get them
back—following a process that is paradoxically both gradual and dramatic all
at once—as people. Reading, writing, adding, subtracting, singing, drawing,
running, jumping, perceptive, curious, precocious little people. Our elemen-

tary school principal—kind, competent, and enthusiastic as she seemed—didn't explicitly say any of this, but it wasn't hard to unearth it—and, once I did, it was even easier to embrace it.

The same, I want to argue, is true of my central premise here—a premise that I suggest all those who are, have been, or wish to be affiliated with liberal arts colleges would be wise not only to believe but also to embrace: *the purpose of the liberal arts is—or should be—less about making better students than it is about making better people.*

From my vantage point, there are three transformative processes that characterize—or might characterize—a student's time at a liberal arts college like Williams, each of which is catalyzed in a different manner. First, there is the process of becoming a better student. This can be *taught*—and, indeed, faculty teach it every day in every office and every classroom on campus, with lectures and discussions and assignments as well as guidance about how to read a novel, write a policy memo, or analyze a soil sample. Second, there is the process of becoming a better citizen. Sometimes this is taught—I have a pair of classes that feature experiential work designed to get students involved in democratic life, for example—but, for the most part, it's a process that occurs because it is *enabled*—by the institution, through opportunities and resources, with the sweat and exhortations of wonderful staff facilitating growth not just in the classroom but in the world. Third, there is the process of becoming a better person. This is the tricky one—we can't teach it, and I'm not sure we can even enable it. But we can *urge* it—chiefly by fashioning a community that takes it seriously, that pays attention to it, and that persuades students to do it for themselves. Taught to be a better student, enabled to be a better citizen, urged to be a better person.

In my own experience as a student at Williams, the first (becoming a better student) was no problem. My professors—two in particular[1]—taught me how to interpret a text, how to find my analytic voice, how to make sense of the political world. They were wonderful in every way. They are not only the reason I wanted to do this with my life but also the reason I'm blessed to be able to do this with my life, and hardly a semester goes by when I don't dwell on the fact that I wouldn't be where I am, holding my dream job, if it weren't for their work—their devotion, their integrity, their standards.

But, thinking back a decade, the second (becoming a better citizen) was a little more touch-and-go, and the third (becoming a better person), well . . . yeah. Maybe decades from now—maybe when I'm closer to my fiftieth college reunion than my fifteenth—I'll look back and realize this occurred in a meaningful way, but, right now, I'm just not sure it did. Don't get me wrong: I absolutely loved my time in college—I found both a career I love and a partner I love—and I learned things about myself I didn't know before, but I didn't seize opportunities to become a better citizen, and I'm not sure I ever explicitly thought, not even for a moment, about becoming a better person. Maybe that was unique to me—maybe I was just lazy and clueless—but I actually think there's something about the nature of how we imagine what it is we do as educators that makes it a problematically endemic feature of the liberal arts. To this very day, my own institution— both my alma mater and my employer—is absolutely stellar at the first, good and getting continually better at the second, but somewhere between befuddled by and uneasy about the third. And that's unfortunate because the third is where we (as academic institutions and intellectual communities) can really excel—and where our students really need us to excel.

The key is to recognize and exploit—to help our students to recognize and exploit—what I want to call "learnable moments." The phrase "teach-able moment" is something of a cliché nowadays in education at all levels, from college to (as I learned at kindergarten orientation) elementary school. If a student really struggles on a paper or says something embarrassing in class, you might think or say to yourself, "that's a teachable moment"—a moment you can step in and try to educate the student about whatever he did wrong so that he might do it better next time. Teachable moments are great, but they're entirely provider focused. That is to say, the idea of teachable moments is an idea about education as seen from the perspective of the educator: something goes wrong, and a sage and seasoned guide steps in to inform and enlighten. But, of course, as anyone older than twenty-two knows all too well, after college, you rarely have such a resource or a luxury; you rarely, in other words, have someone to teach you the teachable moments.

Yet the moments—the moments—continue to come long after you depart campus. They come faster and more furiously, with greater stakes and greater angst, with more options and more bewilderment than you could ever have imagined or could ever attempt to manage. To the extent that these consequential moments are all around you yet unaccompanied by any kind of personal didactic guide, the emphasis on *teachable* moments obscures the fact that what we really need to emphasize are *learnable* moments. Because only by learning from—that is, by deriving discernible meaning from—those moments will young people have the opportunity to compose a life that matters to them. More so than teaching algebra or interest groups, more so than channeling involvement and enthusiasm, teaching how to seize learnable moments is, I want to insist, our chief responsibility in the liberal arts. After all, teaching isn't so much our end goal as it is the means to the end goal of learning. Isn't it? Shouldn't it be? Liberal arts education is about—should be about—teaching how to learn. It's a perverse twist, in my mind: students, our elementary school principal assured me, *want* to learn at any age, yet we need to teach them *how* to learn at all ages.

I'm inevitably reminded here of my former Pomona colleague, the late David Foster Wallace, and his breathtakingly brilliant 2005 commencement address at Kenyon College. One of the many things Wallace does in that speech is unpack the platitude that the liberal arts enterprise is less about teaching you what to think than how to think. Acknowledging that he, an Amherst alum, used to be insulted by hearing this—"The fact that you even got admitted to a college this good seems like proof that you already know how to think," he remarks—Wallace goes on to say that it's not insulting at all because "the really significant education in thinking that we're supposed to get in a place like this isn't really about the capacity to think, but rather about the choice of what to think about." As he writes later in the speech, the freedom of a real education is that "you get to consciously decide what has meaning and what doesn't."[2]

It's an arresting insight—Wallace was blessed with arresting insights emanating from his pores—but it also increasingly strikes me as a partial insight, far more modest than it needs to be. Because even as what Wallace says is totally true, what he doesn't say is equally true as well. Consciousness and awareness aren't merely a function of learning how to think but a function of learning how to live. Those states of mind, as Wallace frames them, aren't solely about what goes on in your mind but about what goes on in your heart and what goes on with your hands, and your feet, and your mouth, and your stomach. They aren't exclusively cerebral virtues; they guide and shape action in addition to belief. Learning how to think is nothing short of learning how to live—how to live a life of learnable moments: how to learn from every moment you live and how to live every moment to learn.

Consider, for example, one class or category of learnable moments, the class of learnable moments faced by Ephraim in my conversations with him—namely, those involving vulnerability. Vulnerability is, in my view, the purest of all human conditions—present from the moment we inhale our first breath until the moment we exhale our last. We enter the world—crying and cold—unsure of where we are or what we're doing or who these strange people poking and prodding us are. We're vulnerable right then and there, and the feeling never really ends. Not completely, at least. We're kidding ourselves if we think it does. We're all vulnerable. We surely don't all have the same vulnerabilities, but we're all vulnerable to someone or something. All of us, all the time.

In theory, there's something unifying and oddly comforting about this notion. Except that we don't admit it to ourselves or to each other: we hide vulnerability rather than discuss it, we conceal it rather than uncover it. But in suppressing our vulnerability, we let it fester in our minds and seep into our souls. We let it consume or control us. We let it distract or dissuade us. Some of us are fortunate enough to convert it into something else—hopefully something healthy—but, for most of us, our vulnerability just sits there, even if in a dormant state, generating a series of potentially paralyzing emotional tics that almost all of us have in some form or another. Our secrets follow us. Our flaws gnaw at us. Our mistakes haunt us. No one ever said vulnerability was pretty.

We know this when we comfort a friend or console a partner—we know that our kind is wracked with vulnerability. But as good as we might be at applying this to others, we are miserable at internalizing it ourselves. This kind of dualistic impulse—reluctant to be vulnerable ourselves yet conscious of the fact that others are naturally vulnerable themselves—seems eminently logical to me. After all, it allows us to project the image of being both strong and sensitive, both confident and caring; it allows us to live a life where we permit weakness but never exhibit any, where we soldier on to help those who simply aren't as "put together" or "centered" as we are.

Of course, if we're being truly honest with ourselves, we know that life is a lie. Moreover, the reality isn't simply that we are vulnerable; it's that we need to be. Despite the potential hurt vulnerability might bring, a life without vulnerability is empty. Most of us, deep down, probably accept this—or, at the very least, could learn to accept it. But accepting it means more than stating it: it means understanding that we will—at some point and in some way—fall prey to it, and it means being ready to forgive ourselves for making the mistakes that result. Because just as a life without vulnerability is empty, a life without self-forgiveness is painful. Yet, assuming the same self-protectionist posture that causes us to hide our own vulnerability even as we tend to it in others, most of us live some version of that life—exhibiting plenty of empathy for others' lots but eschewing self-forgiveness for our own.

I blame the Golden Rule—you know, the aphorism, present in some form or another in almost every culture and every tradition, that you should "do unto others as you would have them do unto you." Don't get me wrong: It's a good precept, and I teach it to my kids. But as a fundamental maxim of everyday ethics, it strikes me as capable of governing only half (if that) of our lives and behavior. Because, as much as we emphasize the Golden Rule, we ignore, forget, or decline to extol its loose converse, a natural corollary I'll call the Platinum Rule: "Do unto yourself as you know you should do unto others." In other words, and I'm drawing from David Foster Wallace again here, treat yourself with the warmth and gentleness you would treat "a really good, precious friend" or a child that you "absolutely loved more than life itself."[3] That's not selfishness, it's self-compassion—and it's integral to learning how to live, how to survive, how to thrive in the world. Distinct from bigger buzzwords but lesser virtues like self-confidence or self-esteem, self-compassion isn't about trumpeting or asserting one's own prerogative and needs and importance in the face of competition or hostility; it's simply about exhibiting the same decency and concern for the ever-present face in the mirror as you would for the ever-changing faces outside the window. Think about it: you spend far more time with yourself and thinking about yourself—weighing your options, wrestling with your emotions—than you ever could with another. Your parents are there at the beginning but gone by the end. Your partner, if you're lucky, might be there at the end but only arrived at some midpoint along the way. Maybe a sibling (or a sibling-like friend) could be there almost start to finish, but no matter how much time you spend together, you also spend plenty of it apart. By contrast, and this goes in the category of things so obvious they probably don't even need to be said, you're never apart from yourself. Not when you close the door or close your eyes, not when you get in the shower or get in your car. Never.

Which is why the ability to forgive oneself—to embody the sort of consciousness and awareness Wallace emphasizes in his Kenyon speech but channeled and directed inward rather than outward, to apply Tami Taylor's declaration in *Friday Night Lights* that "there's no weakness in forgiveness" to your own mistakes—is simultaneously one of the most important and most difficult things a person can learn, outstripping in both value and complexity even the ability to forgive another. It's the thing I most wish Ephraim could learn. Because all of us will need to be forgiven for something at some point in our lives, because all of us will do something we regret—something we're embarrassed about or ashamed of—at some point in our lives. In fact, most of us will do several such things. We'll lie—whether to our boss, our kids, or ourselves. We'll cheat—whether on the golf course, our taxes, or our partner. We'll fail—whether to take out the trash, see the stop sign, or keep our promises. Most of us will—it's the simple, undeniable truth of our fragile and fallible humanity. And you know what? That's okay. I repeat: *That's okay.* I say that not to excuse the behavior and not to lower standards; I say it only to excuse our failure to meet those standards from the eternal judgment of our most stern and ceaseless critics—ourselves.

Unless we have suffered incredible loss of someone close, were brought to the precipice ourselves by some sort of addiction, or are devoutly spiritual, most of us live the first portion of our lives without really grasping any of this—without really understanding mistakes as human and self-forgiveness (in addition to any forgiveness we may seek from others) as divine. Which leaves those of us working with young adults—the vast majority of whom, especially at elite and secular institutions like Williams, probably do not satisfy the aforementioned criteria during their time in college—in a situation where those in our care: 1) are going to commit serious mistakes in life by betraying their moral code, hurting something near and dear to them, or making bad personal choices; and 2) are going to need to learn how to deal with those mistakes lest they become consumed by them; yet 3) will have absolutely no idea how to do that unless we help them develop a propensity for self-forgiveness.

Young adults drawn to small, selective liberal arts colleges like Williams are, I'd argue, even more in need of this sort of help than many others. Not because they're privileged or sheltered or oblivious, but because they are so damn perfectionist. The function of a society that has taught them at every stage that only the best and brightest can thrive, that only those at the top of one mountain are permitted to climb the next, their standards—for others, yes, but even more so for themselves—are invariably far loftier than is either practicable or healthy. Which is, of course, a fact that they have neither the time nor inclination to ponder and debate. Lest they want to tumble down from the high perch to which their hard work has elevated them, they have little choice but to regard cultivating their resume and becoming a better applicant as far wiser—far less amorphous and risky, far more concrete and responsible—than cultivating their soul and becoming a better person.

I reverted to "they" and "them" and "their" just now, but, to be honest, it's really "we" and "us" and "our" because I stand not as some omniscient outsider but as a contemplative insider. I, too, am a product of this culture and this institution, and I, too, wish I could have learned what I so desperately want my students to grasp. For whatever I got from my liberal arts experience—and let me be clear: it was an incalculable amount—I didn't get this: I didn't learn to forgive myself. I didn't have a teachable moment in this genre, and I didn't learn to recognize and exploit the learnable ones. Believe me when I tell you that I wish I had, that I've wished I had at various points in my life where I needed reflexivity and introspection that was less analytic than empathetic. I left college certain to make mistakes but without any real clue how to forgive myself for them, and I'm a lesser person for it: I've both caused more heartbreak and felt more heartache as a result.

When I was a kid, I used to want to be an adult—to have a career, to buy a house, to start a family. I laugh now when I think about that. Not because those things aren't enriching and fulfilling (save for mortgage payments and home repairs, they undoubtedly are), but because the rush to "hurry up and get there already" epitomizes the true purity of childhood for me: the belief that adulthood is more or less just like you've always lived but with more money and more fun and more freedom. Sure, you know about more responsibility and more pressure, but what you don't know—what you can't possibly know—is about the end of innocence. The shattering of naïveté that comes when you make mistakes and struggle to recover from them. The loss of something—a feeling, a disposition, a sensibility—that never really returns. Because when it ends, it's over. There's nothing any of us can do to stop that for ourselves or for others, but just as we, as parents, have the obligation to put our children in the best position to prepare for it, so, too, do we, as educators, have the obligation to put our students in the best position to emerge from it.

It's common to hear people wax poetic about learning from failure and about how, in what is perhaps my least favorite adage of all, "what doesn't kill you makes you stronger." Those things sound dandy, but, despite the fact that saying them is easy, actually doing them is really, really hard. (For me, at least, what doesn't kill me often just makes me weaker.) Scarcely anyone, in fact, instinctually knows how to do them; scarcely anyone doesn't need to learn how to manage vulnerability or survive mistakes. And just as African art or molecular science is infinitely harder to learn after college—on your own, without the benefit of an expert and enthusiastic guide—so, too, is the art and science of being a person in this world, of being comfortable in your own skin, of being able to look at yourself each and every day and be kind to what you see. *All* of what you see—good and bad, pretty and ugly, triumphant and dejected. My favorite recent articulation of this comes from Jennifer Lawrence in *Silver Linings Playbook*. Arguing with Bradley Cooper about her troubled past—a past that saw the death of her husband send her into a tailspin of sexual promiscuity and emotional degradation—she proclaims, "There's always going to be a part of me that's sloppy and dirty, but I like that. With all the other parts of myself. Can you say the same about yourself, fucker? Can you forgive? Are you any good at that?" For most of us, the answer to those questions is a resounding no.

I should be clear that this emphatically isn't about learning right from wrong. Almost all of us—including my students from the moment they arrive—know the difference, and most of us (and most of them) will, more often than not, choose right when faced with the choice. This isn't about that. Rather, it's about the fact that far fewer of us (and even fewer of them) know quite what to do—with ourselves, with our emotions—when the moment comes that we choose wrong.

This can be a wholly shattering experience. I mean, take a minute and really think about it. When you're a high achiever of the kind that matriculants at elite liberal arts colleges are, you're not used to choosing wrong—not on the mundane, certainly not on the momentous. Which means you're not accustomed to needing to forgive yourself for mistakes. Which means that, when you do screw up—and, as I try to tell my students, you inevitably will in your life—the default reaction is a creeping absolutism of failure until self-blame dwarfs, diminishes, and all but destroys any meaningful semblance of self-understanding. The doomsday-ish questions—What will my friends think? What will my parents say? How will I explain this to all those who have supported me?—begin to outnumber the reassuring answers by a factor too great to identify.

Alas, basic liberal arts education doesn't automatically stop this masochistic tendency. It can, of course, if we make it, but it doesn't always do so as a matter of course. In fact, even if not directly responsible, liberal arts education as it's all too often practiced—in a sort of rudderless manner that altogether ignores the goal of ethical (as opposed to intellectual or civic) betterment—is at the very least substantively complicit it. What does liberal arts education do well if not encourage the sort of constant, obsessive pursuit of refinement that forces the mind to search for and linger on shortcoming and inadequacy? Whether in classroom discussions with students, written assignments for students, or evaluative feedback to students, so much of the basic, everyday work of the liberal arts in its more facile form is geared toward deconstructing arguments, dissecting evidence, and disputing conclusions—modes of finding fault all. After four years of this sort of training, our students are—presuming we're good at our jobs!—veritably conditioned and disciplined to do it.

These are important skills. I teach them, I enjoy teaching them, and I'm glad we teach them. But if we're going to rear our students to be so analytic and critical, we also need to teach them how to resist becoming so in all realms and how to survive becoming overly so in their most intimate realms. That is to say, if we're going to equip our students with these sorts of *academic* skills, we also need to impart the *life* skills needed to contextualize and compensate for the dangers of them. Because better students aren't necessarily—aren't inevitably, aren't intrinsically—better people: as comforting a thought as it might be to those of us in higher education, being better in the classroom simply doesn't mean you're necessarily better in life.

Unless, of course, we rethink what we do—or, at least, how we conceptualize, verbalize, and emphasize what we do—in the classroom writ large, going beyond the scholastic virtues of creativity, clarity, and eloquence into ethical ones such as sacrifice, patience, and hope. Make no mistake: in order to embed these values into the lifeblood of a liberal arts education, in order to make a liberal arts education practically overflow with learnable moments, we need to extend its reach into our students' lives until we can both nourish the mind *and* nurture the soul. At its core, this means defining ourselves as more than academics and defining our relationships to one another in more than strictly pedagogical terms. It means setting aside—nay, flatly rejecting—the idea that our project can be reduced to the (re)production of knowledge and achievement and excellence, that our work could ever be faithfully captured in the mechanical terms of a factory.

Far from something so impersonally bureaucratic and methodically efficient, the best descriptor for the best aspects of any liberal arts college isn't just communal but familial. On a personal level, it's a thought legitimized by the fact that I've long called my students—especially my first groups of students at both Pomona and Williams—"my kids."[4] What that meant didn't really resonate with me until I actually had children of my own, but, now that I do, I realize how incredibly meaningful it is to call someone that. I'm sure I originally intended it colloquially, but I've come to feel and attempt to embody it more deeply: to try to teach them like I teach mine, to feel an obligation to raise them as I raise mine—not just intellectually but ethically, in word as well as deed. I want—we need—to instill the notion that the wall of solitary individualism is a menace that leaves you worshiping at the flawed altar of yourself. That when you reach out beyond that isolation for someone equally exposed, someone equally fearful of admitting it more often than not reaches back. That pain shared with another is not only pain halved for you but also pain potentially converted into help for another. I want—we need—to illustrate how you can't learn life's virtues without trial. How the best of those virtues—the best traits any of us possess—are also the ones that only count when demonstrated. How we almost exclusively have the opportunity to demonstrate those virtues following failure, and how our failure to demonstrate them invariably is what compels us to reaffirm their importance continually.

If you think about it, we do, in a way, have the potential to espouse some version of this—this admission and embrace of vulnerability—in the classroom. Take, for example, the student who absolutely bombs a paper because . . . well, because she does. Maybe she loses sight of the prompt and ends up delving into a topic that is at best orthogonal to the assignment. Maybe she simply strings together secondary sources in a haphazard way without really making any sort of novel argument. Maybe she simply misinterpreted a key concept or reading, causing her to anchor her entire analysis on a faulty premise or orient it around false dichotomy. As any faculty member knows, each of these is a fairly common occurrence. Now, after the first semester or two, chances are the student knew not to do these things—knew that writing a good paper required staying germane to the question being asked, developing and substantiating an original argument, accurately employing course material in service of her claims. And chances are that, most times she writes a paper, she manages to do just that. But this time, for whatever reason—ambition, confusion, procrastination, indifference—she didn't. What do we do with that student? What do we say to that student? In the case of the secondary source–dominated, argument-free essay, probably something along the lines of: "It's okay, Ephelia—that happens sometimes. I assume you know what went wrong here because your last paper was quite strong. And, indeed, this paper had its moments, too. You just didn't foreground and develop your analytic points as you need to, instead getting lost and hiding behind the secondary sources. That doesn't mean, of course, you're a bad student, and it doesn't mean you're going to fail the course, though it does mean you're going to need to work extra hard on the final paper to dig yourself out of this hole. But I have every confidence you can do that, and you should, too. Just remember to keep that argument front and center—and stop by during office hours if you want to show me a draft or ask any questions." There are standards, and there are consequences, for sure, but there's no judgment—and, in fact, there's even tenderness and comfort. There is, in a sense, an urge to the student not only to look at what went wrong and to do better next time but also to forgive herself for having not done so this time.

So, we're already equipped to model some of the quasi-familial self-forgiveness I'm talking about in the classroom; we just don't firmly entrench it there, let alone show our students how they might apply and extend it or any number of other deserving virtues to their lives beyond the classroom. But that's exactly what we need to do in turning a fairly narrow and incon-sequential teachable moment into the catalyst for a series of sweeping and substantial learnable moments. Because it's not about the paper but about what comes out of and after the paper—about knowing who you are and what you're about and knowing both how to deal and where to turn when faced with your occasional inevitable failure to be or live up to it. Those things are hard to learn at any point, but they're even harder to learn on the fly when the stakes are high. Which is precisely why we need to urge students to learn them now—when the stakes are lower, when the margin for error is greater, when the chances to practice are more plentiful. And precisely why we should aim to help each and every young man and young woman who walks through our college gates to be not just a better student or a better citizen but a better person.

As anyone who knows me could attest, I'm a liberal arts boy through and through. When it comes to this sort of education, I'm a partisan and an ideologue—a true believer of the deepest sort. So it should be no surprise that I think the sort of work—real work, difficult work—I'm describing is uniquely performed by institutions and communities—by *families*—such as this one. I said at the beginning that we can't teach or even enable the transformation of a better person, but we can urge it. In fact, I dare say we in the liberal arts are designed to urge it, what with both our emphasis on questioning, discovering, and experimenting and our small-scale, close-knit community where accountability is inescapable but support omnipresent. We *alone* are destined to do that, in fact. Most colleges and universities make better students, and some make better citizens, but few are even capable of making better people. UConn and UMass can't. Harvard and Yale won't. This is both our opportunity and our responsibility. And I firmly believe it's an opportunity and responsibility we should embrace as part of our vision and mission—as who we want to be and what we aim to do. Obviously, I'm happy if my students leave knowing more about American politics and the Constitution and the Supreme Court, and I'm delighted if they leave more likely to go to town meetings or join civic organizations, but both those outcomes are, in a sense, a means to a larger end. The former (the knowledge) will prove irrelevant to most of them in short order—*Brown v. Board of Education, Roe v. Wade*, someone v. someone else. And the latter (the engagement) could well prove fleeting—elections are periodic, life sometimes gets in the way of citizenship. But the humanity of becoming a better person is far more likely to be enduring, even forever.

Why are liberal arts colleges the best kinds of colleges? Because we alone have the means, motive, and opportunity to perform this task. Because we alone have the scale and the resources, the intimacy and the community to make it an institutional commitment and institutional priority. Because we alone have the gravitas—the tradition, the credibility, the insulation, the courage, the ambition—to ignore the nearsighted preoccupation with preparing our charges for the workforce in favor of the infinitely more crucial task of preparing them for what I'll call the *life*force. It takes time, and it takes effort—it requires both—to make someone a better person. But if we truly want to harness the power of this institution to make the greatest possible difference in the lives of those who love it, I dare say it's less an option than an imperative. Because, at the end of the day, it's what's necessary to make this place the best version of what we aspire it to be.

It's also why, incidentally, so many of the opponents of the online education craze supposedly sweeping American higher education are, if anything, understated in their criticism. It's not simply that online education "isn't what we do here"—after all, what we "do" here is continually evolving and improving; it's that online education is so much less than what we do here and, as a result, unequivocally beneath what we do here. What we do could be so much more, what we aspire to do should be so much more than what so-called massive open online courses allow. Because if the liberal arts experience—if my college's legendary Mark Hopkins and his log—is about anything at all, it is about seeing the whole person, educating the whole person, transforming *the whole person*. Not just the student, not just the citizen—the person. About teaching Ephraim to learn—not just how to read and write and analyze, not just how to argue and reason and participate, but how to live and how to learn and how to learn to live a life of learnable moments. And if you think any of this business about instructing in the ways of a life well lived mind-bogglingly overwhelming, well, welcome to the club. But it's also worth it—it's worthy of us and the model of education we hold so dear.

And, besides: ain't nothing compared to what they face in kindergarten.

Notes

I thank "Ephraim" for inadvertent inspiration, Darlene Berryman for a necessary nudge, and Vera Cecelski and Billy Glidden for their deep investment, their thoughtful critiques, and—most of all—their compassionate souls.

1. Gary Jacobsohn (now of the University of Texas at Austin) and the late Tim Cook.

2. David Foster Wallace, 2005 Kenyon Commencement Address, May 21, http://web.ics.purdue.edu/~drkelly/DFWKenyonAddress2005.pdf.

3. Quoted in David Lipsky, *Although of Course You End Up Becoming Yourself: A Road Trip with David Foster Wallace* (New York: Broadway Books, 2010), 292.

4. Two such kids, Vera Cecelski and Billy Glidden, deserve credit for many of the ideas—and even some of the words!—that follow in this paragraph.

(What Is Meant to Be) Straight Talk
on Intellectual, Cultural, and Moral Formation

•◦•——•◦•

JASON PETERS

Jason Peters holds the Dorothy J. Parkander Chair in Literature at Augustana College (Illinois), where he has taught British and American literature since 1996. He is also a faculty member in both the Honors and Environmental Studies programs. In 2013 he was recognized with the Jaeke Award for excellence in teaching. His work has appeared in the Sewanee Review, South Atlantic Quarterly, English Language Notes, Orion, Explicator, Shenandoah, The Review of Politics, First Principles, University Bookman, American Notes & Queries, The Journal of Religion and Society, *and* Christianity and Literature, *among other publications. He is the editor of* Wendell Berry: Life and Work *(2007).*

ॐ

Henry Adams defined a schoolmaster as someone who educates himself at his students' expense. He also said that three years of teaching would unfit a man for any other kind of work.

Whatever straight talk you can find in this racket is worth latching on to, and I think Adams, though he had a pile of irony in him, was talking straight here. The author of *The Education of Henry Adams* had his doubts about the education of anyone—he's the one who said a generation of Harvard graduates tested the worth of their education on the

85

battlegrounds of Shiloh, Antietam, and Gettysburg—but you get the feeling that this self-deprecating historian was not a man given to mendacity or self-aggrandizement.

Yet look around you. You sometimes feel as if no one can earn a PhD anymore who hasn't earned six credit hours of graduate work in mendacity and self-aggrandizement. I knew a man of small irony and less self-knowledge (he was a biologist) who had as one of his many email tags something to this effect: "I am a teacher. A teacher is someone who leads. There is no magic here. I do not walk on water. I do not part the sea. I just love my students."

Now if you teach, and if you teach well—there are many people in liberal arts colleges who do this, all worthy of our respect and admiration—then you know that with such respect and admiration come certain temptations, one of which is to think more highly of yourself than you ought. But it is probably a sign of some kind of psychic disorder—and certainly evidence that too little of the Adams family irony runs through your veins—if you must constantly remind yourself, *to other people*, that you are not Jesus Christ or Charlton Heston.

I begin with Adams and The Biologist for the sake of making a brief gesture in the general direction of humility, because I'm about to turn around and do the opposite. What I mean to say as a matter of first business is that a professor's effect, even in the context of the liberal arts, and regardless of his or her talent, must surely be a small thing. We teachers build on the work of many predecessors, not to mention on the mysterious and native stock of each student. We introduce a scene or swell a progress, but we're not Prince Hamlet—nor were we meant to be. So let us begin by admitting that whatever good we do is probably always a little less, and maybe a lot less, than what we'd like to think it is. It was said of the beauty queen caught wearing a padded undergarment, "There's less here than meets the eye." And no one is impressed if Mickey Mouse floats down the river on his back shouting, "Raise the bridge! Raise the bridge!"

But so much for humility, because the truth of the matter is that many of us—and I'm going to go ahead and include myself here—are pretty good at what we do. If called upon to substantiate this claim, we can point to the official "measures" and "outcomes" that the Lords of Assessment obsess over—as well as to a great deal of unofficial (and more reliable) evidence. If we also agree that confidence has something to do with being good at pretty much anything, like hitting a tee shot down a narrow fairway or shooting a free-throw with no time left on the clock or explaining the *analogia entis* to thoroughgoing materialists, we nevertheless feel obliged not to equivocate on the ancient dictum *gnothi seauton*: true self-knowledge is what it is. The boasts at the end of a Shakespearean sonnet are, after all, warranted.

So if really good teachers are truthful with themselves they will have to admit that, just as they were once well taught, so now they are teaching well. They can see plain as day that the lives of their students are intellectually exciting—just as their own lives were many years ago. It is true the good teachers have had to destroy the books in which they preserved their early sophomoric marginalia. Comte is no longer so comely, nor Barth so brilliant. They are not so swindled by Swinburne. But like the man in the gospels, and as the result of someone's good work in the classroom, they know that at some point they were obliged to say, "I was blind but now I see"—even if through a glass darkly. I remember clearly how the poetry of John Donne (he of the "gold to airy thinness beat") first struck a match that gave me heat and light, and I can remember in whose class this happened. (And I once had a colleague, a man of considerable irony and infinite jest, who used to smile wickedly and say of this or that student, "She has run *afoul* of the metaphysical poets!" or "They've limned her!") From my first encounter with the Holy Sonnets what I remember most is a kind of blessed shipwreck, a kind of happy entanglement, a cured blindness, a hunger and longing, a longing that proved to be its own satisfaction. And now, thirty years later, having seen my former self played out again and again in young men and women who are learning to read as if they're small children eagerly unwrapping presents on Christmas morning, I have no real choice but to see my current self playing out in the men and women who taught me. My role is probably, as I said, less than what I think it is. But there's a danger in underestimating its worth and importance. No one knows what "the marriage of true minds" is going to mean to a student ten years, fifteen years, thirty years down the road. No one knows how long an operation of grace can go underground before popping up unexpectedly to vex, and in vexing save, a lost soul.

I spoke just now of unwrapping presents, which implies a certain attendant wonder and surprise. But I would like to think differently for a moment about the enterprise of teaching in a liberal arts college and admit to a little more of that danger of which I also spoke, of a ground less firm. I am thinking about that uneasy and maybe uneven balance a good professor learns to strike between instructor and guide. For at a certain point questions will come that have nothing to do with the tidy dates that delimit an author's life or a world war. At a certain point explaining the *filioque* will fail to satisfy a good many students who haven't yet shaken off the curiosity education is so good at destroying. Sooner or later a student will say, "Yes, but what do *you* think?"

As in, where do you stand on the virgin birth or the hopeful monsters or upward mobility or a father's insistence that his son keep the family tradition alive and choose the most prosaic pre-professional major available?

(Honor your father, but learn your Aristotle.)

I am perfectly at ease going on record and saying I believe there is a necessary middle ground between the professor who shows no cards, who plays everything coyly, and the one who is naught but a windbag of ideological bombast. We all know both types, and so do the students—better, maybe, than we. I think the coy approach is mostly cowardly and the ideological mostly abusive. But in between those two, in the *via media*, much of the difficult but also rewarding work of a liberal arts professor gets done.

To clarify this point, I must emphasize something I think is fundamental to the educational enterprise: no student should pass through a liberal arts college without undergoing something like a crisis of conscience. (Those who do should probably receive a full tuition refund—with the exception, perhaps, of the impervious students who arrive on campus already sure of what they "want to be." Such students are careerists. They have already stopped learning and have entered not college but an apprenticeship.)

I am not talking here about a crisis issuing from the self-assured assistant professor of New Testament who, having decided that holy writ is the sole property of the academy, sets out to show the inter-varsity crowd why they are wrong, wrong, wrong. Still less am I talking about a crisis visited upon the sociology major whose capacity for moral outrage (in accordance with his or her training) begins and ends with the school's mascot, which if it is a Viking, a Chieftain, or a Longhorn is clearly offensive to the self-appointed Offense Monitors of Scandinavians, Native Americans, or Vegetarians, respectively.

I am talking, rather, about what must necessarily happen when young people accept their responsibilities as heirs of human culture and when they struggle to take seriously the moral and intellectual demands that descend upon them from the past. I believe students should engage passionately— that they should wrestle Jacob-like with—the art and thought of which a liberal education is composed. But I highly doubt that they can accept their responsibilities as heirs of human culture, or struggle to take seriously the moral and intellectual claims made on them by the past, or cultivate any passion for the liberal arts, without some measure of crisis. Getting messed up isn't only for Friday nights. Can you see a brave new world and not, like Miranda, marvel? Can you really arrive at the readiness without first doing something akin to picking up poor Yorick's skull and meditating on death—as all the sages recommend?

Students who do this, students who ask, "Where be your gibes now? Your gambols?" are, many of them, going to put questions directly to their professors. And, as I say, much of the work, much of the most satisfying work, is giving these students straight answers, answers, let us say, of confident circumspection, or circumspect confidence.

What this means is that, whether we like it or not, we are involved in the messy business of intellectual, cultural, and moral formation. And that whole business, like marriage, is not to be entered into lightly.

I tremble a bit to say this, because I find the moral vision of some of my colleagues as horrifying as they find mine (a better word for theirs is *immoral*, but I'll leave that be): we couldn't think one another more wrong than we do, and yet each of us is in a position—and a fearful one it is—to change a student's mind or be part of that change. But there's no getting around this except by cowardice or bombast. It is the fire with which we must play. So let us play with it—with dignity and with fear and trembling. And let us remember the parents behind it all who, God help them, apparently trust us to do no harm.

It is sometimes said, perhaps with too much self-satisfaction, that one of the advantages of teaching in a liberal arts college is that "you get to ask the big questions." This expresses a dubious exclusivity. We can ask the big questions (whatever they are) in a walk-in beer cooler if we want to—with or without tenure, and I think we should. If our friends in big R1 institutions aren't doing this, they should get with the program. They should—if it's not too late—unspecialize what they do and find the context for the small things their institutions and funding agencies force them to stare at all day long. The reason is plain: the best college students are after more than an education; they also want guidance, meaning, and purpose. It would be a shame not to direct them toward the Virgils and the Beatrices that may lead them to the paradisiacal heights.

Once after one of my lectures on the poetry of George Herbert, specifically on the influence of St. Augustine and the famous restlessness that inaugurates the *Confessions*, a student walked by me and said in a muted voice, almost as if he wasn't sure he wanted me to hear, "Great class."

Maybe, maybe not. God knows I've laid my share of eggs. But I think what happened that day is that a few shapeless, unarticulated sentiments found expression in the mind of a student desperate for a momentary stay against confusion. Those sentiments were given a local habitation and a name. A young man learned not only that he isn't alone but that he hasn't been orphaned. Herbert is there. St. Augustine is there. And like the man from whom I learned the seventeenth century, I was there too, educated at the lad's expense, or at the expense of his forbears, and, if unfit for any other kind of work, nevertheless doing what I'm supposed to be doing: talking straight.

Robert Frost, Symbolical Teacher

Robert H. Bell is Frederick Latimer Wells Professor of English at Williams College, where he was founding director of the Project for Effective Teaching. He is winner of two national teaching awards, the Robert Foster Cherry Award for Great Teachers and the Carnegie-Case College Professor of the Year Award. Author of many scholarly works, including Jocoserious Joyce: The Fate of Folly in "Ulysses," *(1991), his most recent books are* The Rise of Autobiography in the Eighteenth Century *(2012) and* Shakespeare's Great Stage of Fools *(2013).*

I should awfully like a quiet job in a small college where I should be allowed to teach something a little new on the technique of writing.

—Robert Frost, correspondence to Sidney Cox, 1914

I hate academic ways. I fight everything academic.

—Robert Frost in Edward C. Lathem,
Interviews with Robert Frost, 1916

On his annual tax forms, Robert Frost recorded his occupation as teaching or farming. In fact he devoted far more time to teaching than to farming. No major poet writing in English taught longer or more variously, "every darn year from kindergarten to graduate school."[1] Almost continuously from 1915 to his 1963 death, Frost was formally affiliated with institutions of higher learning. In 1917, he became America's first poet-in-residence at Amherst College, where he spent most of his academic career, except for two stints at the University of Michigan and several years at Dartmouth College. He was also a founding father and regular attraction at Bread Loaf in Middlebury, Vermont. Frost was always teaching, obliquely in his poetry and conspicuously in his public "talks": "My poetry and my teaching were one."[2] Biographers recount Frost's appointments and disappointments at academic institutions, while alumni magazines recall the great man's life-transforming visitations. Less publicized are Frost's lifelong dissatisfaction with institutionalized learning, his ambivalence about higher education, and his strife with colleagues and administrators.[3] As he recollected, "I'm imperfectly academic," and late in life he publically wondered whether he ever taught anybody anything. As a college freshman, he abruptly left Dartmouth in mid-semester, and he would later tell Dartmouth boys, "I ran away from here."[4] He tried Harvard College, where he lasted a year and a half. In 1963 Frost's last talk at Dartmouth touted *extravagance*, a favorite word derived from the Latin, "outside wandering." On principle and by temperament restless and unruly, Frost preferred to wander outside the groves of academe. He felt most himself, in some ways most at home, making things up, while wandering outside, or while "in flight."[5]

Without a BA and with a family to support, Frost taught school. Recognized as a radical innovator and model educator, he addressed several conventions of New Hampshire teachers in 1909. Though he was not a Deweyite progressive, his concept of education was more student oriented than subject centered. In the Pinkerton Academy catalog of 1910–1911, Frost defined the twofold aim of the course in English: to bring students "under the *influence* of the great books, and to teach them the *satisfaction* of superior speech." For the next fifty-four years Frost justified liberal arts "to get the impression fixed for life that there is a book side of everything."[6] For his own course syllabi, he didn't much worry *what* books, as long as they were well written and "influenced" him. He assigned mostly English literature, though not always canonical texts or "Greats." The point was not to learn something about a subject but to subject oneself to wonderful writing, lots of it, without organizational plan or educational agenda. He believed in books.

Frost saw college as "one more chance to learn to read in case we haven't learned in High School."[7] Frost's educational mission was always to bear witness to poetry's power and glory: "Poetry *is* the liberal arts. It's the whole business."[8] Studying poetry, the "profoundest thinking that we have," one learns better taste (no trivial pursuit) and sharper judgment; at home in poetry, one reads and hears more astutely an editorial or political speech—or spots a specious proposition. A proselytizer for poetry, Frost was a seminal teacher of teachers who learned from him what to *do* with a poem in class and how to talk about it.[9] Frost modeled enthusiastic joy in close reading and acute listening. His pedagogy wasn't theoretical but a cluster of interests and practices he could display to reporters and interviewers, Dartmouth and Amherst students and alumni. He rejoiced to address the common reader.[10]

Frost's poetics highlight "the figure a poem makes"—its imaginative designs and linguistic subtlety. A poem's resources are *words*, language as dramatic utterance, with intricate metaphorical and aural components, cooperating to heighten reading pleasure. Poetic language is highly charged, meticulously arranged, connected, and varied, to suggest complex meanings and multiple possibilities. Notably, Frost insisted, "Everything written is as good as it is dramatic," signifying that a poem enacts a character in a dramatic situation listening to himself and/or addressing an interlocutor. With all the prowess he can muster, the poet plays a part or performs a role. The speaker or persona—frustrated lover, bemused observer, or prophetic bard—projects attitudes, ideas, and feelings.

Paramount is a compelling speaking voice, comprising different tonal registers, perhaps trying on various attitudes and feelings or competing intonations. Thus Frost construes a poem not as a product but as a process of internal debate, the ongoing play of point/counterpoint, an encounter of competing possibilities in conjunction or competition. Poetry is a form of dialectic. If style "is with outer seriousness, it must be with inner humor," he said. "If it is with outer humor, it must be with inner seriousness. . . . Neither one alone without the other under it will do."[11]

Poetic language is vitally metaphoric, the "attempt to say matter in terms of spirit, or spirit in terms of matter, to make the final unity." Poetry is "one permissible way of saying one thing and meaning another."[12] There may be a central, governing metaphor, connected (for example) by different sensations, sight, touch, hearing, or situated in different times or places. Frost emphasized that "education by poetry is education by metaphor" and insisted that metaphor is the "whole of thinking," including scientific idiom: "Unless you are at home in the metaphor, unless you have had your proper poetical education in the metaphor, you are not safe anywhere." For Frost, all discourse, including quantum mechanics and cosmic physics, is metaphoric. Thinking, after all, "is just putting this and that together; it is just saying one thing in terms of another." Astronomers say that matter is "something like" curved in space; biologists deploy *evolution* as an organizing metaphor, so that the universe is "like unto a growing thing." But a poem always exposes the *limits* of its metaphors; therefore, readers of poetry know better "how far you expect to ride [a comparison] and when it may break down," for "all metaphor breaks down somewhere. That's the beauty of it." Though a poem tends or aspires (more or less) toward a resolution, it can only achieve "a momentary stay against confusion."

Frost maintained that poetry is distinguished by alertness to sounds, especially the rhythm of a line, conceived as a perceptible pattern of sounds and pauses in sequence. A poem's particular aural effects, such as irregular rhythm, elaborate its pattern or adumbrate its overall design. Frost underscored "the sound of sense," heard as rhythm, alliteration, rhyme, and other aural "events." Hence we're not really reading a poem unless we're reading aloud, experiencing the *sound* of sense.

Frost's pedagogy also highlighted the uses of form, the poem's organizing principles: "There is at least so much good in the world as admits of form and the making of form. And not only admits of it, but calls for it."[13] Frost's focus on aesthetic form, though not unprecedented, "calls for" elaboration. Asking readers to hear the sounds of sense, the variegated rhythms, linked elements, to notice the movement from here to there, to contemplate the degree of closure and the intricacy of a poem's architectural structure—these concerns distinguish the literary study of poetry from casual reading, foregrounding subject or content and seeking "meaning." Poets gesture toward meaning, to be sure, but they also play with words—"revel in felicities of language."[14] As Frost attested in poems and from bully pulpits, "All the fun's in how you say a thing" ("The Mountain"). A poet explores and exploits the vast resources of language.

Professor Frost was puckishly mischievous. He once claimed that the book that influenced him "most" was *Piers the Ploughman*—"yet I never read it." His account doesn't seem facetious: "When I realized how much the book had influenced me I felt I should read it" but "decided against reading it," lest the book prove not to be "what I had thought when I started out to do what I have since done—what the book, unread, inspired me to do." There in the canon he places Langland's fourteenth-century dream vision, a poem probably chosen for its alliterative title and pastoral evocations. Frost liked to be preposterous: "And this is intended to offend you. I hope it offends a few."[15] Making mischief he justified as fundamentally educative. What others called Socratic method Frost called education, "raised to a higher plane of regard."[16] His classes and conversations he envisioned as debates with one's self, speculating and revising perceptions: "Anybody with an active mind lives on tentatives rather than on tenets."[17]

The systole and diastole of thinking were the movement and countermovement of possibility. Actively wandering and wondering, the perennial contrarian advocated nothing—except skepticism, perspectivism, and pluralism. Robert Frost was a galvanizing force in twentieth-century teaching of literature, though he was neither a scholar nor quite a New Critic. He doubted the usefulness of research and disdained inert pedantry. Splendidly learned, he carried his learning lightly. Once asked (at the last minute) to teach a colleague's class on Milton, Frost astonished the Milton scholar by "saying" all 193 lines of "Lycidas." Frost could recite from memory thousands of lines of poetry; he could also discourse confidently about astronomy, botany, or physics. Yet, with all that poetry on tap, the poet distrusted and disparaged the solemn tendentiousness he found in academic analysis. He disliked "professionally literary" commentary that "analyzes itself—and the poem—to death" or defined meanings or qualities as if criticism were a science. Famously, he said that "poetry is what is lost in translation," and added, "It is also what is lost in interpretations."[18] Though Frost urged reading a poem "in the light of all the other poems ever written,"[19] his methods were less academic and systematic and more openly subjective. Frost strove to awaken and extend the student's sensibility, her capacity to respond. Far less important was the determination of any single interpretation or definitive reading.

Frost taught almost constantly to underwrite his primary mission, writing poetry. Amherst undergraduates a century ago met Frost, as one former student recalled, "a sturdily built man in his early forties, wearing rumpled clothes and a celluloid collage, with unruly brown hair, blunt features, and eyes of a seafarer's blue that had a way of magically lighting up." Many students were enchanted by Frost's spell: "He spoke slowly, often rolling up a phrase with many heaves as though it were a stone to be placed in a wall that needed mending." Frost speaking was "an arduous creative triumph, the shaping into form of ideas drawn from the dark abyss of the unconscious mind. It was a dramatic, a memorable hour."[20] A tireless talker, Frost was a remarkably generous mentor, talking with his "boys," or at them, long into the night. "I can stay with a student all night if I can get where he lives, among his realities." But "Professor Frost" also dreaded being "invaded" by students or consumed by dreary busywork. As a member of the faculty, his involvement was minimal—no committees, departmental business, or personnel decisions. He rascally proposed to abolish all academic committees except the Committee to Abolish Committees. To write as much and as well as Frost did, a poet must be alone and self-absorbed.

Relationships with any institution were bound to be tense. Naturally unruly, stubbornly independent, Frost chafed at institutional protocols and academic requirements. He seems to have reckoned himself an *agent provocateur*. Even on the bucolic campuses of Amherst and Dartmouth, Frost was a perennial maverick and restless spirit; as he recalled, "I ran away twice and I walked away a good many times." Frost epitomized William James's "undisciplinables"; his first book of poems was titled *A Boy's Will*. Fiercely unfettered and "dangerously skeptic" ("The White-Tailed Hornet"), Frost delighted in puncturing reputations, interrogating conventional wisdom—

including the value of liberal arts education. He frequently surprised students by asking, "Why do they have classes anyway?" or advising them to leave school. "Then," he said, "if they insist on coming to school it is not my fault. I can teach with a clear conscience."[21]

As Frost's fame burgeoned, the teacher of tentatives and advocate of nothing became more monumentally imposing, the lionized bard and prophet, illuminating the state of poetry, the country, and the world. Just as his later poems sometimes lapsed into verse homilies or parochial proverbs, without the vital equivocation of "For Once, Then, Something" or the sly self-irony of "The Most of It" or the scrupulous nonpartisanship of "Home Burial," Frost the iconic teacher occasionally delivered aphoristic maxims or takeaway points. More often, then, in his celebrity, Frost spoke in "a personal voice which for all its official embracing of skepticism," William Pritchard observes, was "not notably skeptical about its own prejudices and the weight of authority they commanded."[22] With colleagues and peers he was the king holding court and pronouncing judgments; it's unlikely that he was less sublimely marmoreal with undergraduates.

The great gray eminence was an egregious prima donna who loved to be feted: "I only go / When I'm the show," he would say, as if self-ironically, when invited to perform with other poets. Always the cynosure, he refused to share the platform or limelight. Even in small groups of faculty, Frost did all the talking, perhaps fielding questions and usually radiating an "essential goodness and humanity,"[23] suitable for America's apostle of poetry, as Dartmouth poet and professor Richard Eberhart recounts.

Robert Frost's powers to catalyze and mesmerize audiences were entangled with troublesome and troubling instincts. In his truly Sophoclean family history, Frost was markedly un-innocent. By several accounts, Frost was a "monster of egoism": irritable and irascible, paranoid and vindictive.[24] A shameless gossip, Frost cruelly assailed rivals and "abused even teachers close to him on the campus; but always with a fine turn of phrase," recalls Pritchard, "the lines of a brilliant entertainer."[25] Anyone expecting a beneficent, magnanimous spirit was startled by his "violent prejudices and hatreds." Frost proclaimed himself firmly "mounted on [his] prejudices," which he regarded as judgments of value and matters of principle. Sometimes he could appear to be anti-intellectual, or as it were, insufficiently deferential to scholarly erudition. He seems to have disliked teaching young women at Michigan, especially those "advocating feminist ideas made popular during" World War I; female students who challenged his authority he referred to as "little she devils."[26] At Amherst in the 1920s, he resisted and protested President Meiklejohn's "inquisition to compel liberality."[27] Students were often surprised to discover that this professor was no liberal; he thought that FDR's New Deal encouraged "sentimental humanitarianism." In our egalitarian times, Frost would be termed an elitist, teaching the talented tenth, whom he regarded as the "free-born students," distinct from the drones and "slaves."

Some forms of Frost's aggressiveness were harmless and amusing. He was a fiercely combative softball player into his seventies. Frost was more congenial when he won, like old Henry VIII jousting against his young knights. Any performance was a demonstration of *prowess*, another cherished word he often employed to characterize sports and poetry. Frost performing Frost—"the Great Act," in Robert Lowell's phrase—was charismatic, "me myself in the summer heaven godlike" ("For Once, Then, Something"). Frost wasn't the least reticent or queasy about theatricality in art or teaching. "I look on the poet as a man of prowess, just like an athlete. He's a performer. . . . Every poem is some sort of achievement in performance." What Frost felt about writing poetry applied, usually, to his teaching: "What do I want to communicate but what a hell of a good time I had writing it? The whole thing is performance and prowess and feats of association."[28] Once a shy, tongue-tied speaker, Frost labored to produce his great act. "While gesticulating he would habitually rumple his thick white hair and produce his characteristically uncombed appearance."[29]

Frost reflected on "education by presence," stressing the "deep potential value" to the students of "communications" with a larger-than-life figure, a "power outside" the academy, "known all over the country."[30] The professor's "own work," Frost emphasizes, "must say that." Of his own teaching, the fifty-year-old Frost remarked, "I am an indifferent teacher as teachers go, and it is hard to understand why I am wanted around colleges unless there is some force it is thought I can exert by merely belonging to them. It must be what I stand for does my work." To teach is to provide access to one's extraordinary presence, as Frost acknowledged, "to give students a claim on me, so that they may come at me at any time, outside class periods."[31] Frost does include in his pantheon of Venerables, "distinguished research scholars," who, like poets, "see life large." Frost urged colleges to build an "upper tier, of teachers who offered themselves or were offered thus" for students wise enough to seek out luminaries and paradigm shifters.

Paradoxically or perversely, Frost endorsed teaching by absence. Defining three modes of teaching—"by formal contact in the classroom, by informal contact, socially as it were, and by virtually no contact at all. And I am putting the last first in importance—the teaching by no contact at all."[32] It worked for Robert Frost, college dropout, wandering and wondering on his own. Fundamentally, Frost believed that "the only education worth anything is self-education."[33] Frost's students were on their own, without any handholding or guidance. In this sense Frost accurately dubbed himself a "symbolical teacher."[34] His teaching was avowedly nondirective: "if you'll let a guide direct you / Who only has at heart your getting lost" ("Directive"). Such teachers put students in the presence of great writers, demonstrate enthusiasm toward and faith in books, and get out of the student's way: "Once we have learned to read the rest can be trusted to add itself unto us."[35] What about the conventional student, or the diffident youth unable or unwilling to "press his claim" to individual audience? That poor lad must take an examination. "But he has already lowered his estimation," that is, "been found wanting." Woe betide the boy daunted by the charismatic prowess.

The educator, Frost said, should "give people the things that will make them say, 'Oh yes, I know what you mean.' It is never to tell them something they don't know, but something they know and hadn't thought of saying. It must be something they recognize."[36] Described metaphorically, it sounds like Socratic dialectic: Frost said he put students "on the operating table and proceeded to take ideas they didn't know they had out of them as a prestidigitator takes rabbits and pigeons you have declared yourself innocent of out of your pocket trousers[,] legs and even mouth."[37] Usually, Frost's courses were one-man shows, not real discussions. One signal toward his students was to distribute slips of paper on which students wrote remarks or posed questions; Frost would begin the next class with reactions to the students' inquiries and observations.

Frost's pedagogy was touch-and-go, or inconsistent. He told students he never "put too much store in the virtue of finishing a book once you had started it. Why? Why even finish a chapter? The interesting thing about reading was what a book made you think about." Books provided "ways of getting you to think, ways of getting you to quit studying, to go off on your own in quest of some sort of original idea, to become more yourself."[38] The charismatic presence of a genius rendered unnecessary lesson plans and teaching tactics. There he was—"talking and talking, a mischievous grin playing over his strangely wrinkled face, his big hands, rough on the backs and smooth on the palms, making rhythmical chops in the air like someone splitting kindling with a hatchet, a gesture at once emphatic and lyrical, as though he were conducting his own music."[39]

Frost's students were unlikely to learn through practice how to reconsider ideas and emend articulations. Student *writing*—on which we liberal arts profs toil arduously—was not nearly as significant or conscientiously appraised by Frost as one would expect. At Amherst Frost required hardly any papers. He didn't believe you could teach writing, and he thought corrections and comments a waste of his time. "To learn to write is to learn to have ideas."[40] He might not read his students' papers, and he hardly ever assessed them. Essays were seldom returned.[41] Once, Frost recalled, after giving a class a chance to say if there was anything in the bunch of themes on my desk they wanted to keep and satisfied myself there wasn't I threw them unread into the waste basket while the class looked on. If they didn't care enough for the themes to keep them I didn't care enough for the themes to read them. I wasn't going to be a perfunctory corrector of perfunctory writing.[42]

Shades of Robin Williams in *Dead Poets Society* excoriating the textbook, tearing it to pieces flung anywhere. It is one way to seize their attention and win their applause.

Frost was equally casual or irresponsible about examinations. As a high school teacher he often distributed blue books and instructed students to write about anything that interested them—while he read. At colleges, he was perfectly happy to administer occasional exams but ignored them conspicuously. He once gave an A to a blank exam; a student, suspecting her blue books weren't being read, submitted a deliberately ridiculous response—and never heard back. One exam he was "compelled to give" instructed students to "Do something appropriate to this course which will please and interest me." This seems to be a question not to be asked, at least not in such bald terms. Frost expected a few boys to read the question and leave, mindful that "I already knew them well enough, that I already had their grades ready anyhow." Perhaps some students would "come to me, a little later, and take it out in talk." Instead, every student appeared one-by-one in the professor's office "to say something pleasant to me in parting." To Frost what was notable was how "they understood the word 'please' in my leading question,"[43] not that his "leading question" encouraged undergraduates, like Lear's older daughters, to utter formulaic pieties. In high school classrooms, Frost neglected discipline, unless the restless boys became flagrantly disruptive. Even at Amherst in the 1920s, his classes were loosely managed and weirdly undisciplined: he ignored the wise guys playing cards in the back row. Frost acknowledged that "half the time I don't know whether students are in my classes or not."

In midcentury America, Robert Frost was in effect poet laureate for life, admired universally and regularly honored. He won four Pulitzer prizes, represented the country as international ambassador, adorned the cover of *Life* magazine, read at JFK's inauguration, sold forests of books, lodged his poems in school curricula, logged countless miles—teaching, talking. Perhaps Frost's most successful mode of teaching was his campus "talks," as he called his lectures and frequent public appearances. Usually unscripted, they focused on long-meditated subjects, such as poetry or reading or education.

He didn't like to speak after a formal dinner because he wanted to withdraw, husband his resources, and percolate in private. His ruminations, reiterating favorite themes, appeared improvised, as if he were thinking aloud, just wondering. He might begin, as he did in 1954, "What am I thinking about now, at eighty? Well, I'll tell you what I'm thinking about. I'm thinking about Freedom a good deal."[44] This brought him to a pet peeve, free verse, and to his preference for form, leading ultimately (if not inevitably) to Frost's cherished distinction between "freedom from" and "freedom to." He disregarded logically developed argument and always insisted he was there to "advocate nothing." "An Evening with Robert Frost" dramatized the play of perspectives and danced around subjects. He enacted the process of contemplation, "the mind skating circles round itself as it moves forward."[45] As if extemporizing, he might ask the audience to help him find the right word for a distinction or comparison. A lecturer like a poet fails (or bores) when his conclusions only reprise what he already knew at the outset. Better to pursue a possibility "more felt than known," a discovery to surprise the author as well as audience. In the 1950s, when he was an annual event at Dartmouth's Great Issues Program, Frost's great issues might be anything unrelated to the ostensible topic and could go anywhere. No one minded; audiences were entertained and inspired by Frost's vibrant presence.

Although critics such as Randall Jarrell and Lionel Trilling found in Frost a much darker, disquieting "modernist," to the public Frost appeared refreshingly healthy, morally bracing, easily accessible, and quintessentially American—our favorite uncle, pausing from apple picking or flower gazing to set us right and cheer our spirits. My wife and I received as a wedding gift a leather-bound edition of Frost's poetry, inscribed, "A happy poet for a happy day." More readers are now attuned to Frost's equivocations and self-questioning, how often his poems are cannily hedging bets and deftly tergiversating:

You could not tell, and yet it looked as if ("Once by the Pacific")

We dance round in a ring and suppose,
But the secret sits in the middle and knows. ("The Secret Sits")

As one who shrewdly pretends
That he and the world are friends ("A Drumlin Woodchuck")

Earth's the right place for love;
I don't know where it's likely to go better ("Birches")

No American writer, save perhaps Mark Twain, so vigorously espoused the efficacy of play or maintained the primacy of pleasure. His mantra was

"The play's the thing. Play's the thing. All virtue in *as if*." In several senses, play's the thing Frost loved, sanctioned, and promoted, as if "From sheer morning gladness at the brim" ("The Tuft of Flowers"). Reading aloud was fun his students learned to enjoy, or ought to have done. What his students and those adoring throngs remembered best were Frost's galvanizing enthusiasm and wry humor. Yet Frost's birch could also swing the other way, for he was constantly, as he himself said, "fooling my way along."[46] "Fooling" licensed mischief, enabling the poet, "imperfectly tamed,"[47] to ruffle feathers and raise hell. As he reflected in one ditty, left in a notebook, "Nothing ever so sincere / That unless it's out of sheer / Mischief and a little queer / It won't prove a bore to hear." Many supposed "oracularities" from on high were accompanied by a wink or uttered tongue-in-cheek. Characterizing his own irony, he said it was "simply a kind of guardedness. So is a twinkle. It keeps the reader from criticism."[48] Reiterating that he was "only fooling" might cover a multitude of sins, transgressions, and improprieties. "Behind light words that tease and flout" ("Revelation"), the old trickster could be mischievous or malicious.

Wary of the extraordinary, Frost was always keen to dislodge anything highfalutin. A favorite tactic was to express and parody high and mighty pretensions. No poet since Dryden and Pope played this game more drolly or subtly. Hence, he writes in "A Wishing Well" (1962), "It takes all kinds of in and outdoor schooling / To get adapted to my kind of fooling." How he must have loved that rhyme between *schooling* and *fooling*! Frost sometimes donned the Fool's cap and bells. Like the sad clowns of Shakespeare, he would say, "I am a jester about sorrow."[49] Some of his discourse resembles the sophistry of Lear's Fool, Touchstone, and Feste—or the antic disposition of Hamlet. "Let's play confusion," he'd suggest to a friend: "Are you confused?" "Yes," agreed his interlocutor. "I'm not. I win," Frost proclaimed, grinning triumphantly. Like any fool worth his keep, Frost entertained and exasperated, by mocking conventional beliefs, turning things topsy-turvy and mixing extravagant nonsense with bitter truths.

For Frost, "The more I say *I* the more I always mean somebody else."[50] Frost's role-playing tempts readers into identifying the poet with his speaker's extravagant faith ("And that has made all the difference" in "The Road Not Taken") or dubious simplifications ("Good fences make good neighbors"). Usually the poem is more many-minded. Maybe, he mused, he was just "too cussedly non-conformist to trust even his own words as texts five minutes after he has uttered them."[51] To Untermeyer, Frost wrote, "You get more credit for thinking if you restate formulae or cite cases that fall easily under formulae. But all the fun is outside, saying things that suggest formulae but won't formulate—that almost but don't quite formulate. I should like to be so subtle at this game as to seem to a casual person altogether obvious."[52]

Frost liked to say he was a dualist in his thinking and a monist in his wishing. The dualist juxtaposes contrasting voices or tones, vernacular and oracular or gravity and levity. It's the simultaneity of competing attitudes that distinguishes Frost: "No matter how humorous I am I am sad. I am a jester about sorrow."[53] He sought "improbable possibilities."[54] He believed a poem to be the play of perspectives, "a kind of fooling."[55] Again, "Play no matter how deep has got to be so playful that the audience are left in doubt whether it is deep or shallow."[56] Poems such as "Mending Wall" conflate teaching and playing seamlessly. An authoritative narrator and his laconic neighbor annually collaborate to rebuild their common wall. The poem splits, or, rather, fragments, by far the greater proportion owned by Frost's speaker, the speaking "I" who dominates the discourse and acts like a teacher, wondering, "If I could put a notion in his head." It's the teacherly speaker who raises the stakes and ponders the ramifications: "Before I built a wall I'd ask to know / What I was walling in or walling out." And it's this pedagogic farmer who qualifies and corrects himself: "But it's not elves exactly" upsetting that wall, as he "could say." And very like a Socratic mentor, he confides, "I'd rather / He said it for himself." This speaker appears to be a surrogate for the poet.

But the boundary between speaker and neighbor, self and other, proves porous, gap-filled, and frost shaken—a tentative "line" rather than a sturdy tenet. "Mending Wall" belies any single belief. It urges nothing, contrary to what poetry sometimes "has to bear in the teaching process," that is, being treated "as something other than poetry."[57] Though he doesn't quite say that a poem *must* not advocate anything, Frost stresses that poets don't necessarily mean what they say, at least not in any straightforward way. Hence, Frost often stages a dialogue between one's selves, so that monologue becomes a lyric debate. In "Mending Wall," Frost's "neighbor," one might observe, is no mere straw man; on the other side he holds his ground. Perhaps he stands for a countervailing attitude within the speaker, who hints: "He moves in darkness as it seems to me," obscurely doubled, "Not of woods only and the shade of trees." There may be an essential half-truth in the neighbor's simple recapitulation: "He says again, 'Good fences make good neighbors.'" In this half-light, it's not gratuitous that the neighbor gets the last word— and utters the memorable adage. Conversely, Frost's speaker is both the source and object of humor—half of which he well knows: "Spring is the mischief in me . . ." Projecting his impish humor, Frost's speaker muses that their wall might discourage "Elves." Seen whole, "Mending Wall" contains without endorsing proverbial lore, however quotable; like the play of mind that animated Frost's teaching and talking, this education by poetry is play for mortal stakes.

Notes

1. Edward C. Lathem, *Interviews with Robert Frost* (New York: Holt, Rinehart and Winston, 1966), 269.

2. Frost, cited by Peter J. Stanlis, "Robert Frost's Philosophy of Education: The Poet as Teacher," *Roads Not Taken: Rereading Robert Frost*, ed. Earl J. Wilcox and Jonathan N. Barron (Columbia and London: University of Missouri Press, 2000), 78.

3. For biographical accounts, see Lawrance Thompson's three-volume biography, *Robert Frost: The Early Years: 1874–1915* (New York: Holt, Rinehart and Winston, 1966); *The Years of Triumph: 1915–1938* (New York: Holt, Rinehart and Winston, 1970); *The Later Years: 1938–1963* (New York: Holt Rinehart and Winston, 1976). There is also a one-volume version, *Robert Frost: A Biography*, by Lawrance Thompson and R. H. Winnick (New York: Holt, Rinehart and Winston, 1981). Another biographer who treats Frost's academic career in some detail is Jeffrey Meyers, *Robert Frost: A Biography* (Boston and New York: Houghton Mifflin, 1996). The best account of Frost's "literary life" is William H. Pritchard, *Frost: A Literary Life Reconsidered* (Amherst: University of Massachusetts Press, 1993).

4. Lathem, *Interviews*, 56.

5. Richard Poirier, *Robert Frost: The Work of Knowing* (New York and London: Oxford University Press, 1977), 158.

6. Edward Connery Lathem and Lawrance Thompson, *The Robert Frost Reader: Poetry and Prose* (New York: Henry Holt, 1972), 459.

7. Ibid.

8. Robert Frost, *Robert Frost: Speaking on Campus: Excerpts from His Talks 1949–1962*, edited by Edward Connery Lathem (New York: W. W. Norton, 2009), 38. Frost's conception of "poetry" was capacious enough to include masterful prose by his beloved Gibbon and William James.

9. See Reuben A. Brower, *The Fields of Light: An Experiment in Critical Reading* (New York: Oxford University Press, 1951). Brower elsewhere describes "Reading in Slow Motion." See *In Defense of Reading: A Reader's Approach to Literary Criticism*, ed. Reuben A. Brower and Richard Poirier (New York: Dutton, 1962). See also Richard Poirier, *Poetry & Pragmatism* (Cambridge: Harvard University Press, 1992), especially chapter 4, "Reading Pragmatically: The Example of Hum 6," and William H. Pritchard, "Reuben A. Brower," *American Scholar* (June 1985): 239–247, and in *English Papers: A Teaching Life* (Amherst: University of Massachusetts Press, 1995), chapter 6, 85ff.

10. "Education by Poetry," for instance, was originally presented to the Amherst Alumni Council in 1930 and published in the Amherst alumni journal. Available at the Robert Frost Periodicals Collection at Amherst College, www.amherst.edu/media/view/79303/original/frost-periodicals.pdf.

11. Robert Frost, "Introduction to E. A. Robinson's 'King Jaspar,'" in *Collected Poems, Prose, and Plays*, edited by Richard Poirier and Mark Richardson (New York: Library of America, 1995), 746. Hereafter *CPP&P*.

12. Robert Frost, "Education by Poetry: A Meditative Monologue," *CPP&P*, 719. The other citations in this paragraph are also from "Education by Poetry." Subsequently cited as EBP.

13. Frost, "Letter to *The Amherst Student*," *CPP&P*, 740. Has any college newspaper ever published a more striking letter to the editors?

14. Frost, "E. A. Robinson's 'King Jaspar,'" *CPP&P*, 747.

15. Lathem, *Interviews*, 38.

16. Frost, *Speaking on Campus*, 156.

17. Cited by Lisa Seal, "Original Originality: Robert Frost's Talks," *Roads Not Taken: Rereading Robert Frost*, edited by Earl J. Wilcox and Jonathan N. Barron (Columbia: University of Missouri Press, 2000), 109. Seal cites Frost, "Heritage One, Program Nine: An Intimate Conversation between Mr. Frost and Dr. Jonas Salk."

18. Cited by Louis Untermeyer, *Robert Frost: A Backward Look* (Washington, DC: Reference Department, Library of Congress, 1964), 22.

19. Lathem and Thompson, *Robert Frost Reader*, 459.

20. George Whicher was speaking in 1946 at Amherst. See Pritchard, *A Literary Life Reconsidered*, 124.

21. Quoted by Irving Yevish, in "Robert Frost, Campus Rebel," *Texas Quarterly* 11.1 (1968): 49–55.

22. Pritchard, *A Literary Life Reconsidered*, 204.

23. Richard Eberhart, "Robert Frost: His Personality," *Southern Review* 2.4 (October 1966): 786.

24. Lawrance Thompson's three-volume biography (1966–1976) was highly provocative and controversial.

25. Pritchard, *A Literary Life Reconsidered*, 130–131, cites Henry A. Ladd, "Memories of Robert Frost," *Touchstone* (February 1939): 15.

26. Frost, cited by Meyers, *Robert Frost: A Biography*, 169.

27. Thompson, *The Early Years*, 119.

28. Frost, "*Paris Review* Interview, with Richard Poirier," *CPP&P*, 890, 892.

29. Meyers, *Robert Frost: A Biography*, 236, cites Peter Davison, "Robert Frost," *One of the Dangerous Trades*, 81.

30. Frost, interviewed by the *Christian Science Monitor* on December 24, 1925, at age fifty, since 1917 on the faculty of Amherst College, and about to begin a stint at the University of Michigan. Reprinted as "Education by Presence" in Lathem and Thompson, *The Robert Frost Reader: Poetry and Prose*, 341.

31. Lathem and Thompson, *The Robert Frost Reader: Poetry and Prose*, 343.

32. Ibid., 342.

33. Robert Frost, *The Letters of Robert Frost to Louis Untermeyer* (New York: Holt, Rinehart and Winston, 1963), 376. Subsequently cited as Untermeyer, *Letters*.

34. Ibid., 289.

35. Published in *Atlantic Monthly* June 1951 and reprinted in Lathem and Thompson, *The Robert Frost Reader: Poetry and Prose*, 459.

36. Robert Frost, *Selected Letters of Robert Frost*, edited by Lawrance Thompson (New York: Holt, Rinehart and Winston, 1964), 111.

37. Robert Frost writing Louis Untermeyer, cited by Pritchard, *A Literary Life Reconsidered*, 124.

38. Peter Davison, *One of the Dangerous Trades: Essay on the Work and Workings of Poetry* (Ann Arbor: University of Michigan Press, 1991), 65–66.

39. Davison, "Robert Frost," *One of the Dangerous Trades*, 81.

40. Frost, *EBP* 724.

41. In "Education by Poetry," Frost laments that teachers must be "markers." His own procedure, to estimate how close a student has come to a poet or poem, he says, is to "mark" students based on their "remarks." He would countenance twenty "fool remarks if he made one good one."

42. Frost, *Letters of Robert Frost to Louis Untermeyer*, 289.

43. See Lathem and Thompson, *The Robert Frost Reader: Poetry and Prose*, 344.

44. Lathem, *Interviews*, 48.

45. Thompson and Winnick, *Robert Frost: A Biography*, 292.

46. Pritchard cites Frost, *A Literary Life Reconsidered*, 128.

47. As his friend and sometime colleague Sidney Cox described the young teacher at the Plymouth (NH) Normal School; cited by Pritchard, *A Literary Life Reconsidered*, 64.

48. Frost, "To Louis Untermeyer" (March 10, 1924), *CPP&P*, 702.

49. Frost, writing to his daughter Lesley in 1917. See *Family Letters of Robert and Elinor Frost* (Albany: State University of New York Press, 1972), 210.

50. Frost at Bread Loaf, in 1955.

51. Frost, cited by Thompson and Winnick, *Robert Frost: A Biography*, 288.

52. Frost to Untermeyer, January 1, 1917, *Letters of Robert Frost to Louis Untermeyer*.

53. Frost, *Family Letters of Robert and Elinor Frost*, 210.

54. I owe this last phrase, and much else, to Pritchard. As Frost once wrote a correspondent, "I state this in the extreme. But relatively I mean what I say." See Frost, *CPP&P*, 729.

55. Frost, "On Taking Poetry," *CPP&P*, 818.

56. Frost, Notebook in Dartmouth College Library, Hanover, New Hampshire, Robert Frost Collection.

57. Untermeyer, *Letters* 194.

The "Job Definition" of a Faculty Member at a Liberal Arts Institution

⋅⋅•⋅——⋅•⋅

ELIZABETH J. JENSEN

Elizabeth J. Jensen is Professor of Economics at Hamilton College. She earned her bachelor's degree from Swarthmore College and PhD from MIT. Jensen is co-author of Industrial Organization: Theory and Practice, *a leading industrial organization textbook developed in part from experiences teaching students at Hamilton. Her recent work investigates pedagogical questions arising in teaching industrial organization, the predictors of academic success in college, and student course choice. Jensen teaches courses in industrial organization, antitrust and regulation, American economic history, and microeconomic theory. She has twice been honored for her teaching, having been chosen as the Christian A. Johnson Excellence in Teaching Professor for 2011–2014 and having received the Class of 1962 Outstanding Teaching Award in 2002.*

๖

As a senior at Swarthmore College, I was trying to decide whether to apply to law school or to PhD programs in economics. Fortunately for me, I was chosen as a student assistant in economics statistics, a position in which I worked with students on problem sets and led help sessions. This experience showed me the joy teaching could bring and solidified my decision to apply to graduate school. And when I was on the job market five years after that,

I focused my search on liberal arts colleges where excellent teaching was valued and expected. However, even thirty years ago, more than excellent teaching was required at selective liberal arts colleges; during the decades since then, these schools have formalized expectations with regard to the dimensions of the job and the bar for scholarship has been raised at these schools. Now, as a senior faculty member involved in hiring, mentoring, and evaluating junior colleagues, I think about these expectations, leading me to the question, what is the "job definition" of a faculty member at a selective liberal arts college? Or, another way of asking the question, what are the requirements to earn tenure at such an institution? In order to get an idea of the responsibilities of faculty members who work with students at these colleges, I examined faculty handbooks from small liberal arts colleges listed in the top twenty-five in *U.S. News & World Report* (recognizing the fallibility of any such list). The bars at these schools are set high; undergraduates are being taught by faculty members committed to both teaching and research.

Teaching

Not surprisingly, all of the schools expect excellence in teaching. Although they make different statements about the importance of teaching relative to the other criteria for tenure and promotion, no college or university assigns a *lower* weight to the quality of teaching than to any other faculty responsibility. Simply put, one cannot earn tenure at a small liberal arts college without demonstrating a commitment to and skills in educating and working with undergraduate students.

Let's look first at the statements about importance of criteria—at the relative weights given to different dimensions of the job. At some institutions, teaching and scholarship are explicitly identified as the more important considerations, with no distinction made about the importance of one versus the other; service is the third, and less important, criterion. For example, at Bowdoin College, "two [criteria] are of paramount importance: candidates for tenure will be expected to have excelled in their teaching and to have achieved a level of professional distinction recognized by members of their guild outside the College."[1] Similarly, Vassar College "seeks excellence in its faculty in both teaching and scholarship or creative activity."[2] Other institutions indicate that teaching is of primary importance: Amherst College states that "effective teaching is regarded as a prime factor for reappointment and promotion";[3] Carleton College notes that "Carleton is primarily a teaching institution. Thus, demonstrated excellence in teaching is the most important concern in the consideration of a candidate for tenure";[4] and Harvey Mudd College indicates that "ability as a teacher is of prime importance."[5]

These statements lead to two questions: What does it mean to be an effective/excellent teacher at a liberal arts college? And, what evidence is used to evaluate teaching effectiveness? The characteristics listed in handbooks as defining excellence in teaching are not surprising: institutions mention knowledge of the subject, enthusiasm for the material, organization, and the ability to present abstract ideas or theoretical material clearly. In addition, schools are interested in growth of the students as a result of interactions with the professor. Thus, an effective faculty member encourages students to think for themselves, helps students to write clearly and logically, and incites students' intellectual curiosity. Also, several institutions look for accessibility of the faculty member outside of class, fairness in grading student work, flexibility, reliability, and willingness to try new concepts, both in terms of course offerings and use of technology. Excellence in teaching requires preparation, communication skills, and dedication to working with undergraduates outside of class time.

Because of the importance of teaching in reappointment, tenure, and promotion decisions at liberal arts institutions, and because of the recognition that teaching is a complex and multifaceted task, several types of evidence are used in evaluating a faculty member's performance. Typically, a candidate for tenure and promotion submits a personal statement addressing issues related to teaching, such as objectives for each course, pedagogical methods used during class, and types of assignments and expectations for the students. Materials such as syllabi, lab assignments, problem sets, and exams can supplement and support the candidate's personal statement. Student assessment of teaching effectiveness is important and expected; although the specific details of the forms vary, all of the colleges use student evaluations of teaching forms as part of the reappointment and tenure process. Many also solicit letters from students. At Bates College, for example, letters from twenty students or former students are part of the files; Macalester suggests the inclusion of letters from ten to twenty students or alums; at Hamilton, the faculty member provides names of ten to fifteen students and the Registrar's Office randomly selects fifteen students. Finally, assessment from colleagues—based on classroom observations, attendance at seminar presentations given by the candidate, and class materials—is part of the personnel file at some schools.

A Walk Down Memory Lane

But hasn't teaching always been important at liberal arts colleges? How have expectations changed over the past decades? The *Hamilton College Faculty Handbook* from 1957 (the earliest handbook in the archives) states, "Good teaching is the primary and indispensable function of every member of the

Hamilton College faculty" and "effective teaching is [their] basic and central interest, the superior teacher [their] pride." Interestingly, aspects of effective teaching listed in that handbook were the same in 1957 as today, including enthusiasm, mastery of the subject, skill in organizing material, and careful class preparation. Yet, several important changes have occurred. Indeed, both the evidence gathered to document good teaching and the procedure used to assess a faculty member's effectiveness as a teacher seem to come from a different world. At Hamilton, promotion from assistant professor to associate professor in 1957 required "skill in instruction, evidence of which shall be obtained from the best available sources," with no discussion or list of what might constitute such sources.[6] Further, there is no description of promotion policy. In fact, the handbook goes further, arguing that it is not possible to have a policy:

> Promotion of a faculty member to higher rank is contingent upon many factors, tangible and otherwise; each instance is obviously weighed upon its own merits. Accordingly, no statement of official promotion policy is possible, beyond that adopted by the Board of Trustees in 1956 to the effect that no member of the faculty shall normally be considered from promotion to the rank of Associate Professor unless he possess the Doctors Degree.[7]

Today, APT procedures (appointment, promotion, tenure) at all schools have to be codified, routinized, and transparent in order to conform to professional (and legal) standards.

The biggest change at liberal arts colleges, however, is that in order to be successful, a faculty member today must also maintain an active research agenda, so we turn now to scholarship.

Scholarship

As discussed, several of the top liberal arts colleges state that teaching and scholarship are the primary aspects evaluated for tenure and promotion. Even at the schools that give the most weight or highest priority to teaching effectiveness, however, scholarship is a close second. Amherst places "great weight" on "continued scholarly growth of faculty members,"[8] and Colgate University explains that while excellence in teaching is "necessary, it is not alone sufficient for retention or advancement; it cannot compensate for scholarship that is not of high quality."[9] Similarly, Hamilton weights quality of teaching most heavily but adds that "research is both encouraged and expected."[10] At Scripps College, which "emphasizes, above all, the teaching ability of its faculty,"[11] tenure requires "evidence that the candidate has made a significant contribution to her/his discipline or area, and shows promise of continuing to do so."[12]

Why do liberal arts colleges, with their commitment to undergraduate education and teaching effectiveness, expect their faculty members to be active scholars? While some faculty handbooks do not discuss this explicitly, stating just that scholarly accomplishments are required for tenure, several tie continued effectiveness as a teacher to work as a scholar. As Carleton explains, "Teaching effectiveness and the quality of a faculty member's inter-action with students and colleagues over the long term of a career depend on a commitment to and a capacity for scholarship and continuing intel-lectual growth,"[13] and Hamilton "believes that effective teaching and sound scholarship are mutually reinforcing."[14] Wellesley wants its faculty members to use their scholarship "to enliven discussion in the classroom and within the college community and beyond."[15] At Swarthmore, strong teaching is not "regarded as probable in the absence of strong scholarship."[16] Other institu-tions note that scholarship is valued in and of itself: Claremont McKenna College seeks faculty members "whose scholarly activity is of genuine profes-sional value to his or her discipline."[17] Washington and Lee University values intellectual activity and achievement as a valuable characteristic of a faculty member because it "can contribute to the learning and teaching that the University seeks to foster."[18] And Scripps College recognizes that professional engagement contributes to teaching but also states, "Through professional achievement faculty become part of the academic community at large."[19]

A few schools make no explicit statement about what constitutes evi-dence of scholarship or make only minimal statements. Amherst, for exam-ple, mentions "research, publication, and creative work,"[20] and Swarthmore explains that "scholarship will be considered in the light of publications, effective research, or other activities (such as professional consulting and advising) that contribute to the advancement of knowledge."[21] It is clear that all look for research in the form of publications or the equivalent for creative disciplines. Several handbooks include statements such as Pomona's: "The most obvious form of such work is scholarly productivity in the form of books, significant articles, the completion of publishable manuscripts, or artistic creation or performance."[22] Similarly, Hamilton notes that "original research and its equivalent expression in the performing and creative arts are the principal forms of scholarship,"[23] and Smith expands on the value of published work in the statement, "Published written work is usually the best guide to a faculty member's scholarly capabilities, since publication enables peers in the profession, outside as well as inside the College, to judge the quality of scholarship."[24] Additional indicators of scholarship are explicitly considered at several schools; presentation of work at professional conferences, consulting, and receipt of awards and grants indicate active and ongoing scholarship. Middlebury looks for "a pattern of related professional activities";[25] Swarthmore recognizes that the tenure decision is ultimately a forward-looking decision, adding that "it is ultimately an integral decision about performance and potentiality."[26]

In order to assess the quality of the scholarship, institutions rely on external reviews as well as evaluation by the senior members in the candidate's department or program. Typically, the candidate compiles a list of potential reviewers and the department compiles a separate list, with stipulation that one or more reviewers must be chosen from each list. At several institutions, the dean or provost seeks additional reviewers not on either list. The numbers of outside reviews specified ranges from four to eight; processes require senior colleagues of the candidate in the department or program to include consideration of the reviews in their recommendation. This process, of course, provides peer reviews of scholarship, including both published work and work in progress.

Service

As discussed, several institutions explicitly indicate that service is the least important of the three general dimensions of the job. Smith College, for example, states that "the primary criteria for reappointment, promotion, and tenure shall be the individual faculty member's accomplishments as a teacher and scholar. Service to the College also shall constitute a criterion for advancement."[27] Amherst College explains, "In addition, the College takes account of a faculty member's general contribution to the life of the College community,"[28] and Grinnell's handbook states, "An important element, although less weighty than i. [teaching] and ii. [scholarship], is a demonstrated commitment to the College."[29]

As Grinnell's statement makes clear, however, even though service is weighed less heavily than teaching and scholarship, a faculty member at a liberal arts college is expected to participate in some service. Thus, at Claremont McKenna, "Service, in the sense of sharing in the administrative responsibilities of institutional life, is an integral but lesser part of the teacher-scholar's relationship to the College. Lack of service can, however, play an important role in the denial of promotion and tenure."[30] And for Colgate, "Service to the University is the third area of consideration. Different candidates may contribute to the University in different ways, but service of high quality is expected of all."[31] So, clearly, junior faculty members must juggle all three aspects of their jobs, while making sure that service does not take up an inordinate amount of time.

Most of the handbooks recognize that service to the college or university can take different forms and that, as stated by Bates, "the nature and extent of these contributions may vary from individual to individual." Among the activities that can count as service are membership on committees—at the department, college, or program level—lectures, performances, or exhibits for the college community; advising student organizations; arranging lecture or performance series; and "myriad other activities that aid in faculty and college governance and enhance the intellectual and artistic life of the community."[32] Several institutions recognize service beyond the campus as valuable. Here, examples include serving as an officer in a scholarly organization and advancing primary or secondary education.

Putting It All Together

As this essay makes clear, a faculty member at a liberal arts college must meet many professional responsibilities, and it is a challenging occupation. But it is a rewarding path. As the president of Washington and Lee University, Kenneth P. Ruscio, writes in the introduction to its faculty handbook, "But in a busy career as a teacher-scholar burdens are borne out of love of learning, a passion for seeking and expressing the truth as best we can, and a commitment to serve an institution with a long and distinguished history of introducing young people to the responsibilities of the professions and the life-long enrichment of the liberal arts."[33] A quote from a thank-you note I received from a student who graduated in May 2014 shows the rewards of this profession: "You've helped me not just with problem sets and Econ homework, but with life and guidance about the future. I look to you as a role model, whose advice and words of wisdom will guide my footsteps throughout life." What a privilege to have a career that provides this kind of opportunity! Like Chaucer's cleric, we faculty members would "gladly learn, and gladly teach."[34]

Notes

All of the websites documented in the following notes were accessed multiple times, most recently between August 18 and August 20, 2013.

1. Bowdoin College, *Faculty Handbook, 2012–13*, http://www.bowdoin.edu/academic-affairs/forms-policies/policies/pdf/12-13FacultyHandbook.pdf, IV.E.2: 22.

2. Vassar College, *Faculty Handbook*, http://deanofthefaculty.vassar.edu/docs/Faculty-Handbook.pdf, C.III: 80

3. Amherst College, *Faculty Handbook*, https://www.amherst.edu/academiclife/dean_faculty/fph/fachandbook, III.E.3.

4. Carleton College, *Campus Handbook*, https://apps.carleton.edu/handbook/facultyapp/?a=faculty&policy_id=864379#865953.

5. Harvey Mudd College, *Faculty Notebook, May 2010*, http://www.hmc.edu/about1/administrativeoffices/deanoffaculty1/faculty-notebook-2012.pdf, 4.41: 45.

6. Hamilton College, *Hamilton College Faculty Handbook*, 1957.

7. Ibid., 10.

8. Amherst College, *Faculty Handbook*, III.E.3, https://www.amherst.edu/academiclife/dean_faculty/fph/fachandbook/facstatus/fulltimetenure.

9. Colgate University, *Faculty Handbook 2012–13*, http://www.colgate.edu/docs/d_offices-and-services_deanoffacultyoffice_currentfaculty/faculty-handbook-09-13-12.pdf?sfvrsn=4, III.D: 41.

10. Hamilton College, *Faculty Handbook, 2012*, http://www.hamilton.edu/documents/Faculty%20Handbook%202012.pdf, VI: 28.

11. Scripps College, *Faculty Handbook, 2012*, http://www.scrippscollege.edu/offices/faculty/files/2012%20faculty%20handbook.pdf, 3.5.II.A: 1.

12. Ibid., 3.5.II.A: 1.

13. Carleton College, *Campus Handbook*, https://apps.carleton.edu/handbook/facultyapp/?a=faculty&policy_id=864379#865953.

14. Hamilton College, *Faculty Handbook, 2012*, http://www.hamilton.edu/documents/Faculty%20Handbook%202012.pdf, VI.E.2: 32.

15. Wellesley College, *Faculty Handbook, 2012*, http://www.wellesley.edu/sites/default/files/assets/departments/provost/files/facultyhandbook.pdf, I: 3.

16. Swarthmore College, *Faculty Handbook*, III.A.7: 150, http://www.swarthmore.edu/Documents/academics/provost/Faculty%20Handbook.Revised.pdf.

17. Claremont McKenna College, *Faculty Handbook, July 2010*, http://www.cmc.edu/dof/policies/Faculty_Handbook_July_2010.pdf, 3.2.1: 49.

18. Washington and Lee University, *Faculty Handbook, 2013*, http://www2.wlu.edu/documents/provost/Faculty%20Handbook%20July%202013%20mw(0).pdf, 7.

19. Scripps College, *Faculty Handbook, 2012*, http://www.scrippscollege.edu/offices/faculty/files/2012%20faculty%20handbook.pdf, 3.5.II.A: 1.

20. Amherst College, *Faculty Handbook*, https://www.amherst.edu/academiclife/dean_faculty/fph/fachandbook, III.E.3, https://www.amherst.edu/academiclife/dean_faculty/fph/fachandbook/facstatus/fulltimetenure.

21. Swarthmore College, *Faculty Handbook*, III.A.7: 150, http://www.swarthmore.edu/Documents/academics/provost/Faculty%20Handbook.Revised.pdf.

22. Pomona College, *Faculty Handbook, 2013–14*, http://www.pomona.edu/administration/academic-dean/guidelines-policies/faculty-handbook.pdf, II.B: 28.

23. Hamilton College, *Faculty Handbook, 2012*, http://www.hamilton.edu/documents/Faculty%20Handbook%202012.pdf, VI.E.2: 32.

24. Smith College, *Policy of Appointment, Reappointment, Promotion, and Tenure at Smith College, 2012–13*, http://www.smith.edu/deanoffaculty/policy/tpa12-13.pdf, II.A.2.b: 9.

25. Middlebury College, *Faculty Handbook*, http://www.middlebury.edu/about/handbook/faculty/Faculty_Rules#review_eval_scholarship.

26. Swarthmore College, *Faculty Handbook*, III.A.7: 150, http://www.swarthmore.edu/Documents/academics/provost/Faculty%20Handbook.Revised.pdf.

27. Smith College, *Policy of Appointment, Reappointment, Promotion, and Tenure at Smith College, 2012–13*, http://www.smith.edu/deanoffaculty/policy/tpa12-13.pdf, II.A: 8.

28. Amherst College, *Faculty Handbook*, https://www.amherst.edu/academiclife/dean_faculty/fph/fachandbook/facstatus/fulltimetenure, III.E.3.

29. Grinnell College, *Faculty Handbook*, http://web.grinnell.edu/dean/Handbook/FacultyHandbook.pdf, IV.E.1.b.2: 38.

30. Claremont McKenna College, *Faculty Handbook, July 2010*, http://www.cmc.edu/dof/policies/Faculty_Handbook_July_2010.pdf, 3.2.4: 54–54.

31. Colgate University, *Faculty Handbook 2012–13*, http://www.colgate.edu/docs/d_offices-and-services_deanoffacultyoffice_currentfaculty/faculty-handbook-09-13-12.pdf?sfvrsn=4, III.D: 41.

32. Bates College, *Faculty Handbook 2012–13*, http://www.bates.edu/dof/files/2010/09/1-Faculty-Organization-and-Procedures-2012-132.pdf.

33. Washington and Lee University, *Faculty Handbook, 2013*, http://www2.wlu.edu/documents/provost/Faculty%20Handbook%20July%202013%20mw(0).pdf.

34. Geoffrey Chaucer, *The Canterbury Tales: General Prologue*, line 310.

How Liberal Arts Colleges Have Shaped My Life

·•——·•·

Akila Weerapana

Akila Weerapana is Associate Professor of Economics at Wellesley College. His teaching interests span all levels of the department's curriculum, including introductory and intermediate macroeconomics, international finance, monetary economics, and mathematical economics. He was awarded Wellesley's Pinanski Prize for Excellence in Teaching in 2002. His research interests are in macroeconomics, specifically in the areas of monetary economics, international finance, and political economy.

ঙ

I grew up in Sri Lanka during a tumultuous period in the country's history. I was fortunate in that none of my immediate family, and only a few of my close friends, were affected by the unrest and violence. At the age of sixteen, however, I found myself wanting out of the country I had grown up in for all but a year of my life. So, like many of my peers, I decided to apply to a university in the United States. There was no Internet or *College Insider* websites, but we had two important ingredients: the library at the American Center, with its thick college guides full of statistics and descriptions of colleges, and a well-tended grapevine that provided names of universities where other Sri Lankan students had received the magical "full scholarship" that was essential for most of us who were applying. Information was not hard to come by since most Sri Lankan parents were not bashful about telling all their friends and acquaintances about these "full scholarships."

Thinking back, I now see that my sixteen-year-old self had little idea about the difference between a research university and a liberal arts college, other than the obvious fact that the latter had only undergraduates. My dreams, and my peers' dreams, were of Harvard, Stanford, Princeton, Yale, and MIT, those magical names that accepted only the best of the best. As a teenager I was not short of self-assurance: I knew that I was one of the best students at my high school, which was clearly the best high school in the country. So I dreamed big. But even then I had embers of self-doubt about whether I would get into any one of these storied establishments. The source of that self-doubt lay in my academic interests. In Sri Lanka, after the tenth-grade "O-Level" examinations, all students had to choose their stream of study for their advanced-level examinations, which in turn would determine the field into which they could enter the Sri Lankan university system. Blood, gore, and dexterity comprised an impossible trinity for me, so medicine, the glamour field of parents, grandparents, and relatives all over Sri Lanka, was not an option. Almost by default, that meant the engineering track, the "Avis" to medicine's "Hertz" in the hierarchy of academic norms in Sri Lanka. Following this track meant that pure mathematics, applied mathematics, physics, and chemistry were to be my subjects. I was good at these subjects, but I cared only about applied mathematics; I had no passion for pure mathematics, physics, or chemistry. And so even though I tried to tell myself that I deserved to go to Princeton or Yale, in my heart of hearts I was beginning to fear that even if I managed to get into such a university, I would never be able to succeed in these subjects.

I was not ignorant about the difference between American universities and Sri Lankan universities. I knew that I was not destined to study these subjects and could choose others, but I had no idea what those other fields would be. So I wrote "Computer Science" in the place on my application form that asked me for fields of study. I did this even with no formal high school education in that field, and my informal computer skills were limited to writing Lotus 1-2-3 macros and doing simple BASIC coding taught to me by my dad's friend, who was the head of the Computer Science Department at a Sri Lankan university. Once I made that choice, I knew that my chance of getting into the glamour schools was shot. But I had made my decision that I was not going to continue pretending to be interested in things in which I had no interest.

Just as I feared, or maybe expected, the rejections from the research universities arrived at a steady pace. To my surprise, however, there were acceptances, too. But these came from liberal arts colleges. These colleges did not really seem to be too concerned that I wanted to study something I had not studied before and also seemed perfectly content that I did not want to study something that I had studied before. So with little geographical awareness but a lot of excitement, I arrived at Oberlin College to begin my college education. Every international student has an educational culture-shock story; mine was the time I stood outside my first-year advisor's office for forty-five minutes waiting to be invited in before seeing another student breeze in with a casual "hey there." In Sri Lanka, marching into a teacher's office with a breezy "hi" would get you some good old-fashioned corporal punishment honed through many generations of colonial rule! Once I had acclimated to the new environment, it was time to choose courses. I wish I was eloquent enough to describe what I felt when I first got my hands on the course catalog, something that I had never seen at the American Center in Colombo. A list of hundreds of courses in dozens of fields, and I could choose any course that had no prerequisite! For someone who had been itching to break free of the restrictive A-Level curriculum, the natural reactions to this intellectual smorgasbord were indulgence, gluttony, awe, and relief.

Finally, I had arrived at a place where I could choose, a place where no one was going to be looking over my shoulder saying I could not (or should not) choose this field or that field. So I chose the familiar (calculus), the ostensibly mandatory (computer science), and the new (English literature). I was great at the familiar and bad at the unfamiliar, but I did not care because they were subjects I chose. And then, if I needed a reminder that education is not just something we received from a professor in a classroom, I was assigned a roommate who grew up in an American army base in Okinawa. He loved economics and politics more than anyone I had ever met and always wanted to discuss what was happening in the world around him. I grew up as one of those kids who watched US presidential debates at the American Center and learned all the capitals of the world before I was ten, so this was catnip for me. However, I kept losing arguments to him because I did not really understand economics, at least not as much as my roommate seemed to know. So the following semester, I chose Principles of Economics as one of my courses. It was my way of obtaining a fighting chance to win some dorm-room debates.

I find it difficult to describe how eye-opening that first economics course was. My most similar previous "eye-opening" experience was of a more literal variety, having occurred during a visit to the optometrist when I was a teenager. I remember the doctor asking me to describe what I saw in a pastoral painting and then slipping on a new lens that revealed all the little creatures previously hidden in a blur of shadows. Similarly, as the hours in the classroom flew by, answers to questions that had long perplexed me began to emerge. I soon understood why my parents had to endure long waits in line, ration cards in hand, to receive my baby food. I understood why even a Sri Lankan middle-class family like mine could afford someone to cook and clean, while my affluent American dorm mates had grown up washing their own clothes and dishes. I understood why my father was so eager to save his earnings in dollars rather than rupees. From that semester on, I immersed myself in economics. The fascination never dwindled; there was always more to know. When the papers I read for my senior thesis became impenetrable, I decided to go to graduate school. I simply could not stand not knowing enough economics. I had come full circle, an opportunity to go finally to one of those glamour schools—Stanford University—for which I had pined four years before.

I was, and still am, a slow learner about life. When I went to Stanford, I was deeply appreciative of Oberlin and what it had meant to me, but now my focus was on finishing my PhD and getting a job at the IMF or the World Bank, the jobs that Sri Lankan parents wanted their kids who were studying abroad to have. Job security, travel, a salary drawn in dollars, home leave every year—what job could offer a more complete checklist than that? I was almost a decade older than when I first thought about applying to college but apparently not much wiser: I was being drawn to a path that was more about pleasing a social norm or ideal rather than following my intellectual passion. The wakeup call this time was the opportunity to teach my own class in my last year of graduate school. That experience was the time when everything clicked for me. Only then did I understand not only how liberal arts colleges had shaped my life up to that point, but also how liberal arts colleges could shape the rest of my life as well.

So, equipped with the tools of the trade, I arrived at Wellesley College as an assistant professor eager to share my passion for economics with bright, motivated students. I was utterly convinced that a significant number of them had the same latent passion for economics that I had as a first-year college student. Since the very first day I arrived at Wellesley, I have done my utmost to inspire my students to love economics as much as I do. I want to show my students the range of economic applications in my introductory courses, to guide them through the mathematical rigor and sophistication of economic theory in my intermediate courses, and to expose them to the joys of research and the awaiting challenges of graduate school in my advanced courses. All the work I have done in research, teaching, and service at Wellesley has been driven by my belief that all of my students' lives can be transformed by their Wellesley experience, as profoundly as my life was transformed by my own college experience. It is the work I want for the rest of my life.

As a professor at a liberal arts college, I have come to believe that the essence of teaching is discovery. Even when I am teaching a course for the fifth time, conveying concepts utterly familiar to me, I continually remind myself that most of my students are seeing the material for the first time. It is my job and, more importantly, my passion to share those ideas and discoveries with my students. Some students will have always loved these types of ideas and eagerly consume them. Others will be seeing them for the first time and come away captivated. Yet others will find that these new ideas are not as enthralling for them as they are for some of their classmates. All of that, a process or journey of trial and error, is part of my learning while teaching.

What I live for are those rewarding moments that often arrive unannounced on a nondescript Tuesday afternoon in early fall. These are the times when I notice a spark in the eye of a student suddenly aware that she is looking at the world with the eyes of an economist, and enjoying the view! These moments never arrive as often as I would like, and sometimes they pass without ever progressing into anything more meaningful. Occasionally, however, the spark ignites and catches, and a student is transformed by the discovery of a new intellectual passion. That is the moment that captures what it means to be in a liberal arts college.

I imagine that perhaps someday this book, or possibly an electronic version of it, will find its way into the hands of a motivated sixteen-year-old student somewhere in Cambodia or Kazakhstan, maybe even in Detroit or Fresno, who is worried or uncertain about what to do with her life after high school. I can only hope that this sixteen-year-old will be motivated by reading the essays and stories in this book to apply to a liberal arts college and begin her own life-changing journey.

PART THREE

The Curriculum

Liberal Education as Respecting Who We Are

PETER AUGUSTINE LAWLER

Peter Augustine Lawler is Dana Professor of Government at Berry College, where he has taught for thirty-four years and won several teaching awards. He's also executive editor of the acclaimed refereed quarterly Perspectives on Political Science. *He served on President Bush's Council on Bioethics and received the Weaver Prize for distinguished writing in popularizing the idea of human dignity. He's written or edited seventeen books, including, most recently,* A Political Companion to Walker Percy *and* Modern and American Dignity. *He has written well over two hundred articles and chapters for a very wide variety of venues, and he's spoken at well over one hundred colleges and universities.*

I teach in a small, residential college in semi-rural Georgia. It's not really a liberal arts college in the mode of Pomona or Centre. There are lots of students who major in business, education, animal science, and communications. And the college, in truth, is not oriented toward "enhancing" its "traditional" majors; those traditional majors we have—such as political science, English, psychology, French, history, philosophy, and religion—are holding their own in the face of benign institutional indifference. Benign indifference is, of course, punctuated by periodic enthusiasm for educational fads—both "politically correct" and techno-vocational, but those episodes are usually pretty episodic. Still, our administrators remain entranced by the latest studies and what the foundations are saying, and they want to do better in bringing Berry in line with what the experts are saying.

Over the last year, I've been paying more attention to what the educational experts are saying. And while I am, to a point, all about what political correctness—what diversity, multiculturalism, and all that—has done to trivialize American higher education, producing, for example, identity politics majors such as women's studies and film studies that manage to be neither liberal education nor vocational education; however, I don't think political correctness is the great danger we face. It's the so-called disruptive innovation that wants to hold higher education completely accountable to the logic of the market and measurable productivity. In this sense, "the sixties" have lost and capitalism—or at the least the form of capitalism we find in Silicon Valley and other havens of our proudly meritocratic "cognitive elite"—has won.

Listening to our administrators, it was impossible to miss a telling contradiction. There's anxiety about each college having a distinctive mission that easily morphs into a "brand." Liberal arts colleges have to explain why they're different from and even better than their rivals in order to flourish in the increasingly competitive educational marketplace. They have to justify the rapidly rising cost of the residential private college "experience," which includes inducing a good number of students to borrow big for the credential they could, in Georgia, actually get for free at the state school down the road.

To their credit, our administrators at Berry College might be clearer than most that it would be best if what the college actually accomplishes corresponds to its branding about what it accomplishes. The danger is that the "substance" might be transformed with the brand in mind. The even greater danger is that the quest for distinctive or even extraordinarily excellent substance will be deemed futile. So many colleges have reached that conclusion that they sell themselves according to the amenities that grace their residential experience, and there's nothing more shameful and silly in American education today than the resulting amenities arms race.

But the desire for "substantial" distinctiveness (that drives St. John's in Annapolis/Santa Fe or Thomas Aquinas in California or Morehouse in Georgia)—which can be at the service of the genuine diversity that's the best point of American higher education—is mitigated by the desire to correspond to "best practices" as articulated by accrediting associations, foundations, and government bureaucracies. And best practices are, these days, pretty much about attending to method or form at the expense of content or substance. What we need are "measurable student outcomes" that are abstracted from content. You can't say these days that every student needs to study this or that period of history or body of literature. That would undermine student choice and privilege mere information over marketable skills. Administrators are somewhat slow to see, for example, that if the goals are critical thinking and analytical reasoning, they might correspond to the *disciplines* of history or philosophy. Our allegedly disruptive thought that learning only occurs if it is measurable competency—which has become banal management-speak dogma—would standardize education everywhere with the acquisition of the skills and competencies required for our the twenty-first-century global competitive marketplace. Education that's method abstracted from content knows no standard higher than productivity or power.

Education for Sophists

The democratic, technocratic slogan is we don't want to teach you "what to think" but "how to think." And there are easier ways, surely, of becoming a methodical critical thinker than messing with history made by or literature written by dead white males who had lots of personal "issues" that often prevented them from living productive and responsible lives. So at the allegedly cutting-edge college being founded by Ben Nelson's much-touted Minerva Project, students won't read "great books." Instead they will learn debating skills, practical writing, formal logic, and behavioral economics straight on.

Now it's true that guys like me hate Nelson for working so hard to replace the liberal arts college with the bookless and placeless (the students will change their location often so as not to get tied down or be less than cosmopolitan) training of a merely cognitive elite—specialists without spirit or heart, as someone said. But it's also true that Nelson understands that if the study of history is for "critical thinking," then educational efficiency means dispensing with tedious content and getting right to the thinking. History, after all, is merely information that can be Googled when you need it. And true philosophy is nothing but analytical philosophy, a method for thinking clearly or logically. The content "Plato" is perfectly dispensable and certainly not worth obsessing about. That's why rigorously analytical programs think of "history of philosophy" in the same way physics programs think of "history of physics"—a somewhat instructive record of errors that occur when you haven't quite figured out how to think of the proper method for inquiry. That's why analytical graduate programs have sometimes followed physics graduate programs in that they no longer require the study of foreign languages. Everything you really need to know was written recently and is available in English. And, of course, an upside of writing following the logical rigor of mathematics is that there's little danger of something really fundamental getting lost in translation.

But Nelson's university—with its training in "debating skills" and "behavioral economics"—isn't really about the production of analytical philosophers or theoretical physicists. *The Big Bang Theory*'s Sheldon Cooper would be laughed out of the seminar room as the socially clueless nerd that he is. This university—which aims to replace Harvard as America's top educational "brand"—means to produce sophists. Now, Plato gave the sophist an undeservedly bad brand. Socrates said that sophists—unlike poets, politicians, and perhaps even parasitic philosophers such as Socrates himself—use what can be learned from natural science to solve problems people really have. Sophists are technicians or experts or consultants. And because their knowledge is scientific, it's valid everywhere; they can get and really do deserve the big bucks wherever they go. The reason Nelson will have his students change locations so often is so that they will understand themselves as rootless cosmopolitans—or freed from the prejudice that some local belief or concern trumps wealth and power in determining what needs to be done. So they will always give sensible advice when it comes to "calculating probabilities" about how to sustain oneself or one's institution in a fundamentally hostile environment.

Professors, in this view, become nothing more than sophists themselves. They are to be evaluated according to their measurable productivity, and they too will work only if they have what it takes to flourish in the competitive marketplace. One downside of this way of thinking, of course, is the residential liberal arts college will disappear, as will any educational arrangement based on what we now call Socrates's "humanistic" objection to, on behalf of both truth and virtue, the sophists' technocratic focus.

Defending the Humanities?

So you would think that professors in "the humanities" would have enough class-consciousness—the class-consciousness shared by Socrates himself—to oppose with powerful arguments and rhetorical effectiveness this reduction of liberal education to sophistry. The American Academy of Arts and Sciences did issue a report defending the humanities. It wasn't a very resolute defense, and it seemed somewhat desperate. The result was all kinds of articles that were more about recording than resisting the humanities' decline and fall in our techno-scientific time. It reads like it was written by a committee, and it only rarely transcends the level of the management-speak of the sophist. Most of all, by calling the humanities "a matter of the heart," it actually reinforces the technocratic distinction between real knowledge (the head) and emotional responses (the heart). The report's overall effect is somewhat between special pleading and abject capitulation.

Lee Siegel, in a thoughtful essay in the *Wall Street Journal* ("Who Ruined the Humanities?"), gave an optimistic spin on the humanities' inability to defend themselves.[1] What we might be witnessing is the liberation of the humanities from the stultifying confines of today's institutions of higher education. As a political scientist, I, like Aristotle himself, find myself caught between the categories of humanities and science—or what Aristotle would call poetry and philosophy. So I can't help but find myself asking what's worth defending about "the humanities" anyway. Here Siegel turns out to be a lot of help.

It's hard to know what "the humanities" are exactly, as opposed, I guess, to the sciences. The center of the humanities seems to be the study of literature. And allegedly the key sign of their decline is the fading away of the English major, despite the real evidence that most of that fading took place a generation ago. Just as grade inflation has apparently stabilized at a very high level, the number of English (and philosophy) majors seems to have done the same at a low level.

When committees and commissions tell us about such trends, it is always in terms of a crisis, such as the crisis of civic literacy or scientific literacy or just literacy. We're told that the study of literature is indispensable for literacy, which it surely is above a certain level. But there's a lot more to this crisis. The lack of a formal humanistic education, as Siegel observes, allegedly "leads to numerous pernicious personal conditions, such as the inability to think critically, to write clearly, to empathize with other people, to be curious about other people and places, to engage with great literature after graduation [branded "lifelong learning"], to recognize truth, beauty, and goodness."

Now no one really thinks that people who weren't English majors or minors suffer from all those pathologies, nor does it make sense to think that English majors—because of their reading literature for credit—are free from them. Taking a couple of courses in literature as part of a "core curriculum" couldn't possibly make that much difference.

I do think that people who fill their leisure time by reading "real books"—literature, philosophy, and such—do have qualities of the soul that are in short supply in our middle-class techno-world. We're talking here about people who read for intellectual pleasure and not just for stress-relief recreation. One downside of our digital age is that they're probably more than ever the exception to the rule. In the film *Liberal Arts* (about Kenyon), we see a student for whom college is being obsessed with a single huge book. We also see that he's not fitting in with his fellow, better-adjusted students. In the HBO series *Girls*, we see a young woman who majored in "film studies" at a school in Ohio we know to be Oberlin, struggling (well, not struggling as much as she should) to earn a living as a writer in New York City. She has a decent prose style, but it turns out she has nothing to write about. One reason: she managed to get through college without reading any "real books" with real care.

Siegel reminds us that literature wasn't taught in our colleges until the end of the nineteenth century because reading novels and poetry "were part of the leisure of ordinary life." That's what an educated person did, and not, of course, for college credit. Thoughts and imaginations were shaped by literature as much as anything else. Sometimes they may have been silly thoughts and romantic imaginations—such as the chivalrous South-erners who were moved by Sir Walter Scott to choose a very bloody and very optional war. And sometimes, as in the case of Abraham Lincoln, Shakespeare and the Bible almost all alone were enough to discover and "communicate" both the urgency and poetic/theological significance of the seemingly prosaic American proposition.

The study of literature for credit became common as the twentieth century rolled on. It was, in part, compensatory, to make up for the declin-ing quality of educated leisure and for a waning of religious authority. The search for meaning in a bourgeois world, as part of higher education, became focused on the genres of novels, poetry, and plays.

There was, as Siegel suggests, a kind of "existentialist" moment that began after World War II and persisted through part of the sixties. The focus on one's personal destiny in a world distorted by technology and ideology—a world that produced unprecedented mass slaughter—privileged literature over other forms of "communication." Insofar as philosophy was existen-tial—and so obsessed with Camus, Heidegger, and Sartre—even it seemed more like literature than a technical or "theoretical" discipline. The goal was to save reflection on the truthfully irreducible situation of the particular person from the clutches of theory. The predicament of the person born to trouble—or at least a brush with absurdity—is what novels are about. And the insufficiency of philosophic prose to display that predicament explains why Sartre, Camus, and Walker Percy, for philosophic reasons, wrote novels. It is close, at least, to why Plato wrote dialogues and why St. Augustine wrote his *Confessions*.

As the great critic Lionel Trilling pointed out, it might have been near ridiculous to teach books that should make us radically discontent with our ordinary lives in the newly standardized format of American higher educa-tion in the 1950s. And it increasingly became doubly ridiculous to have those books taught by careerist professors without the spirit and heart of specialized scholars. It might be triply ridiculous to expect administrators, bureaucrats, and other certifiers of competencies to be able to understand—much less articulate—a credible defense of "the humanities."

The existentialist point of "the humanities" is to experience the mysterious singularity of the particular being stuck for a moment between two abysses, born to love and die, to be moved by the sometimes inexpressible suffering of the being who must love and die, and to experience the joy of "insight" with others, an experience that has nothing to do with "collaborative learning." As Siegel puts it, it's to experience "transcendence" of our everyday world, and transcendence can generate issues of "reentry" into that everyday world, issues that can negatively affect productivity and ordinary effectiveness.

One such issue is that the noncareerist teacher of literature—including philosophy understood as literature—can't possibly explain why what he or she does might be good for critical thinking, effective communication, empathy, or "diversity." Siegel is right that most literature is not the place to look for writing that is clear in the business or technical sense. And empathy, of course, is a pitiful substitute for love. The preference for diversity over truth and the common good depends on the detached attitude of the tourist. It is something to be transcended, not affirmed as some educational bottom line.

Most experts today have figured out that the so-called suicide of the humanities began when they succumbed to the temptation of trendy theory. It was too hard to remain "inward," and so they turned outward, to moralizing on issues of "social justice," to finding the racism, classism, and sexism that discredits the claims to truth of the "canonical" books of the past. "Political correctness," of course, is meant to stifle "man's search for meaning." That's not because the person experiencing the hell of "pure possibility" of our high-tech world longs to be a racist, but because the issues of race and class and all that have been already resolved, so today's "leftover" being can't be told who he (or she) is and what he's supposed to do. Professors of literature decided to confine their moralizing to politics, the area of human life in which they could claim neither competence nor a recent tradition of responsibility. The turn outward in the name of relevance actually made the humanities seem more irrelevant.

Before their capture by theory and political correctness, the inwardness of the humanities included the experience of the misery of man with God. That experience might be authentically affirmed as part of the absurdity of being the displaced or homeless being. Or it might be that the experience of transcendence might find good-enough satisfaction in losing oneself in the aesthetic experience of beauty for its own sake. Or anxiety in the face of the lonely nothing that is oneself in God's absence might be understood, as Walker Percy and other Catholic, existentialist sort-of Thomists did, as the prelude to the wonder that might lead us to intimations, at least, about the goodness and gratuitousness of a created being.

In those days, "the humanities" weren't hostile to religion, although they did highlight how difficult belief is in our radically untraditional time. It was also in those existentialist days that the humanities seemed genuinely bohemian—even in the sense of Russell Kirk, bohemian Tory—or not merely bourgeois bohemian. They were about concerns that should animate one's whole life. But today, we sadly say, the humanities aren't typically a refuge from either the despotism of fashion or the despotism of theory, much less the despotism of careerism. That's one reason among many they seem like a boring waste of valuable time for most students.

Given what most of our institutions of higher education are really like today, Siegel celebrates their abandonment of the humanities. Now literature is free to flourish somewhere else. It's true enough, I can add, that Socrates never taught for money. And he never could have gotten tenure. He didn't publish, and his student evaluations would have been uneven. It's far from clear why it would help a great writer to get any degree at all and certainly not one in "creative writing." Someone could argue, of course, that things were different when people routinely read real books outside of class. But there's no reason why they can't do so again.

Siegel's understanding of the humanities is perhaps too existentialist, too animated by contempt for the alleged diversions of ordinary life. The study of great books probably flourishes best when "contextualized" by the relational responsibilities of free persons. Liberal education through most of our history was somewhat "Stoic" or connected to the relational duties of ladies and gentlemen located in a particular place. And it was also, of course, usually somewhat religious or conditioned by what we can know and must do as beings made in the image of a loving God. The humanities, properly understood, are about who we are and what we're supposed to do as beings born to know, love, and die.

This is emphatically not an exclusively conservative conclusion. The politically liberal and proudly neo-Puritanical novelist Marilynne Robinson (*When I Was a Child I Read Books*) recalls the original antebellum, abolitionist, Christian mission of Oberlin: liberal education was available for everyone, including blacks and women. Everyone studied, and everyone—including the professors—worked. The egalitarianism with condescension that motivates our noblest defenders of liberal education is often—even typically—of Christian and liberal inspiration. I could add here, of course, a commentary on the fearless Christian responsibility that Martin Luther King Jr. said was taught to the proud men of Morehouse. The point is, of course, that because we're essentially neither black nor white, male nor female, Jew nor gentile, liberal education—as opposed to, say, women's studies—is for us all.

There is probably something to Siegel's perception that the effort to defend the humanities everywhere in our educational system might be misguided. Maybe the focus should be on "countercultural" (which doesn't mean all about the sixties) institutions that exist in a communal context and that have what it takes to resist standardization, trendy theory, and the understandable but still excessive focus on techno-productivity. Maybe they can in some indirect way elevate us all.

Or maybe we should just ask that there be a lot more celebration of the diversity that still characterizes higher education in America, even in particular institutions and sometimes within particular departments. The enemy of this diversity is standardization—what comes from shamefully intrusive accrediting agencies, government bureaucrats, the use of "branding" and various forms of management-speak to describe liberal education, the adoption of the skills-and-competencies model (which is okay for tech schools) to evaluate higher education, and the insistence that the standard of productivity should drive all educational funding. The enemy of diversity is the reduction of education to sophistry.

One advantage of standardization, of course, is that it holds slackers accountable. But we shouldn't work too hard to get rid of all those slackers (such as those "tenured radicals"). Otherwise, we'll too often mistake leisure for laziness. We might even mistake metaphysics, theology, poetry, and so forth for self-indulgent pursuits that don't prepare students for the rigors of the competitive twenty-first-century marketplace. More than ever, it seems to me, it is essential to hold members of our "cognitive elite" to a standard higher than productivity. All Americans' lives would be less pathological— and so, for one thing, more productive—if imaginations were, once again, filled with what can be loosely called the romance of the soul.

Studies show, E. D. Hirsch (the cultural literacy guy) has reported, that the key to flourishing in the world as someone with a strong personal identity in touch with the world as it actually is and ready to take responsibility for himself or herself and others is to have a huge vocabulary and an exact and imaginative understanding of what those words mean. The only way to achieve this competency reliably in primary and secondary school is through reading lots of "real books." And another study shows that a very reliable clue to how a child will fare in school and life is the number of bookshelves his parents have at home or, in other words, whether he or she has been raised in a seriously bookish environment where reading is privileged as a form of civilized leisure. It might well be the case that the best argument for the residential liberal arts is cultivating future parents who will keep themselves and raise their children in such a home.

Let me now say something about the teaching method we do or ought to find at those colleges, which is, partly, conversational. But it's not merely or simply conversational. The "Socratic method," for us, isn't much without "respect for texts." The point of the Socratic method, even today, is to help students gain the confidence to reasonably and erotically enjoy "real books."

The Socratic Method and Its Limits

Martin Heidegger called Socrates "the purest thinker" in the West, which, I gather, doesn't necessarily mean the best thinker. The sign of Socrates's purity is not writing down his thoughts, for fear they would become ossified, misunderstood, vulgarized. What you say always depends on the character of the person to whom you are speaking. Books speak to no one in particular, violating the common-sense principle that your teaching style ought to vary according to the learning style of your student.

One trouble with taking the purely Socratic approach too seriously is really believing that a great teacher is one who leads his students to the truth dialectically, with no books or other "outside authorities" needed. We have no firm evidence that approach really worked that well for the "historical Socrates"—as opposed to the idealized character Socrates, who shows up all the time in Plato's dialogues (or really wordy plays). It is highly unlikely it really works for the teachers these days who pride themselves in using that teaching method. We even see in Socratic dialogues that his really smart interlocutors don't have memories good enough not to be flat-out tricked by Socrates, who often reminds them about—by changing up—what he said before.

Now I don't try to trick my students that way, although I constantly remind them how easy it would be to do. When I say, "Remember we just said . . . ," they know it's because I'm saying something different—either because I screwed up before or to provocatively change my position for instructional or entertainment reasons. When I say, "I have to take a controversial stand," I follow with a stand that nobody would find controversial at all. "I do think women these days should be able to work." Or: "Slavery is just wrong." What passes for my pedagogical intention is to show that professors who preen about "being radical" or offensive are usually being quite conventional. It would be genuinely radical to say in class: "Religious liberty makes most people more unhappy than they should be." I do regularly put the latter, genuinely thought-provoking opinion in the mouth of Marx, when talking about "On the Jewish Question."

Another pedagogical point that I hope I make is that there are always limits to free speech. There are some things that Socrates dare not say straight out, like believing in the gods is stupid. But Plato does sometimes lead us to assume he must really think something like that. Once students make that assumption, it's time to remind them that Socrates also taught that those who are proud of their atheism—the sophists—also stupidly thought they knew more than they really did. Socrates doesn't make the mistake of feeding the sophists' vanity and needlessly corrupting the already-arrogant youth by openly dissing the gods. He seems to use reason to make religion better.

Socrates shows us time and again that it's impossible to say everything you really want to say. A teacher has to think some about what his audience wants to hear. Socrates has to watch what he says to the strong and idealistic young men in the Republic. He says, for example, he knows he can't walk away without giving them some positive account of justice, even though he actually believes such a confident account is above even his pay grade. It would be bad for them, given their reluctant but real openness to tyranny. It would be bad for Socrates, who might get the stuff beaten out of him or have charges brought against him for impiety and corrupting the young. It would even be unfair to the young men. Socrates had "dialectically" taken the religious and poetic defenses of being just off the table. Without saying more, he would have rendered them defenseless before clever sophists who believe that money and power are the bottom line. It was his responsibility to convince them it makes sense to be good, to be just, because tyranny and wisdom aren't "on the same page."

No decent young person really wants to believe that money and power are the bottom line. And, you know, they aren't. Part of the Socratic method, more than ever, is to keep students from surrendering what they really know about who they are to those clever sophists. In this sense, classroom conversation is, in part, a polemic—even a shameless polemic—against the sophist's two weapons of scientism ("studies show") and relativism ("that's only your opinion").

So it's always important to remind students that justice always imposes responsible limits on free speech. The reigning view of justice is always somewhat tyrannical. As Socrates shows in the *Crito*, "the Laws"—the dominant view of who we are and what we're supposed to do—always demand more of people than is reasonable. In American democracy, as Tocqueville insistently reminds us, there's sometimes "the tyranny of the majority." A secular liberal would add here immediately, of course, that that tyranny explains why American political leaders can't be openly atheistic, and why President Obama had to feign being opposed to same-sex marriage until recently. A libertarian would add, of course, that's why no politician can tell the truth that entitlements on which an overwhelming majority of Americans depend are unsustainable.

Socrates points out that the democratic prejudice is to exaggerate both the goodness and the real possibility of individual liberation. The "moral majority" is actually a popular prejudice against pure democracy; it's the spirited and pious prejudice that produced the trial of Socrates. Pure democrats claim to be all about an easygoing acceptance of diverse lifestyles, including, of course, Socrates's. But radical democrats—meaning those who are extremists when it comes to "Doing your own thing" being the bottom line—readily get angry and vicious when it comes to those who say that freedom must be limited by virtue, by coming to terms with the responsibilities necessity—beginning with the necessities of birth and death—imposes upon us.

The argument over same-sex marriage today should be a reasonable and friendly discussion of the relationship between freedom and virtue. But it's not: Partly because even the Supreme Court says that all the words coming out of the mouths of those on one side of the discussion are motivated by animosity toward homosexuals as a class. That's a conversation stopper, if ever there was one. Faculty members these days in mainstream institutions can only say what they please about same-sex marriage in class if they agree with the dominant view of sophisticated Americans—our "cognitive elite"— today. That's not to say that view is wrong but that it's become a dogma.

It's easy for me to be fair-and-balanced and acknowledge that most people on both sides of that issue and plenty of others are pretty dogmatic. Faculty members teaching at evangelical and seriously Catholic colleges have to watch what they say too, if they want to educate their students "from where they are," not to mention avoid being fired.

Professors, like Socrates, can't really educate without taking into account the reigning dogmas, including dogmas that exaggerate our personal freedom, as well as dogmas about who God is and what He requires of each of us. Free speech that moves minds and hearts is always fairly tricky. That's why, as I've already suggested, the freedom of speech is enhanced by respect for texts. And it's that respect that's most missing among our technocratic experts. It's not after all either a democratic quality or a technological quality. It depends on the conviction that there's a personal standard that trumps money and power. So the main thing wrong with education in America today is that texts have lost their authority to move us with their wisdom and beauty. In every area of life, we've forgotten that respect—respect rooted in our anxious longing for what we have not been able to supply for ourselves—is an indispensable prelude to wonder.

Respect for Texts

Someone might say—and libertarian skeptics often do—that classes in philosophy and literature are given quite an arbitrarily inflated value by being accorded with credit. Do away with the credit system and give degrees based on real demonstration of measurable competencies valuable in the twenty-first-century marketplace, and you'll find out what studying Plato's *Republic* is really worth. I admit that's a humbling thought, one that I'm sure my college's administrators would like me to have at least once in a while. And I've heard that our professors of finance and accounting and computer science (and even the political scientists) think I should be having such thoughts a lot more often than that.

Now, to be fair to libertarian techno-skeptics, they almost all believe (and many have discovered for themselves) that it's really worthwhile to read the *Republic* or Shakespeare. It's just that you can do that on your own time and for free. Well, I agree you should do that on your own time and for free. But it's pretty hard—if not quite impossible—to know why you should spend your precious time that way without a good teacher. It turns out that openness to books—and so openness to the truth—usually depends on trusting a personal authority to some extent. That person—your teacher—has to earn your trust. And in some ways that's harder than ever.

Alexis de Tocqueville explains pretty well why Americans have an "issue" with trusting personal authority—especially personal intellectual authority. The Americans, he says, are Cartesians who've never read a word of Descartes. They hit upon the "Cartesian method" because it's identical to the "democratic method." If you want to reduce that method to one word, it would be "doubt." That means being really, really skeptical of the words of other persons. If I trust you, then I let you rule me. And ruling myself is what democracy means for me. I have to think for myself.

Thinking for myself, so understood, is a mixture of antiauthoritarian paranoia and a kind of unwarranted or excessive self-confidence in one's own "critical thinking skills." We techno-Americans tend to believe there's a method for everything, even or especially, as Descartes said, for thinking. But the question remains: What should I think about? Surely I'm stuck with thinking about who I am and what I'm supposed to do. And just as surely it's asking too much for me to answer that "who" and that "what" question all by myself. Even God himself didn't create himself out of nothing.

Now there's something admirable and something ridiculous in this "hermeneutic of suspicion." It has a noble Protestant origin, after all, in the determination to trust no one but myself—and not those Satanic deceivers who call themselves priests—in interpreting the word of God. But even choosing to read the Bible depends on taking someone's word that the Bible is God's word. And to submit even to the word of God, after all, is undemocratic. Christianity might teach we're all equal under God, but we won't really be liberated as "autonomous persons" until we free ourselves from being under God's personal thumb.

So at a point certain democrats dispense with the Bible and other people and try to find God in themselves. But the religion of me—all alone—turns out to be pretty empty and certainly not the foundation of much "critical thinking"—toughly judgmental thinking—about who I am and what I'm supposed to do. It's this personal emptiness, Tocqueville explains, that causes democratic religion to morph into pantheism—or the denial of real personal identity.

Obviously we'd know more about ourselves if we read the Bible as if it might be true—or not from the point of view of detached tourists who believe that what this or that "culture" once believed has nothing to do with us these days—or, more precisely, with me these days. And obviously Americans would know a lot more about what genuine critical thinking requires if they read Descartes. But to privilege his book on method over others requires submitting to the personal authority of those who have read and recommend it. We democrats really see the despotic danger of such submission. We've all read, for example, that Leo Strauss got his "neocon" students to read Plato to impose his own personal agenda on them.

It's easy to respond that not to read the Bible or Descartes is to even be more thoroughly or thoughtlessly dominated by those books. The personal egalitarianism that drives most moral thinking today is full of biblical premises, and to think with those premises with no awareness of their foundation is, obviously, not really to think for yourself. We defenders of "human rights" assert that every human person is unique and irreplaceable. But we have no idea why. Certainly most of modern science is incapable of even beginning to explain why.

The same goes, of course, with Descartes's audacious choice of the modern technological project. Every transhumanist is a Cartesian, whether he knows it or not. If you become liberally educated, you can actually start to make connections between the Bible and Descartes. Then you will actually start to think clearly about how techno-liberation depends both on the Bible's view of the person while being a rejection of the Bible's personal and relational God. A critical thinker full of theological and philosophical content might exclaim: "How reasonable is that!?"

The big point here is the excessively resolute determination to doubt personal authority doesn't really lead to freeing oneself altogether from authority. What rushes in, in the absence of personal authority or relational personal identity is impersonal authority. It's too hard—too dizzying and disorienting—to think all by yourself. Because you don't know who you are, you really don't know what to do. So what fills the void and makes action possible, Tocqueville observes, is usually either public opinion—or trendy opinion—or the impersonal expertise of science.

When we defer to public opinion, we, in fact, become relativists. We say there's no standard—when it comes to truth, beauty, justice, and so forth—higher than what sophisticated public intellectuals assert these days. When we defer to experts and what their "studies" or "data" show, we find ourselves in the thrall of scientism. We too easily believe neuroscience or evolutionary psychology or rational-choice theory as explorations for everything, as the definitive sources of knowledge of who we are and what we're supposed to do. It's not denying the truth and utility of science to be aware of scientism. It's the ideology that's the result of popularizing scientists speculating authoritatively beyond the limits of what they can really know through their methods.

Both deferring to public opinion and deferring to "popular science" are ways of denying what you really can see with own eyes about who you are and what you're supposed to do. It's, as the philosopher Heidegger and the novelist Walker Percy observe, surrendering oneself to what "they"—to what no one in particular—say. It's freeing oneself from the "they" that's the point of existentialism. It's also the point of the efforts of both Socrates and Jesus.

Public opinion, let me emphasize, doesn't only mean what the majority thinks. It means the opinion of your public. As Rousseau incisively pointed out, sophisticated intellectuals in democratic times flee from "the vulgar" by being witty and fashionable—and so by not being critical of what the witty and fashionable believe at any particular time. We can see now, for example, that neuroscience as a comprehensive explanatory system—that incorporates, for example, neurotheology and neuro-humanities—peaked out as scientism around about 2008. But the progress in the real science of neuroscience continues, even if it's given less attention by the witty and fashionable.

Here's a beginning to teaching respect for texts: There should be nothing in the classroom except a professor, students, and a great or at least really good book (a Supreme Court opinion or a classic political speech count as a really good book). No PowerPoint, no laptops, no smart phones, and so forth. And the professor should be calling constant attention to the text, reading aloud and dramatically, from time to time. At least the occasional class should be devoted to a single page or even a single paragraph, just to make clear how much there is for us to know.

Respect for texts, let me conclude, is, among other things, about overcoming the distinction between the humanities and the science. My biggest objection to the Academy's report on the humanities, it turns out, might be that not only does it do an injustice to the humanities, it does the same to science, or especially to what the humanities and science as they're now understood share in common. There's nothing in the report about the joy of discovery and sharing the truth with others across time and space. There's nothing about "the community of knowers and lovers" that should include theoretical physicists, philosophers, novelists, poets, theologians—among others. Plato, we remember, excelled in all those specialized disciplines, because he thought that the discipline of specialization was at the expense of the comprehensive inquiry required to know who we are and what we're supposed to do. So the division of human inquiry into the humanities and the sciences is artificial and alienating. It's clearly at the expense of the humanities. Theology and philosophy, for example, are sciences—for science is nothing but genuine knowledge of the way things really are. And there may be no human mode of communication more empirical—not to mention more diagnostic—than a great novel. Dostoyevsky, for example, had a clearer insight than Darwin or Hegel or Marx about what the twentieth century would be like.

Berry College's Contribution to Our Educational Diversity

A respect for texts—and a respect for conversation and even a respect for method—is finally all about the foundation of the community of knowers and lovers that include us all. The residential liberal arts college deserves a future only if it's set up to be a home for a small and intimate part of that community. Let me conclude by explaining why Berry College has some singular features that allow it to provide a "safe space" for that kind of welcoming home.

The "Berry College advantages" don't include an enlightened and sympathetic administration; they don't even include colleagues to whom I can tell the truth and share the joy of discovery. I have to be trickier with them than with the students, and let me tell you: I'm too often not tricky enough. The Berry advantages are, in fact, wonderfully accidental. They weren't chosen by anyone at all.

The first is that Berry is a vaguely Christian school not connected with a denomination. There are a lot of seriously religious students (and a lot who are not religious) and a pretty typical, mostly secular, or at least liberal Protestant faculty. The result is a kind of freedom of speech and intellectual openness not found in either a strictly secular or narrowly denominational school. The Berry classroom (or mine, at least) is a safe space for both devoutly observant and complacently skeptical students. If I'm careful, it's even possible to have a real discussion about whether *Roe v. Wade* was rightly decided. When I gave a talk at Pomona in California, I asked students about the place of religion in higher education; they were almost uniformly amazed that anyone could think there was any. At Berry, that issue is a real bone of contention.

Our more bookish evangelical students often really become seekers and searchers, wonderers and wanderers, alive with the predicament of having a personal destiny open to a variety of possibilities. The evangelicals— say, Southern Baptists—are often equally dissatisfied with the superficiality of their churches and the relativism of the reigning secularism. And they sometimes have actually been raised to have respect for texts. They're open to the Bible teaching the truth, and so they're very open to the suggestion that the only reason to read any "great book" is that it teaches the truth. They want to hear about, say, Nietzsche, from Nietzsche's point of view. They're surprisingly reluctant to be satisfied with concluding, as evangelicals in general sometimes do, that "according to my 'worldview' Nietzsche is wrong." One reason, of course, is they're quick to get on board with his criticism of liberalism as a kind of inauthentic Christianity without Christ.

Another reason some Berry students are strikingly undemocratic in their respect for texts, of course, is that the South is more about personal respect, about even the authority of parents, and having good manners, than most of the rest of the country. So on my best days, I'm able to be alive to the mixture of Southern Stoicism, believing Christianity, and modern existentialism that makes liberal education—or serious inquiry concerning who each of us is and what each of us is supposed to do—possible in my particular place. I'm grateful that Berry affords me the space and the students to do what I think I'm supposed to do.

Note

1. Lee Siegel, "Who Ruined the Humanities?" *Wall Street Journal*, July 12, 2013, http://online.wsj.com/articles/SB100014241278873238230045785958032967 98048.

Humanizing the Subject

·•——•·

Toward a Curriculum for Liberal Education in the Twenty-First Century

JEFFREY FREYMAN

Jeff Freyman is Professor Emeritus of Political Science at Transylvania University in Lexington, Kentucky, where he taught courses in comparative and international politics until his retirement in 2014. He received a B.A. in political science from Williams College and a Ph.D. in political science from The George Washington University. He was the recipient of the Bingham Award for Excellence in Teaching in 1988. In 2005, Jeff founded and served as the director of the Center for Liberal Education at Transylvania. The mission of the Center is to stimulate discussion within the academy—both at Transylvania and nationally—about the meaning of liberal education and its contemporary relevance. In association with the Phi Beta Kappa Society in 2006, the Center began offering "The Transylvania Seminar: Twenty-first Century Liberal Education as a Contested Concept" each summer for faculty members from liberal arts colleges throughout the United States. He has given talks at colleges across the country on the subject of liberal education.

۶۹

The Transylvania Seminar invites faculty members from liberal arts colleges across the country to come together to discuss the nature of liberal education and its prospects in the twenty-first century. It asks its participants to think seriously about the meaning of liberal education in order to understand how the tradition can be preserved in the face of ever-changing contemporary circumstances. Despite the seminar's insistence on the need to distinguish liberal education's purpose throughout its history from its specific historical curricular modalities, I am sometimes asked by participants to please be more concrete about the sort of curriculum I envision for liberal arts colleges in the future. Here is what I tell them: I don't know and I don't care. Needless to say, few are especially satisfied with my answer. So I suppose that I should explain myself, and fast.

I don't know what curriculum is best for any particular liberal arts college. When asked to specify the arrangements of a future socialist community, Karl Marx would respond that he was unwilling to write recipes for socialist cooks. For Marx, socialism meant those circumstances in which human beings were able to realize their essential freedom. So its specific arrangements would be nothing more (nor less) than whatever the people living in socialism decided to make of it. It would be presumptuous, indeed contradictory, for him to tell free socialist citizens how to live their lives in socialism. He saw that any specific prescription might become reified and, as a consequence, that socialism would suffer from a "displacement of goals."

In a somewhat different context, I, too, would prefer not to identify specific elements of a liberal education curriculum for the future. Like Marx's conception of socialism, my conception of liberal education has something to do with essential human freedom. This notion has an ancient pedigree, going back to classical Athens, subsequently transplanted in classical Rome. The word "liberal" (from the Latin *liberare*, meaning "to free") refers to that education which is appropriate for free human beings. (Back then, human freedom meant not being a slave and not having to work, presumably because one owned slaves who did the work instead. It means something different today.) It would certainly be very presumptuous for me to prescribe a curriculum for you. Just as one's education is uniquely appropriate to each individual learner, so too the educational experience offered by each individual college is uniquely appropriate for that institution. A particular college's curriculum defines and reflects who its members are as an academic community. The curriculum instantiates what the college believes to be important for its students to learn and to become. It is thus an act of collective self-fashioning, for both faculty and students. As such, the college defines itself, its identity, its mission.

What Liberal Education Is Not

I don't care what curriculum another college constructs. (At least, not within certain limits anyway, which will be made clear shortly.) I don't care, because a given curriculum does not define the nature of liberal education. Please don't get me wrong. Of course liberal education must have *some* curriculum. It must be about something. The life of the mind must have something in mind. It's just that a lot of different pedagogical experiences will do the trick. And I know that some curricula are more conducive to liberal learning than others. My point is that liberal education should not necessarily be identified with any particular one of them.

First, consider the *substance* (content, subject matter) of the curriculum. Largely because liberal education got started in the classical world, it was identified with Greek and Latin literature for a very long time. Not until the nineteenth century did educators find this course of studies too narrow. Consequently, a number of modern proponents, wishing nevertheless to maintain the tradition as a fixed canon, have identified it with a limited set of Great Books that represent "the best that has been thought and said" throughout the course of Western civilization from Plato to NATO. A similar impulse has led others, proponents of liberal education as "cultural literacy," to identify a set of facts that should be known by every educated person. But however extensive such lists of works or facts might be, by virtue of their necessarily being finite, they must exclude many important aspects of the Western tradition, not to mention the numerous other voices that are also part of humanity's great conversation. There is something far too restrictive about such a project for it to be considered truly "liberal."

Sensitive to these issues, many educators have come to identify liberal education not with any set of specific works or facts but with a set of specific academic fields of study called the "liberal arts." These disciplines in the humanities, the arts, the social sciences, and the natural sciences are characterized largely by what they are not—namely, they are not *primarily* vocational. Rigorous study in one of these fields, it is thought, constitutes a liberal education. It is, admittedly, sometimes difficult to differentiate vocational subjects from nonvocational ones. While acknowledging these ambiguities, the Phi Beta Kappa Society nevertheless has concluded, "It is not difficult to distinguish between broad cultivation and technical competence."[1] I agree, but their claim begs another question. If liberal education is defined by "broad cultivation," then how does concentrating in any one specific discipline—even if it is one of the liberal arts—constitute liberal education? Rather, it is suggested, what is needed is a general education cast broadly across all subject matters. Harvard's Charles Eliot took the idea of breadth to its logical (or illogical) conclusion by arguing that if liberal education is about freedom, then we should let students take whatever they want. By the second half of the twentieth century, these various positions reached an uneasy compromise in what is academe's now widely accepted Trinitarian formula: students spend about one-third of their time either fulfilling requirements in their liberal arts major field, in general education, or in electives. (It is hard to imagine Socrates and Isocrates arguing over the precise number of credit hours to be dedicated to each of these three areas with the same intensity as do faculty members today.) But while liberal education can occur within any of these different curricula, it is not necessarily identified with any one of them.

Next, consider the *form* (instructional style, pedagogical methods) of the curriculum. It is common, for instance, to identify a liberal education with the academic setting in which it takes place. I often hear comments to the effect that colleges like Middlebury or Transylvania offer a liberal education because of their small size, which encourages personal interactions and individual attention. Our two colleges may do these good things, but that is not what makes us liberal education institutions. After all, there are some much larger and more impersonal schools—say, Harvard—that do a pretty good job of liberal education. And there are some far smaller places that do not. What is more, many think that liberal education is best achieved when students engage in off-campus experiences like internships, service-learning activities, or study-abroad programs. So liberal education is not necessarily the same thing as learning in a close-knit community. More generally, over the course of the past several centuries, liberal education has been identified with a variety of widely divergent pedagogical techniques, from recitation and disputation, to tutorials and seminars, to blogs and webcams. Some educators insist upon the intensive, introspective, and individual nature of the enterprise, while others emphasize the importance of social interaction between students and teachers or collaborative learning among students themselves. Again, my point is that all of these approaches can work, but liberal education should not be identified with any particular one of them.

What Liberal Education Is

To identify liberal education with the content or form of its curriculum is to commit the analytical error of conflating a thing with those factors that are (arguably) conducive to bringing the thing about. Liberal education is not defined by its instrumentalities. What makes education liberal is its distinctive purpose. Aristotle noted, "In education it makes all the difference *why* a man does or learns anything; if he studies it for the sake of his own development [n.b., *not* "for its own sake"] or with a view to human excellence, it is liberal."[2] Liberal education aims at the fullest development of the person as a human being. You would think that people don't need much instruction in being human; it ought to come fairly automatically to them just by being born. But the truth is that being human is rather different from being almost anything else. Who we humans are is not precisely fixed either by our genes or by our physical environment. Biology is not destiny. As human beings, our lives are, to some important extent anyway, whatever we make of them.

And while we are at it, we might as well make the *most* of our lives. This has meant different things to different people throughout time. History has witnessed many changes in the conception of the "good life." What has remained fairly constant, however, is the idea that whatever the "good life" is, it is worth pursuing and it does not just happen. It requires a bit of effort and guidance. People make themselves, but not in circumstances of their own choosing. We can't do much about the limitations imposed on us by physical reality, including our mortality—although God knows we keep trying. The freedom to shape our lives as we imagine is also limited by our imagination. It's the lack of vision thing. That's where education comes in.

The long tradition of liberal education has been marked by different conceptions of what human beings can and should become. Each age has defined for itself its ideal of the fully human life and has designed its own particular *paideia* by which that ideal might be achieved: from the noble statesman of classical Greece and Rome, to the self-fashioning individual of the Renaissance, to the "Christian Gentleman" of early America, to the democratic and global citizen of today. The essence of liberal education lies in none of these particular historical instantiations but, instead, in what all of them have in common. Their commonality is a pursuit of what it means to be fully human. All of these conceptions, each in its own way, represent examples of humanity's capacity for self-reflection and self-definition. We today can reflect upon that evolving tradition and liberate it from any of its specific historical expressions. Understanding liberal education in this new way would also suggest a new way for understanding what it means to be human. This, it seems to me, is our task as liberal educators in the twenty-first century.

"Know thyself," commanded the Oracle of Delphi. "The proper study of mankind is man," wrote Alexander Pope. Whatever the subject matter, the real objects of study in liberal education are the students themselves. Socrates noted that the unexamined life is not worth living. Self-examination is not just navel-gazing. It is not done for its own sake but in order to lead a richer and freer, more human, life. Liberal education is the lifelong examination of the big questions in our lives: Who am I? What does it mean to be human? What can humans accomplish? What is freedom? Thus, not the Great Books, but the Great Questions. The questions define a liberal education, not the answers. Answers will differ from person to person and from one time period to another, but the questions are those that all humans face. Asking them of ourselves is the mark of our humanity. It is something that, as far as I know, only we humans do. People hunger for answers to these questions in order to better understand themselves. As Richard Light notes, "The most common hope expressed by students when they embark on a new class is that it will somehow change them as persons."[3] Liberal education is a type of soul food.

The sad thing is how much of life's richness is unexamined. Let me give you an illustration. My wife and I visited Rome several years ago, during which we toured the Vatican, including a stop inside the Sistine Chapel. Decorating its walls and ceiling is a series of frescos painted by Michelangelo that are among the world's greatest artistic masterpieces. The center vault of the ceiling depicts the iconic "Creation of Adam." In it, God extends a pointed finger toward Adam, who mirrors his creator by extending his finger back to receive the divine spark. This panel expresses both the divinity of God and the godlike nature of humans, who are created in God's image. Just as God created human beings, so do humans create masterpieces (including those depicting God) like the frescoes in the Sistine Chapel. From overhead, Michelangelo calls upon the viewer to appreciate our humanity in all its glory. It is discouraging how many of my fellow tourists were so distracted by more mundane activities that they failed to notice that inspiring message. Many never even looked up at the ceiling.

Many people just don't "get" it. They sell their lives short by living only a part of it. We play roles written by authors other than ourselves. Many years ago at a party with my then fellow graduate students and their families, I was introduced to the wife of a colleague. In answer to my question, "So, what do you do?" she replied, "I'm *just* a housewife." Over the years, I came to know this woman rather well, and what I discovered was a remarkable, multitalented human being who could not be defined by any social role. She was so many wonderful things, not *just* any one of them. Or, consider the case of Anna Sam, who worked as a cashier to pay her way through college. Anna was thoroughly alienated by her menial job until one day, largely to occupy her mind at work, she decided to mentally collect anecdotes for a future book about her experiences as a cashier. Even before ever writing a word, Anna began to see herself and her world with new eyes. She realized that she was not *just* a cashier; she was a human being who had something profound and witty to say. Subsequently a runaway best seller, her book *Tribulations of a Cashier* transformed many lives, not just Anna's.[4] Other cashiers who read the book told her how much it had changed their perceptions of themselves as well. And members of the public related how they had begun to perceive and therefore treat cashiers differently, like real human beings.

Liberal education seeks to reveal and unleash our inner human being. Its central lesson is: *Ecce Homo.* We are all potentially so much more than our conventional selves. And whatever this quality is, we share it with our fellow human beings.

A Concrete Example

"This all sounds really inspiring," I suspect some of you are thinking, "but really it's just a lot of hand-waving. What would 'revealing the human' look like in the courses that I actually offer?" It is certainly easier for some disciplines (such as those in the humanities, the social sciences, and the arts) than in others (namely, the physical sciences). But ironically, much of the teaching in the former is not liberal, while the latter lends itself quite well to the purposes of liberal education.

Too often the more "humanistic" disciplines are taught in ways that are decidedly illiberal, in that their disciplinary focus becomes an end in itself. Each field walls itself off from others and sees its mission as training students to become as accomplished as possible in it. So, for instance, the goal of artistic or historical or anthropological education is often taken to be producing effective artists or historians or anthropologists. But the goal of liberal education is to produce flourishing human beings. Liberal education seeks to transcend the constraints imposed upon us by conventional social categories and social roles—whether these are conceived in terms of race, gender, class, nationality, occupation, or, as in the case of the academy, discipline. These categories can become prisons of our own making. "In a school of liberal education," writes Charles Bailey, "we are not trying to produce an artist [for example], but a human being who has some understanding of the arts as a great and persuasive human practice. I should add here that another characteristic of the place of art . . . in a liberal education is that the particular practice is to be seen in the light of, as shedding light on, all the other practices studied."[5] The same may be said of all fields in the liberal arts. Liberal education makes use of their particular subject matter, but it insists upon treating that material in a *new way* that transcends disciplinarily.

Let me give you a concrete example. But rather than using a field that readily lends itself to the study of people, I'm going to stick my neck out and look at the natural sciences, which are conventionally seen to be in tension with humanistic culture.[6] In what sense can we say that, regardless of the particular subject matter of the natural sciences, the subject under investigation is our (and our students') humanity? Well, in the most trivial sense, the human body is subject to the same physical, chemical, and biological processes as is everything else in the universe. Stated more grandly, we humans are composed of the "star stuff" that is shared by the entire cosmos. But that's not good enough. While humans are undeniably natural beings, humanism insists that humans are not totally reducible to the physical material of which we are composed. Hannah Arendt expresses this idea by her distinction between things that are understood in terms of *what* they are, and humans who are understood in terms of *who* they are.[7] Does natural science reveal anything to us about how we humans are interconnected with and yet different from every other thing in the world? That is to say, what does science say about our *distinctive* humanity? *Ex hypothesis*, this aspect of scientific education, namely, its revelatory potential regarding the human condition, is what makes science part of liberal education.

Let me emphasize that the purpose of this exercise is not to prove anything about science but rather to use science as an illustration of what I mean by liberal education. Nevertheless, not being a scientist or historian of science or philosopher of science myself, I approach this task with some trepidation. I'm really operating without a net here. But in for a penny, in for a pound. So here goes.

Such an answer proceeds from the obvious distinction between *nature* and *natural science*. Science is not nature: it is what we know (or think we know at a given time) about nature and the processes by which we gain that knowledge. What is taught in schools is science, not nature itself. Unlike nature, science is a human activity. Humans did not create nature (although we have altered it and done our best to destroy it), but we are the creators of science. What we know about nature reflects the attributes not only of the object of our knowledge but also of the subject doing the knowing. For the astrophysicist S. James Gates, science lies at the intersection of physical reality, human imagination, and human technology.[8] The answers given by science are always replies to questions asked by humans. And to the extent that those answers rest upon observations made by scientists, they are always limited to the possible range of human perception. Of course, technology continually extends that range of possibility, but technology is itself a human product. Arthur Zajonc, who teaches physics at Amherst, observes, "Science is actually not about a pre-given, hidden, microscopic world existing completely independent of us, but it is about what we can know through experience and reason."[9] What humans know (and can know) about nature thus has our fingerprints all over it. This is what Werner Heisenberg meant when he wrote, "Modern science gives us the impression that we always confront ourselves . . . , that we in a certain way seem to find only ourselves everywhere."[10] While the physical reality of nature does not change (the nature of nature is that it is unchanging), our theoretical constructions of it do. Scientific theories are always provisional and paradigmatic.

Science is a human activity in other ways as well. As much as is the case with art for the artist, science for the scientist offers a vehicle for self-expression and self-transcendence. The scientific enterprise is probably the best example of Aristotle's comment on human nature that "humans have a natural desire to know." And knowing things can change us. While watching a *Nova* program, "The Fabric of the Cosmos," on PBS recently, I was struck by the comment of the physicist who said, "After you learn quantum mechanics, you're never really the same again."[11] Science also offers a profoundly aesthetic experience. As Henri Poincaré observed, "The scientist does not study nature because it is useful to do so. He studies it because he takes pleasure in it; and he takes pleasure in it because it is beautiful . . ."[12] If art is the disciplined pursuit of a passion, then science might be seen as the passionate pursuit of a discipline. Or is it the other way around?

Aristotle also said of human nature that "man is a political [i.e., of the *polis*, or social] animal." Science is a *collective* human enterprise. It transpires within a scientific community. Scientific knowledge is communicated in a scientific language (often some dialect of the human language of mathematics), transmitted to other scientists through social media such as scientific journals and conferences, and its conclusions are subjected to the process of peer review. Like every other community, the scientific one possesses a social structure, whose organizational features include aspects of both bureaucracy and democracy. Members of the scientific community are socialized to adopt normative roles in such a community. After all, scientists are not born that way; they are trained to think and act like scientists.

The scientific method for establishing truths about the natural world is itself a human construct, and the objectivity of observations, which it requires for establishing these truths, is constituted by the intersubjectivity of those who practice it. Scientific knowledge progresses over time as a cumulative process, one that both builds upon and revises the perspectives of others in the past. In this way, it is analogous to other cultural traditions from, say, Catholicism to liberal education. Like these other living traditions, scientific development is characterized by both change and continuity. At the core of its evolving understanding of the natural world is an unchanging set of fundamental assumptions—a modern "scientific worldview" resting upon the philosophical principles of realism, determinism, rationalism, and empiricism—about how the world works and how human beings can know how it works. Its most basic premise is that the cosmos is orderly in a way that humans can understand it. As far as the scientific community is concerned, these shared core commitments define what it means to do science and to be a scientist. Because science is a social enterprise, questions of ethical conduct become relevant. Despite the conventional wisdom that science is value free, the reality is that it requires the commitment by scientists to certain moral and intellectual virtues, such as honesty and integrity.

The scientific enterprise is an institutionalized practice (like business or religion or politics), which is affected by its wider social environment (with its commercial and religious and political influences). Such nonscientific factors often—many scientists would say too often—distort scientific research agendas. The causal arrow goes the other way as well: science also has a profound impact on the rest of society. The scientific worldview, new scientific discoveries and theories, and the technological advances deriving from them have all had a dramatic effect on how the rest of us go about our business. What's more, science has had a tremendous influence on what it means to be human. By contributing to humanity's understanding of the natural world, science has enabled humans to use that knowledge in order to partially overcome its physical constraints. Science has also transformed humanity's self-understanding about what it means to be human. Its understanding of the natural world has helped emancipate humanity from our misconceptions about our place in it. Much like the works in philosophy or literature or art, the results of scientific inquiry point to profound insights about the human condition. For one, we can take justifiable pride at the amazing achievements of which human beings are capable. Or another, we should remain humble in the face of our ultimate powerlessness in confronting a vast, incomprehensible, and uncaring cosmos. Or still another, we ought to feel a reverence for the unfathomably beautiful and awe-inspiring universe that is our home. Such is the stuff of any course in the humanities worth its credit hours.

Let me reassure you that I am not offering an epistemological critique of the merits of science. I am no constructivist, and my essay is not a salvo in the "science wars." Rather, I am trying to reconstruct the teaching of science in light of my ideas about liberal education. Although you may not articulate these notions in the same way as I have done, I suspect teachers of science really agree with me to a substantial degree. I bet that you already address many of them, if only implicitly, in your courses. That's undoubtedly one reason why you require labs: students need to *do* science, not just master its conclusions. However, "doing science" is crucial not only because it is a more effective method for *teaching science*, but also because it *teaches about science* as a human activity. That human activity, like all human activity, reveals a great deal about the humans doing it. Is there a more quintessentially human activity than designing and conducting a rigorous, controlled experiment? What does that activity say about *us*? This is why Emerson told his fellow American scholars to "study nature": not only in order to learn about the natural world but, by seeing themselves in nature (including observing and thinking about it), to learn about themselves.[13] Teaching science in this spirit is demystifying and de-reifying. What I am proposing is a critical pedagogy, which reflects critical thinking about the nature of science and the nature of liberal education.

Means and Ends of Liberal Education

Let me return to my thesis. We should not confuse the means of liberal education with its ends. This distinction is not merely pedantic. It has very practical consequences. We live in a world where technological imperatives, the "creative destruction" of market forces, and the totalizing logic of instrumental rationality reduce human beings to the status of things. In the face of modernity's dehumanizing prospect, a humanizing liberal education is perhaps needed more now than ever.

We liberal educators have a responsibility to protect liberal education from those things that threaten it. Many of these are well known, such as the financial exigencies faced by many liberal arts colleges and their students. A less obvious, but perhaps more insidious, threat comes from the "displacement of goals," in which means replace ends, and instrumentalities replace purposes. Contemporary America is enthralled by "the ineluctable modality of the instrumental." Instrumentalism devalues the human. Humanism is the notion that human beings are "ends in themselves" (whatever that means), whereas instrumentalism reduces all ends to means useful in achieving other ends. Correspondingly, educational instrumentalism devalues liberal education. It comes in many guises today. Consider the discourse on *education as an instrument* (as in vocationalism or the concern over international competitiveness). Or witness the fixation on the *instrumentalities of education* (as in the culture of assessment or the reliance on instructional technologies for greater teaching effectiveness). A "nuts-and-bolts" approach to the curriculum is another aspect of educational instrumentalism. At the very least, a focus on curricular "improvements"—especially those that are thought to be valuable by virtue of being innovative or entertaining or attractive to sources of funding—can be awfully distracting. The latest high-tech gadget or engaging activity can too easily deflect the teacher's effort to "get the soul out of bed, out of her deep habitual sleep."[14]

Losing sight of our purpose may have an even more pernicious consequence. The displacement of goals sometimes entails more than the substitution of means for ends. It might also result in the desired end being replaced by an altogether different, indeed antithetical, one. Let me give you a historical example. In their interpretation of the Italian Renaissance entitled *From Humanism to the Humanities*, Anthony Grafton and Lisa Jardine examine the discrepancy between the idealized accounts of humanistic education offered by Renaissance schools and their actual pedagogical practices.[15] The authors distinguish between "humanism," a worldview extolling the notion of *dignitas hominis* that served as the end for an education in which "the individual acquired a general fitness for a human existence," and "the humanities," or the concrete curriculum based upon the study of specific texts. Despite overblown inspirational claims for a classical liberal education, Grafton and Jardine note the real drudgery of rote memorization in humanistic schools. The skills of reading and writing in Latin were much in demand for those seeking employment from members of the ruling class. The very pedestrian nature of this pedagogy promoted the personality traits of obedience and docility that rulers found attractive in their servants. Seen from this point of view, they conclude,

> The general approval expressed for [this] kind of humanistic instruction by the Italian establishment has more to do with its appropriateness as a commodity than with its intrinsic intellectual merits. As long as humanist schools turned out such suitable potential servants of the state, they were prepared to endorse the enthusiastic claims of humanist idealists for their literary studies . . .[16]

A similar displacement is occurring today. Of course, the knowledge, technical skills, and attitudes required of contemporary servants of power and wealth are radically different from those of the Renaissance. IT is the new Latin. And the cutting-edge pedagogical modalities of today's liberal arts colleges—including internships, study-abroad experiences, service-learning opportunities, collaborative learning, interactive learning, and creative use of educational technology—are far more edifying than the one described by Grafton and Jardine. After all, today's professional and managerial employees of global businesses need to demonstrate technological capacities, leadership, creative thinking, teamwork, and cultural sensitivities required by corporations as they operate in the new competitive realities of global and flexible production.

I hasten to add that such a dynamic may be especially seductive for selective liberal arts colleges, which educate many of the children of the nation's intellectual and economic elite. It is all the more important that such colleges hold fast to the humanistic purpose of liberal education. I hope that ongoing discussions about curricular innovations at such colleges will not eclipse their continuing commitment to the purpose of liberal education. Stewards, students, faculty, and graduates of these colleges should never confuse what the college is good *at* with what the college is good *for*.

Notes

1. The Phi Beta Kappa Society, *The Founding of New Chapters* (Washington, DC: Phi Beta Kappa, 1990), n.p.

2. Quoted in Richard Livingstone, *On Education: The Future in Education and Education for a World Adrift* (New York: Cambridge University Press, 1954), 63.

3. Richard Light, *Making the Most of College: Students Speak Their Minds* (Cambridge: Harvard University Press, 2001), 47.

4. Anna Sam, *Les tribulations d'une caissière* (Paris: Hachette, 2009).

5. Charles Bailey, *Beyond the Present and Particular: A Theory of Liberal Education* (London: Routledge and Kegan Paul, 1984), 121.

6. The *locus classicus* on this point is C. P. Snow, *The Two Cultures and the Scientific Revolution* (New York: Cambridge University Press, 1961).

7. Hannah Arendt, *The Human Condition* (Chicago: University of Chicago Press, 1958).

8. Sylvester James Gates, "On the Universality of Creativity in the Liberal Arts and the Sciences," http://www.umdphysics.umd.edu/images/pdfs/ontheuniversalityofcreativity.pdf.

9. Arthur Zajonc, "Spirituality in Higher Education: Overcoming the Divide," *Liberal Education* 89.1 (Winter 2003): 56.

10. Werner Heisenberg, *The Physicist's Conception of Nature* (London: Hutchinson and Co., 1958), 23.

11. The comment is by Steven Weinberg. See "The Fabric of the Cosmos: Quantum Leap" on *NOVA*, which aired on PBS on July 25, 2012, http://www.pbs.org/wgbh/nova/physics/fabric-of-cosmos.html#fabric-quantum.

12. Quoted in Subrahmanyan Chandrasekhar, "Beauty and the Quest for Beauty in Science," *Physics Today* 32.7 (July 1979): 25.

13. Ralph Waldo Emerson, "The American Scholar" and "Nature" in *The Best of Ralph Waldo Emerson: Essays, Poems, Addresses*, ed. Gordon S. Haight (New York: Walter J. Black, 1941).

14. Ralph Waldo Emerson, entry for April 20, 1834, in *Emerson in His Journals*, ed. Joel Porte (Cambridge: Harvard University Press, 1982), 123.

15. Anthony Grafton and Lisa Jardine, *From Humanism to the Humanities: Education and the Liberal Arts in Fifteenth- and Sixteenth-Century Europe* (Cambridge: Harvard University Press, 1986).

16. Ibid., 25.

Singing a New History

.•────•.

Pathways to Learning in a Liberal Arts Setting

Steven S. Volk

Steven S. Volk is Professor of History and Director of the Center for Teaching Innovation and Excellence (CTIE) at Oberlin College, where he has taught Latin American history and museum studies for twenty-eight years. He has published widely on Chilean history, US–Latin American relations, contemporary Mexico, and issues in undergraduate pedagogy. In 2011 he was named Outstanding US Baccalaureate Colleges Professor of the Year by the Carnegie Foundation for the Advancement of Teaching and the Center for the Advancement and Support of Education (CASE). In 2012, he was named a Great Lakes College Association Teagle Pedagogy Fellow. In 2003 he received the Nancy Lyman Roelker Mentorship Award from the American Historical Association and was recognized for his teaching leadership by the Northeast Ohio Council on Higher Education. In 2001 he was commended by the Government of Chile for "his contributions in helping to restore democracy" in that country. He has received two National Endowment for the Humanities (NEH) grants. His work in the field of museum studies includes development of a pedagogical model for the integration of academic museums into the broad teaching mission of colleges and universities known as "Crossing the Streets" pedagogy.

৯

It was clear to me that she was floundering in the class. Her papers had a lost-in-the-woods quality characteristic of those who begin writing before understanding what the assignment was about and finish without having discovered it. She was quiet in class and often distracted. Although I recommended many times that she come to my office hours, Jessica (not her real name) never did. Jessica, I said to myself, is not a very strong student; she just doesn't understand history.

The class, Dirty Wars and Democracy, examined the Southern Cone of South America (Chile, Argentina, Brazil, and Uruguay) from the 1960s to the 1990s. During that period, each of these countries lived through a particularly brutal military dictatorship. While the military had cycled in and out of power for most of the twentieth century in Brazil and Argentina, Chile and Uruguay boasted the most stable democratic histories in South America. And yet in Chile, General Augusto Pinochet maintained his grip on power for seventeen years, during which time his government was responsible for the deaths of more than two thousand people and over forty thousand documented cases of torture.[1] In Argentina, an estimated thirty thousand people were "disappeared" by the regime, their relatives deprived of any word of their fate, their infant children occasionally kidnapped and raised by military officers.[2] Students would grapple with questions of why stable civilian democracies succumbed to military dictatorships and how to account for the widespread cruelty practiced by the dictatorships. The class considered the circumstances that ultimately led to the return of civilian governments in these countries and puzzled over how they coped with issues of reconciliation, retribution, justice, and memory in the postdictatorial period.

After I had taught a version of the class the first time, I decided to caution prospective students during the first session of the semester that this would not be an easy journey, but we would be making it together. I expected them to absorb the materials not just intellectually but emotionally as well. This wasn't a class for those who only wanted to listen to lectures, I warned them. They had to engage, and even, to the extent possible, live the hopes and feel the fears of the time.[3] I required this commitment, I explained, because the events we would be studying were not "just" history to me, they were *my* history, *my* life. I lived in Chile in 1972 and 1973, conducting dissertation research. On September 11, 1973 (what many of us would later refer to as "the first 9/11"), I watched in horror from my apartment's balcony in downtown Santiago as air force jets bombed La Moneda, Chile's White House, with President Salvador Allende and his aides still inside. Like so many others, I cautiously felt my way through the early months of the dictatorship, saw friends disappear, and, sadly, identified their bodies in the morgue. After I returned to the United States, I continued working for the return of democracy to Chile over the next seventeen years. And when, after many years, I felt that I had achieved the distance necessary to offer a course on this material, I knew that it would have to be a different kind of course. History is not a reenactment, nor was the course to be a personal narrative, but given my own emotional engagement with the subject—which I never hid from my students—I knew I had to rely on their full commitment for the course to work.

Although my approach to the course was idiosyncratic, I also knew that I wouldn't be disappointed. Having taught at Oberlin College for nearly three decades, I've come to appreciate the kind of teaching and learning that can flourish at a residential liberal arts college. Historically, liberal arts colleges have been defined by a series of factors: a curriculum based primarily in arts and science fields with little focus on vocational or professional preparation; traditionally aged, full-time, mostly residential students; relatively small classes; and a faculty committed to teaching while often engaged as well in scholarship.[4] But it is what the students make of these opportunities that allow liberal arts colleges to be transformational. I had come to appreciate that the students themselves create the conditions for a highly generative learning process. That they are intellectually curious, conscious of the world around them, and feel a deep desire to engage almost goes without saying. My students share with other undergraduates the intellectual flexibility that comes from not yet being disciplined into a discipline. They ask questions that wouldn't occur to professional historians or graduate students. Boundaries are continually crossed, and time can be spent exploring why historians ask questions in certain ways and anthropologists in others. They are continually upending what David Foster Wallace described as "default" thinking in his 2005 commencement speech at Kenyon College. "I have come gradually to understand," he observed, "that the liberal arts cliché about teaching you how to think is actually shorthand for a much deeper, more serious idea: learning how to think really means learning how to exercise some control over how and what you think. It means being conscious and aware enough to choose what you pay attention to and to choose how you construct meaning from experience."[5]

Equally important is the students' location in an environment in which learning is fluid and classroom walls are wonderfully porous. Conversations that begin in class spill over to lunch, dinner, or the dorm. I would only learn about this through conversations with students who were not enrolled in the class: "There must be, like, seven kids on my floor taking Dirty Wars," a student remarked. "They're all just talking about the play you had them read." If issues raised in my class carried over into other settings, I began to think about how those settings shaped the way my students were processing the history we were studying. How were their understandings of themes raised in my class revised or deepened when they read a novel by the Argentinian writer Nora Strejilevich in their Spanish course? How did the philosophy course on justice influence their papers? And what of the biology student studying mitochondrial DNA who could explain how bodies buried by the regimes decades earlier could be identified by forensic anthropologists? As I realized that students were "paying attention," in Wallace's sense, to similar problems from multiple perspectives, and that each of these perspectives shaped their understanding in specific ways, I accepted the folly of thinking of my students as "history students," even though my class approached these problems through the lens of history. They were, in all senses, students of the liberal arts experience.

Which brings me back to Jessica. I read in her papers a lack of engagement with the topic as well as an inability to construct historical arguments. I drew her attention to these points in comments written on her first paper, but the second showed little improvement. It was flat, without affect; I couldn't hear her voice. For a second time I suggested that she come to my office hours to talk about her work, but it never happened. Not a good student, I thought, and turned to the next student's paper.

An interlude: Oberlin houses both a liberal arts college and a world-renowned Conservatory of Music. There are many more liberal arts students, but music infuses campus life. Choosing which of the four hundred concerts a year I would attend presents challenges, but I particularly look forward to the two fully staged operas, fall and spring. The voices of these young conservatory performers rarely failed to thrill.

That spring, Smetana's The Bartered Bride, an opera I didn't know well, was the featured work. I arrived as the lights were going down, which left me no time to glance at the program. The curtain soon rose to a scene of happy villagers at a church fair. Mařenka, however, was despondent because her parents were forcing her to marry a man she never met rather than her beloved Jeník. As these singers exited, Mařenka's parents, Ludmila and Krušina, came on stage . . . and I stared in amazement as Jessica, the student who couldn't find her voice in Dirty Wars, had no trouble finding it as Ludmila; she was a spectacular soprano, bright and expansive. I left the opera marveling at her skills as a singer, wondering why I hadn't discovered these talents before and how I could leverage the confidence she expressed in her vocal practice to pry open strengths in her study of history.

"Educators spend a good deal of energy testing critical-thinking ability," Chad Hanson recently wrote, "and, frankly, are frustrated with the results. One reason we have difficulty producing critical thinking is that we separate thinking from thinkers. We treat critical thinking as if it were a free-floating ability when, in fact, it is a function of oneself or one's identity."[6] I had separated Jessica's work from Jessica, and it was through her identity as a singer that I needed to help her find her critical voice as a student of history. A liberal education promotes a sustained conversation between reasoning about some of the greatest philosophical questions that humanity has faced and their artistic expression, between the precision of scientific experimentation and the ambiguity of historical contingency.[7] A liberal education at its best promotes multiple pathways to scaffold our students' learning. As educators, we bring into our classrooms both an awareness of the literature on multiple intelligences and a cautionary note against "tracking" our students into what we might have identified as their predominant learning style.[8] But the heart of the liberal arts experience, I have found, is not only what happens in individual classes but in our ability to actively exploit a multiplicity of pathways to help students integrate, and therefore take ownership over, their learning.

Jessica and I spoke after class the following Tuesday, and I urged her to come to my office hours to talk about the next paper. This time she came. I proposed that instead of writing a traditional paper, she could, if she chose, compose a song that would address the central theme posed in the assignment's prompt: summarize the experiences of living under a dictatorship. But, I added, she would also have to write *two* papers to complement the song: one in which she discussed the lyrics of the song in light of the history we had studied and how her song advanced our understanding, or illuminated the central challenges, of that history. In the second, she was to focus on the music, offering a melodic analysis that I, a complete novice in music theory, could understand, and how the music formed a part of her overall approach to the history she was exploring.

Jessica was noticeably more alive and active in class after that discussion. Whether it was because she found a way into the material that hadn't existed before or because we forged a connection through *The Bartered Bride*, I couldn't be sure. The result of her efforts, however, left no room for doubt. Jessica turned in her project on time, but rather than a song and two papers, she had written the lyrics and music for a five-song cycle ("Cinco Canciones"). It took her little time to encourage a pianist in the conservatory to accompany her, and, together, they recorded the songs. She sought advice from one of the conservatory's most distinguished voice instructors, which allowed me to collaborate with a colleague with whom I had no previous engagement. Finally she wrote both a melodic analysis of the jazz progressions she employed and a content analysis for each of the five songs. The cycle, she wrote, "traces the life and thoughts of a middle aged woman . . . whose life has been brashly interrupted and disfigured by dictatorship . . ."[9] It was, to put it mildly, breathtaking.

Columbia professor Andrew Delbanco, quoting from Emerson's journals, observes that our work as teachers is to "get the soul out of bed, out of her deep habitual sleep,"[10] a similar sentiment to that expressed by David Foster Wallace when he enjoined students to move from their "natural default positions." College is, as Carolyn "Biddy" Martin, the president of Amherst College, reminds us, "for those who are brave enough to put at risk what they think they know . . ."[11] While such sentiments are often applied to the students who attend liberal arts colleges, my experience suggests that they are every bit as applicable to the faculty who teach there as well.

Schooling and the degrees conferred hold out to students (and to their families) the promise of economic returns, nothing to belittle in an era of mountainous student debt. But *education* as a transformative human endeavor finds its central human values elsewhere. A liberal arts education strives to give students the skills, insight, courage, and perspective to allow them to make themselves according to their own image. In that context, the liberal arts experience is much like travel: *how* one gets to a destination is as important, if not more important, than the destination. "Education," as John Dewey reminded, "is not preparation for life; education is life itself."

And what about this journey? My experience with Jessica suggests that the liberal arts experience broadly mimics the way that learning occurs in the brain itself. Dendrites, the "trees" that branch out from brain cells (neurons), play a critical role in learning. As infants develop, learn to crawl, walk, and talk, the dendrites in their brains lengthen and multiply until, by the time a child is three, the brain has formed about 1,000 trillion connections through these pathways. To extend this analogy, we can think of "instruction," mastering subject matter, a process that goes on in the classroom, as the neurons, the brain cells. But an *education* is all about the dendrites, the complex and multitudinous corridors by which classroom and non-classroom learning can be tied together, with each connection reinforcing a different kind of learning. What is best about liberal arts colleges is that they encourage students and faculty to find those pathways together. Jessica's learning journey took her through *The Bartered Bride*, into the conservatory, through jazz compositions and a recording studio, until finally connecting to my classroom, where she found both the voice of the woman who had been "disfigured by the dictatorship" and her own voice as a student of history. Other students and faculty trace their own distinct pathways. But the end is the same: taking advantage of all a liberal arts education has to provide gives us the responsibility, and the great opportunity, of co-curating an education.

Notes

1. Estimates of the death toll are usually around five thousand, higher than those reported by the National Truth and Reconciliation Commission (Rettig Commis-

sion): http://www.ddhh.gov.cl/ddhh_rettig.html. Information on tortures is contained in the Valech Report, available at: http://www.indh.cl/informacion-comision-valech.

2. Francisco Goldman, "Children of the Dirty War: Argentina's Stolen Orphans," *New Yorker*, March 19, 2012.

3. For one example of how I do this, see Steven S. Volk, "'How the Air Felt on My Cheeks': Using Avatars to Access History," *The History Teacher* 46.2 (February 2013): 193–214.

4. Vicki L. Baker, Roger G. Baldwin, and Sumedha Makker, "Where Are They Now? Revisiting Breneman's Study of Liberal Arts Colleges," *Liberal Education* 98.3 (Summer 2012): http://www.aacu.org/liberaleducation/le-su12/baker_baldwin_makker.cfm.

5. "David Foster Wallace, in His Own Words," http://moreintelligentlife.com/story/david-foster-wallace-in-his-own-words.

6. Chad Hanson, "The Art of Becoming Yourself," *Academe* (January–February 2013): 18.

7. Andrew Delbanco addresses many of these issues in *College: What It Was, Is, and Should Be* (Princeton: Princeton University Press, 2012).

8. Howard Gardner, *Frames of Mind: The Theory of Multiple Intelligences* (New York: Basic Books, 2011), and Harold Pashler, Mark McDaniel, Doug Rohrer, and Robert Bjork, "Learning Styles: Concepts and Evidence," *Psychological Science in the Public Interest* 9.3 (December 2008): 105–119.

9. From "Cinco Canciones."

10. Andrew Delbanco cited in Scott McLemee, "To Get the Soul Out of Bed," *democracyjournal.org* (Winter 2013): 105.

11. Carolyn Martin, "What Is College For?" *Chronicle of Higher Education*, April 22, 2013.

Living Art

Ruthann Godollei

Ruthann Godollei is the DeWitt Wallace Professor of Art at Macalester College in St. Paul, Minnesota. She has served as Chair of the Art and Art History Department as well as Dean of the Fine Arts Division. She has exhibited her prints, drawings, and animations internationally, incorporating political and social commentary. Her work is touring internationally with Posada Centenario, a 2013 homage to Mexican printer J. G. Posada on the centenary of his death. A print was selected for The New York Society of Etchers show, Democracy, at Sacred Gallery, New York City, 2012, and the Clemson National Print and Drawing Exhibition, 2011. Her prints have been included in exhibits such as Political/ Poetical, the International Print Triennial, Tallinn, Estonia; the 2014 Biennial Douro, Lamego Museum and Douro Museum, Alijó, Portugal; and the International Triennial of Graphic Art, Bitola, Macedonia. She has been a seven-time resident artist at the Frans Masereel Centrum for printmaking in Belgium. Her work is in many international collections, such as the Belgian Royal Museum of Art, Antwerp; the Polish National Museum of Art, Poznañ; KUMU National Art Museum, Tallinn, Estonia; the Centre for Fine Print Research, Bristol, United Kingdom; and the Penang State Museum and Art Gallery, Malaysia. She teaches printmaking (intaglio, relief, lithography, screenprint, handset type, digital prints) and the senior seminar at Macalester. In spring 2013 she taught a course titled Dissent. She has taught 2-Dimensional

Design, Performance and Installation Art, Women in Art (cross-listed with women's and gender studies), and co-taught Political Art (cross-listed with political science) and Images in Consumer Society (cross-listed with sociology). She was the recipient of the Thomas Jefferson Award for teaching and service to the college in 2013. Godollei is the co-author with Eric Dregni of Road Show: Art Cars and the Museum of the Streets *(2009) and the author of a DIY printing book,* How to Create Your Own Gig Posters *(2013).*

৯

I teach art at a small liberal arts college in St. Paul, Minnesota. Such teaching has been enormously rewarding. I love my students. My position as professor allows me to talk about what I love—art—to a receptive, ready-to-learn audience. Since I teach studio art, I have the luxury of teaching an all-volunteer group of students, although the school does have a fine arts requirement for general education. As a teacher, I believe in the transformative power of art and am privileged to see living proof of it on a regular basis.

Because my classes are small, I know every student, their aspirations, limitations, and many of the challenges they're facing. Because I'm trying to promote the making of real art, not just empty exercise, many times I'm the witness to genuine struggles as these students are deciding who they want to be and how they want to engage the world. They are at a great age to learn. They are excited about ideas. They can tolerate contradiction and uncertainty. They can hold two conflicting ideas in their heads and not explode. They have not yet set everything in stone. Even though they may have already encountered some setbacks in life, they have energy and enthusiasm and demonstrate an inspiring resilience and capacity for learning.

At Macalester College, we have a combined art and art history program with majors concentrating in studio or history. Such a curriculum makes for well-rounded students: art historians learn hands-on processes in various media, and studio artists benefit from the lessons of our excellent art history scholars. All of these art and art history students bring their knowledge from other courses—in the sciences, humanities, social sciences, and other arts—with them when they come to art classes. This breadth gives the students wide varieties of source material upon which to draw in their art endeavors.

My specialty is printmaking. My studio classes cover etching, screen print, lithography, relief printing, digital print processes, and even handset movable type à la Gutenberg. I teach these highly technical processes as vehicles for presenting ideas. Since I have a penchant for liberal arts thinking, I also have taught and co-taught courses in many different disciplines including design, political science, sociology, and women's and gender studies. In every course that I have taught, I see my students making connections between their liberal arts education and the worlds beyond the campus, as I try to do in my own artwork.

Last spring I taught a topics course titled Dissent. It included the history of art's role in resistance movements, and the class also contained hands-on production components. Students were asked to make artwork in support of movements, groups, or causes to which they belonged or with which they identified, with the stipulation that the art be implemented off campus, in the so-called real world. The students produced spectacularly effective projects, ranging from passionate advocacy to straightforward presentation of useful information. Zoe Bowman made "spoke cards" for bicycle wheels for Bike to Work Week in her Wisconsin hometown. Kenny Bello and Carina Lei, computer science students (Ms. Lei was also an art major) collaborated on a multimedia Android phone application for Hubbs Public School volunteers. Hubbs is a school that specializes in teaching immigrants English, math, and basic computer skills. Alizarin Menninga made two original linocuts to print on the front and back of hundreds of envelopes to send to contacts with a letter explaining her friend's art collective project in Mexico City and requesting donations for it. Phoebe DeVincenzi, Anna Van Voorhis, and Alana Masters made stickers, patches, and postcards (with postage) for EXCO, the experimental college of the Twin Cities. The cards read "education is my human right" and "lean on each other to grow." Laura Levinson partnered with WISE, the Women's Initiative for Self Empowerment, and made bilingual stickers on topics of feminism, immigration, and gender politics with messages such as "Marriage Equality Is Who I Am." Cyrus Hair designed the logo and a poster for New Lens, an urban mentoring society in which African American male college students mentor eighth-grade African American males. Zoe Kusinitz designed "Got Breastmilk?" a poster for La Leche League, informing the public that Minnesota law allows for breastfeeding any time in any location. Tori Lewis made a "know your employment rights" flyer for Second Chance Minnesota, to help formerly incarcerated persons get jobs. Peter Vang used a traditional Hmong textile pattern to design a poster promoting ethnic studies in St. Paul public schools. (Minnesota is home to one of the nation's largest populations of Hmong immigrants.)

These were just some of the impressive projects, but equally gratifying were the shows of interest and support classmates paid to each other's presentations on the last day of class. On display was an incredible inventory of the kinds of sites, organizations, and projects these student-citizens had developed to address social problems. We gained the definite sense that art, in numerous ways, can help make things better. An artist friend of mine and I once cooked up a theory of art as simply, "An artist is someone who sees what needs doing and does it."

The students found themselves implicated in the world outside campus, drawing upon their knowledge of the needs of surrounding communities, rooted in their firsthand experiences—their internships and extracurricular activities—as well as informed by broad-based liberal arts learning. These activist art makers benefited from their classroom exposure to excellent exemplars of effective graphics, design, and art interventions. We read widely in theories of power, nonconformism, deviance, resistance, and histories of social movements, labor, civil rights, revolutions, Occupy worldwide, and the Arab Spring. We held a joint class session with Professor Karin Aguilar–San Juan and students from her American Studies course U.S. Racial Formations & the Global Economy. We had lively class discussions of tactics, strategies, art, communication, aesthetics, resources, sustainability, ethics, audiences, and contexts. We used critiques to help makers rework projects to be their most effective in the contexts for which they were intended. Students had to get feedback from the groups with which they worked, many of which were in real need of good graphics, higher profiles, effective messages, and positive attention for their efforts. These liberal arts students used art in projects that became all the more dynamic precisely because they addressed issues about which the students felt strongly. It was my distinct pleasure to work with motivated students from across disciplines in the making of compelling art. For the three parties involved, it was a win-win-win situation. The best classes (for me and my students alike) tend to be those that require that I, too, work all parts of my brain, so that I continue to learn and grow intellectually. I share what I learn with them, I learn from them, and it feeds back into my own practice. It's fuel for my art and theirs.

When I became the printmaking professor at Macalester College, I inherited a decades-long print exchange for the Printmaking I course; I kept the tradition. In an exchange, students create an edition (multiples of the same print) and trade with others in the class, while one copy of each print is retained for the archives. Students get practice with editioning a print, with a motivating mutual purpose (peer scrutiny makes them want to make extra nice prints); and as a result, the college gains a fantastic and ever-growing art collection thanks to a contribution from each student who has taken Printmaking I. Participating students also get to keep one of their own prints, so they experience the pleasant paradox of keeping while also giving away. We hand-typeset a colophon of their names in Century Schoolbook font, working from the same metal letters used for portfolios dating back to the start of the Art Department. It's a lovely tradition; plus, for their labors of producing a print edition, the students get the added bonus of receiving a big stack of their colleagues' art to take home. Each class member knows and values the effort, thought, and skill that go into these works, and they all experience being both producers and consumers of art.

Upper-level printmaking class members, in addition to continuing to explore self-expression while learning new skills, mixed-media techniques, and digital processes, are also assigned sending prints off campus. They apply for exhibits, enter competitions, participate in a portfolio exchange with other artists or schools, donate prints for benefit sales, or suggest a project of their own devising. Many of these opportunities come across my desk, so it hasn't been hard to find venues to suggest that are compatible with students' interests or inclinations. These opportunities benefit serious art students because they can include such exhibits on their resumés. They will need to learn how to scan, digitize, resize, and upload images for applications to graduate school, employment, or grant opportunities, so it's good to have a real-world situation for which to apply these skills. The print trades let students exchange visual ideas and have a gauge of the capabilities of other students across the country. Some students just want to express themselves, master techniques, explore themes, or be part of an art exhibit, while others seriously want to change the world. I have room for all of them in my classes. Every project is voluntary, original, and open ended. The idea is to send good ideas out of the academic classroom and into the arena of life.

Some of these projects have been extraordinary. One student sent her relief print of an elephant off to an elephant sanctuary in the southern United States, a kind of retirement home for circus animals. Not only did they sell the artwork to raise funds for the sanctuary, they used her prize-winning image on promotional materials. These kinds of experiences encouraged Kate Copeland to continue in the medium of printmaking. (She just completed a Fulbright Fellowship teaching printmaking in India.) Other students hand-screenprinted 250 muslin menstrual cup bags, with the image of a pelvis and a uterus on them, to promote eco-friendly alternatives to other feminine hygiene products. They had come up with the idea working from discussions in their women's, gender and sexualities studies classes as well as environmental studies classes. They eventually donated these decorated bags to the local Family Tree Clinic, which was happy to have them to give out to people who come through their office. The project also afforded an excellent technical challenge to print on unusual surfaces. Likewise, last year my entire Printmaking II class decided to donate prints

to the Art4Shelter benefit fundraiser sale to support Simpson Family Hous-
ing Services in Minneapolis, which helps homeless families. Many of those
students were involved in campus-wide efforts to divest college funds from
foreclosure-prone banking institutions. They perceived a need for systemic,
institutional change as well as local direct action, while also satisfying their
personal need to express how they felt about the situation. There are many
different levels on which to engage students making art inside (and then
outside) a liberal arts environment.

I am very proud of helping facilitate these syntheses of the academic,
intellectual, artistic, and practical. When smart, engaged, creative students
apply what they're learning from the liberal arts generally to the particular
art projects they care about, the work overall becomes exponentially better.
Anyone who wants to go on in art will need this kind of big-picture, compelling self-motivation. Artists in our society face a lot of discouragement,
lack of respect, or even ridicule; they need, therefore, internal resources on
which they can draw, and those internal resources typically require a larger,
informing, overarching vision. Even if most of my students (the nonmajors)
never continue in art, they will retain an insider's understanding of artistic
work, the sheer labor involved as well as the whole process, from ideation to
hypothesis to working model to feedback and finally to execution. Informed
viewers have much more respect for the technical difficulties and plain-old
hard work that art requires. They might also gain respect for different ways
of seeing and knowing, including tolerating uncertainty. "Art thinking" can
provide a counterweight to overly rationalistic, utilitarian, and materialistic
tendencies in society. It can be used to explore identity. It can give voice to
outcast concepts and promote empathy for different points of view. Surely
many of these approaches can benefit non-artistic venues and applications,
and so I propose that the practice of art should be encouraged for all, art
majors and nonmajors alike.

As assessment mania began to overtake the nation in recent years,
my school was not immune to knee-jerk reactions to accreditation questions
such as "How do you know your students are learning what you say you're
teaching?" From an art teacher's perspective, the problem with assessment is
not the questioning itself; rather, the problem is with the inappropriate use
of quantitative measurements derived from social science techniques now
imported to and imposed on art activities in order to assess their worth.
More appropriate would be assessment processes drawing upon qualitative,
subjective, descriptive, and comparative tools. Administrators may disagree,
but I know that the prevalent quantification in contemporary normative
assessment protocols misjudges the realm of art. I know, because I see my
students engaging with, responding to, and trying to change their world,
with art as a primary tool. The intrinsic and ulterior worth of such activity

simply cannot be measured, whether by the pound of sculpture, by the square inches of paintings, or by the number of prints in portfolios. It's not the product of clock hours spent or even the amount of effort applied, although sometimes those things add up and do help. Compounding the difficulty of measuring outcomes in art is that any given art problem doesn't lend itself well to the notion that there's one right answer or one right method as a solution to the problem. Good questions raise more questions. Artists need room for failure; an experiment that didn't work can set the stage for real learning. I tell my students not to be so attached to the product, especially at the outset, but to investigate an idea and let the content drive the process. The difference between an amateur hobbyist and a serious student of art is the willingness to try again, to revise, to reconsider, to do over, and to challenge oneself. I know my students are doing well because I watch them as they work and grow. I track them individually, each according to his or her capabilities, background, skill, and potential. And I care about their progress. Teaching art is like playing catch with a giant, squirming ball of living, changing variables. Teaching art is, in essence, a very good art project.

I also teach the studio art majors' senior seminar, which includes their undergraduate capstone project. In the final semester of their senior year, art students must plan, design, execute and present a finished body of work in a gallery setting. I help them conceptualize, gauge, and make realistic assessments of the capabilities, skills, and available resources they will need, no matter what medium in which they decide to make their project. They also consult with the rest of the studio faculty, all experts in their fields. But our class starts with the premise that these are students who have committed their undergraduate education to being artists. And they're the only ones in this whole school who have made that commitment. It's a big responsibility, for them and for me.

For their senior exhibit, the studio art majors must present work beyond mere classroom assignments. This is not the time for a retrospective or "the greatest hits" from their intro classes. Instead, these seniors must exhibit a set of works they will be able to document and use to gain employment, further opportunities, internships, grants, or admission to graduate schools. For the record, Macalester art students have been admitted into graduate programs in every single medium we teach, which is remarkable considering they must compete with art school graduates from much larger programs with more resources. As well-spoken, well-read, well-written, broad-minded liberal arts students generally, our seniors also tend to write cogent, compelling artist statements in support of the work that they submit. This practice certainly helps with graduate school statements and employment applications. Part of the seminar is devoted to asking students to consider where they fit in the world of art, historically and today. They might draw on their study-abroad experience, as did a recent art and anthropology double major who made beautiful prints based on contrasting Maori hand-fishing techniques with giant commercial trawlers in New Zealand. These senior seminar students, with their wide exposure to different modes of thinking, internationalism, and cultural diversity, have the ability to think of their lives in terms of intention and direction. They are positioned to become producers rather than just consumers of art, now informed by art history, philosophy, literature, environmental studies, gender studies, race and class studies, social science, even economics. They prove themselves capable of making some really exemplary art. They provide me increased conviction that the world needs—by any measure—more smart, liberally educated artists.

Indeed, our studio art graduates go on to be designers, curators, landscape architects, photographers, printers, muralists, public artists, or college professors. These sharp, enterprising individuals have formed collectives, started galleries in their living rooms, and founded their own potteries, print shops, and design firms. Some participate in Teach for America or the Peace Corps; others work at galleries, not-for-profit organizations, museums, and schools.

One of the pleasures of teaching at a small liberal arts college is that the relationships I've formed with my students extend well beyond their day of graduation. They go out into the world, do great things, and come back to share them with me. I benefit, too, from inheriting the legacy of other fine teachers before me. Macalester, like so many of these unique places, fosters caring, intelligent artists who engage the world in thoughtfully creative endeavors.

Alumna Heidi Schumann is an independent photographer. She has made documentary photos in the Democratic Republic of Congo, Iraq, Sri Lanka, and Colombia. In 2007 her work was in the Museum of Pristina, Kosovo, and in Belgrade for the United Nations Displaced Persons Conference; it was also exhibited in Bali, at the 116th Assembly of the Inter-Parliamentary Union. Clark Wiegman is a nationally recognized sculptor. He created a work of public art in St. Louis: Blue Train, commissioned by St. Louis Metro for their Blue Line at Vandeventer Bridge. The illuminated railing acts as a gateway between two neighborhoods, commemorating homeless persons who have died on the streets there. Siah Armajani, born in Tehran, Iran, is a world-renowned sculptor. He designed the Olympic cauldron lit dramatically by Muhammad Ali at the 1996 games in Atlanta. Many of his sculptures combine poetry and literary references, sometimes even with benches gently provided for reading.

Duane Hanson, one of our earliest art graduates, was also a world-renowned sculptor. His hyper-realistic sculptures of everyday people are in most major museum collections. The retrospective exhibit *Duane Hanson: A*

Survey of His Works from the '30s to the '90s was launched by the Whitney Museum in New York. I had the pleasure of spending time with him when our school gave him an honorary degree. He loved his Macalester education and his art teachers and said so in his address. In our discussions he was quite emphatic about his intentions for his work and its basis in liberal arts values. He drew a connection between his depicting ordinary individuals in sculpture to Degas's series of paintings of washerwomen at work. Many of Hanson's models were his relatives. He insisted he was not making fun of his subjects but rather trying to find their humanity. He purposefully dressed the eerily realistic polyester resin sculptures in actual clothing and always displayed them off pedestals, not behind velvet ropes, so that they would share the same floor and space as the viewer. His pioneering work, pursuing a democratic vision via sculpture, sets an inspiring precedent for our students today.

Maybe small college teaching is not for everyone. I've found a few research specialists who can't thrive working so closely with undergraduates, although I find the interaction stimulating for my own practice. And I continually find reasons why I'm supposed to be in such a setting, to wit: the joy expressed by a student from Ecuador, who beamed at my mentioning the murals of Oswaldo Guayasamín in class; the pride in recommending an outstanding African American student for successful internships at the Metropolitan Museum, the Whitney, and eventually graduate school at Goldsmith's in London; the pleasure of inviting Living Proof Collective, composed of Macalester alumni, to a show I curated of contemporary printmaking, and watching them do live giveaway printing to an enthralled audience at a packed exhibit opening. I'm certainly not doing these things in order to tally up and check off some preapproved list of quantifiable objectives on an assessment survey. I'm pretty sure that having to fit each activity into a formalized rubric would change the students' experience and would kill my own pleasure in teaching them. The liberal arts model—changeable, adaptable, flexible, innovative—prepares students to take chances, to step up, to contribute, to mean it, to live it. That's the kind of life I'm trying to exemplify as I teach, learn, and grow as an artist.

Social Entrepreneurship in the Liberal Arts

JONATHAN ISHAM

Jonathan Isham is Professor of Economics at Middlebury College, where he is also the Director of the Center for Social Entrepreneurship. His publications include Ignition: What You Can Do to Fight Global Warming and Spark a Movement. *He was the first recipient of the Marjorie Lamberti Prize at Middlebury, which recognizes outstanding teaching. He holds degrees from Harvard, Johns Hopkins University, and the University of Maryland and served in Benin with the Peace Corps.*

ॐ

In my role as the director of the new Center for Social Entrepreneurship at Middlebury College, I've been thinking a lot lately about the liberal arts tradition. Specifically, I've been asking myself: Is there a tension in the contemporary liberal arts, a kind of tug-of-war?

On the one hand, we want our students to slow down, to reflect, to engage great books and great ideas. In the United States, this kind of "liberal education"—education designed to distinguish you as liberated, as free from binding constraints—has gone on for almost four centuries. The roots of this ideal are even older: they can be traced back twenty-five hundred years to those who were "liberated" by their studies, first in ancient Greece, then later among the Romans, and into the medieval period.[1]

Middlebury is an ideal representative of today's liberal arts. Engagement with great books and great ideas can be found in every corner of our Vermont campus: in our philosophy classes, our classes on political theory, in our laboratories, and on our stages. If you attended a liberal arts college, I'm sure you have in your mind's eye the picture of a professor who personifies this ideal. Picture that professor challenging a new classroom full of sophomores to get to the heart of the Platonic ideal; picture those students struggling, stumbling, only to arrive, by the end of their studies with their demanding professor, to a fresh understanding—their own understanding—of Platonic virtues. In so many ways, this is the liberal arts, as it has been and as it will be.

And yet there is another hand, tugging away. In 2006, Middlebury's Board of Trustees approved a mission statement that concludes with this sentence: "Through the pursuit of knowledge unconstrained by national or disciplinary boundaries, students who come to Middlebury learn to engage the world."[2] Not engage great books, not engage great ideas—engage the world. A cursory glance at mission statements of comparable schools yields much of the same: at Yale, students are called to "lead and serve in every sphere of human activity"; at Amherst, it's to "engage the world around them"; at Spelman, young women are called to "commit to positive social change."[3]

And doesn't this make sense? After all, it's now the twenty-first century, and we couldn't be further in so many ways from the often-inequitable conditions and outdated worldviews that launched and nurtured the liberal arts for centuries. This century has ushered in a celebration of diversity, all for the better. Furthermore, in this century the world faces challenges on unprecedented scales: global poverty, climate change, the denial of basic human rights to many. Finally, today's students—thanks to social networking, the low cost of global travel, and many commonly held cultural norms—can truly be labeled global. Of their own accord, well before they end up at top liberal arts campuses, they have learned to be unconstrained by age-old boundaries.

All of this would seem to call for a new kind of liberal arts, one in which dusty old traditions fall away, making room for the kind of learning that John Dewey presciently called for more than a century ago: hands-on learning, service learning, civic engagement. At Middlebury, as is true at so many other leading liberal arts schools, the contours of this kind of learning are by now very familiar. It features: students in an economics class doing a cost-benefit analysis of a proposed local energy project; students in an education studies course tutoring young grade-schoolers; students in an environmental studies seminar helping to research and write state legislation; and students even designing and building an award-winning solar home![4]

Jeff Freyman, a political science professor at Transylvania University and a scholar of the history of liberal education, points to such experiences when he proclaims that the liberal arts has become what John Dewey envisioned: based less on classical ideas and ideals and more on the premise that what matters is what students learn by doing.[5]

And now along comes the newest manifestation of the Dewey tradition: social entrepreneurship. It's a deceptively simple idea—it's the kind of entrepreneurship that seeks to maximize social value, not just profits—and it's everywhere these days. Sparked in the 1970s by the imagination and vision of Bill Drayton, founder and CEO of Ashoka, social entrepreneurship is spreading like wildfire throughout higher education.[6] Oxford University founded of the Skoll Center for Social Entrepreneurship in 2003. Choose almost any of the world's most storied universities and colleges—Harvard, Stanford, and Wesleyan, for starters—and you'll find a center for social entrepreneurship and/or a program on social enterprise, teeming with students bent on making a difference in the world, well before they finish their undergraduate education. These students are looking to design and build better schools in their native Nairobi; spread vaccination programs in South Asia; address poverty and injustice in places they care deeply about, such as West Virginia or Detroit. A recent example from Middlebury is Sword and Plough, a "quadruple bottom line" company co-founded by Emily Nunez (2012) that "works with veterans to repurpose military surplus fabric into stylish bags."[7] Professor Freyman is right: this is the triumph of John Dewey, who famously wrote in his well-known "My Pedagogic Creed": "I believe that education is a process of living and not a preparation for future living" and that "education is the fundamental method of social progress and reform."[8]

So yes, on campuses worldwide, thousands of students have been lit up with the call of effecting social change, on a large scale, right now. It is therefore tempting to abandon Plato and the great books, tempting to say that the tug-of-war is over: that hands-on-learning is triumphant.

It's tempting, but my students and I have concluded that this would be dead wrong. Every January during Middlebury's four-week "January term," I lead a class entitled Social Entrepreneurship in the Liberal Arts. In studying the literature on social entrepreneurship, my students soon learn that the key to leading the life that they aspire to—a life of meaning in the service of others—has very little to do with technical skills, say accounting skills or project management skills. These are important, but they are secondary. What is primary is to take on and embody qualities that can best be called "humanistic"; to be able to empathize, to listen, to act with deliberateness and grace, to engage.

And to do this well, my students and I have concluded, is to return to a question that has, for millennia, been at the very heart of the liberal arts experience: "What is living for?"[9] Indeed, the "aha moment" that we had in this class was to realize that this question is also at the very heart of the entrepreneurial experience. In David Bornstein and Susan Davis's excellent primer titled *Social Entrepreneurship: What Everyone Needs to Know*, the authors quote Andrew Carnegie, who wrote that entrepreneurs must be willing to endure "the humbling eclipse of self" that comes from "profound learning from others."[10] This is not just a prescription for entrepreneurs of all kind; it is a prescription for a life filled with meaning, the kind of humanistic life that all liberal arts students should be reflecting on and aspiring to. A life of the mind, of the heart, and of the spirit.

In his essay "Only Connect: The Goals of a Liberal Arts Education," environmental historian William Cronon delineates "ten qualities I admire in the people I know who seem to embody the values of a liberal education."[11] As you read them, notice what jumps off the page: this could easily be a list of what makes the best social entrepreneurs.[12] These people, according to Cronon:

> . . . listen and they hear.
> They read and they understand.
> They can talk with anyone.
> They can write clearly and persuasively and movingly.
> They can solve a wide variety of puzzles and problems.
> They respect rigor not so much for its own sake but as a way
>   of seeking truth.
> They practice humility, tolerance and self-criticism.
> They understand how to get things done in the world.
> They nurture and empower the people around them.
> They follow E. M. Forster's injunction from *Howard's End*: Only
>   Connect . . .[13]

So thanks to working with Middlebury students, I've concluded that what at first seems a tension, a tug-of-war between old school and twenty-first-century school, is not that at all. If we get it right at Middlebury and at other liberal arts campuses around the world, we will teach our students that their passion to be agents of social change must include not only connecting, it must also include reflecting, with the care and rigor and vision that have always characterized the best liberal arts experience. To embrace the rise of social entrepreneurship on the world's campuses is therefore not to reject the traditions of the liberal arts; it is rather to reaffirm the importance of those traditions in this challenging new century.

Notes

1. Christopher Flannery and Rae Winland Newstad, "The Classic Liberal Arts Tradition," in *The Liberal Arts in Higher Education*, ed. Diana Glyer and David L. Weeks (Lanham: University Press of America, 1998).

2. Middlebury College, 2006 Mission Statement, http://www.middlebury.edu/about/handbook/general/mission_statement.

3. Yale University, Mission Statement, http://www.yale.edu/about/yale-school-mission-statements.pdf; Amherst College, About Amherst, https://www.amherst.edu/aboutamherst/mission; Spelman College, About Us, http://www.spelman.edu/about-us.

4. Middlebury College, "Solar Decathlon Team Finished Fourth Place Overall," September 20, 2011, http://www.middlebury.edu/newsroom/archive/2011/node/289944.

5. Jeff Freyman, personal correspondence, August 8, 2012.

6. David Bornstein and Susan Davis, *Social Entrepreneurship: What Everyone Needs to Know* (New York: Oxford University Press, 2010).

7. Sword and Plough, About Us, http://www.swordandplough.com/pages/about-us.

8. John Dewey, "My Pedagogic Creed," *The School Journal* 54.3 (1897): 78.

9. Anthony T. Kronman, *Education's End: Why Our Colleges and Universities Have Given Up on the Meaning of Life* (New Haven: Yale University Press, 2007).

10. Quoted in Davis and Bornstein, *Social Entrepreneurship*, 28.

11. William Cronon, "'Only Connect . . .': The Goals of a Liberal Education," *The American Scholar* 67.4 (1998): 73–80.

12. See, for example, Jacqueline Novogratz, *The Blue Sweater. Bridging the Gap between Rich and Poor in an Interconnected World* (New York: Rodale, 2009).

13. Cronon, "'Only Connect . . . ,'" 76–78.

Beyond Cs Getting Degrees

Teaching the Liberal Arts at a Comprehensive University

JEFFREY A. BECKER

Jeffrey A. Becker is Associate Professor at the University of the Pacific, where he teaches American political thought and political theory. He has received the Stephen E. Corson Award for the distinguished teaching of first-year students, and a Faculty Mentor Award from the University of Pacific Alumni Association. His book Ambition in America: Political Power and the Collapse of Citizenship *was published in 2014.*

Part of my job is to teach at a liberal arts college that is one piece of a comprehensive university.[1] What that means is that I have students who pursue degrees in liberal arts disciplines like political science, English, history, and biology and students who pursue pre-professional degrees in business, pharmacy, dentistry, engineering, and education. And while it is true of my pre-professional students, it is true of almost all my students that they feel the pressure to pursue an education that will lead to a tangible payoff. Nervous about their futures, many have already decided to pursue careers they neither understand nor have a passion to practice (I find it difficult to believe that the average seventeen-to-twenty-two-year-old wakes up one morning with a burning passion to be pharmacist—some do, but those students are rare). The disparity between what students think they *should* major in and what they *want* to major in was made vivid to me when

I taught a required introductory seminar for first-year students. During the course organized around the question "What is a Good Society?" I asked my class of twenty-three students the following question: If you never had to worry about money, what career would you pursue? The class was made up of students in engineering, pre-dentistry, pre-pharmacy, business, with one music major and one physics major. Out of twenty-three students only three wanted a career in the field/major they were currently studying. All felt the pressure to select a major that would lead to a well-paying career—or that would at least please their parents. Yet, when students thought about what they wanted to study, without the stress of finding a well-paying job (or what they thought was well paying), students wanted careers they saw as more fulfilling but less financially rewarding.

I encourage my students to ask what they see as the purpose of their education, what they see themselves learning as undergraduates, and "what (for them) is the knowledge most worth having?"[2] These days, I spend more time than ever trying to convince students that questions about what we should do with our lives—questions of purpose and meaning—do matter. Those questions remain central for figuring out what will provide for our future success and happiness. To prompt students to make sense of their education, I assign "On the Wings of Atalanta" by W. E. B. Du Bois in my introductory courses. In that essay, Du Bois uses the myth of the Greek huntress Atalanta to question whether freed slaves are being lured away from the best higher education has to offer. In the myth, Atalanta loses a footrace to her suitor Hippomenes because she chases after enchanted golden apples instead of focusing on winning the race. Writing in 1903, Du Bois sees the myth of Atalanta as prescient of the condition of America:

> Atalanta is not the first or the last maiden whom greed of gold has led to defile the temple of Love: and not maids alone, but men in the race of life, sink from the high and generous ideals of youth to the gambler's code of the Bourse; and in all our nation's striving is not the Gospel of Work befouled by the Gospel of Pay? So common is this that one-half think it normal; so unquestioned that we almost fear to question if the end of racing is not gold, if the aim of man is not rightly to be rich.[3]

Du Bois poses the right question for first-year college students: What is the purpose and end of your education? Is it merely the pursuit of wealth, or is there something more?

Encouraging first-year students to think about the purpose and meaning of their education has become more necessary than ever because of the larger culture in which we live, a culture in which higher education is under increasing scrutiny by those who want a stricter accounting of what we do in the academy, why we do it, and why we aren't doing it more efficiently.[4] While questioning the value of the liberal arts is not new, during this economic transition—when the cost of college tuition has increased 1,120 percent over the past forty years—students are all but compelled to approach college thinking like Atalanta, measuring their education in terms of dollars and cents, searching for those golden apples that might, in the end, make them lose the race.[5]

What Knowledge Should Students Learn?

In my classes, when discussing what kinds of knowledge are most important for college students to learn, I ask a question that was asked of me as an undergraduate in a class on postmodernism: How do you *know* whether the person you love, loves you?[6] The point of this question is to push students to think about *what* they are learning in college. I ask students if the answer to such a question, and the way of finding an answer, is important to living a satisfying life. After all, doesn't living a satisfying life mean thinking about how to live with other people, particularly those other people we love?

To counter the materialism and reflexive narcissism that my students breathe, I work to get students to think about their path to personal happiness as linked to the happiness that comes from sharing a life with friends and fellow citizens, to think about the happiness that comes out of honoring the obligations and chosen bonds you share with others. Antoine de Saint-Exupéry's *The Little Prince* had an elegant way of expressing this concept: "You are responsible for what you tame."[7] When we turn the stranger, the "wild" one, into a friend, someone who is "tame," we create a bond of reciprocal obligation with that person. Teaching students how to think about other people, other time periods, other cultures, other traditions, is the core challenge of small residential liberal arts colleges. It is teaching students about their obligations to those other people, other time periods, other cultures, and other traditions. It is teaching students *not* to become Aristotle's solitary individual: "One who is incapable of participating or who is in need of nothing through being self-sufficient is no part of a city and so is either a beast or a god."[8]

At their best, small liberal arts colleges open up possibilities for students to explore diverse interpretations of texts, of life, of experience in a setting where students can speak with one another. And this does not happen in isolation. Interactions with others bring out what is best in people. For Aristotle, this is what it means to participate in the life of the political community: the ability to work collectively with other people. Small liberal arts colleges bring together strangers to live, eat, sleep, work, and study together to learn and develop themselves as people and citizens. At a small liberal arts college you can get to know all of your students. And getting to know who your students are, and where they come from (not just geographically, but their dispositions and aspirations), by engaging them in face-to-face conversations matters if college is to teach them something that will stay with them, make them think, and possibly change them. To this end, small liberal arts colleges provide "goods of great value" at little to no additional cost. "They supply, just by existing, what Edmund Burke called 'the unbought grace of life,' they supply the graces of friendship, of shared memory, of mutual discovery and recognition of self and other, of connection and affection."[9] And these are goods that cannot be replaced by online instruction, no matter how technologically sophisticated the audio-visual elements. Technology will not replace such spontaneity. Knowing students at the levels needed to teach most of them takes place at the small liberal arts college.

For students, coming to a *residential* liberal arts college means leaving behind a place where people know them, their families, friends, and their histories, places where people care for them. Students leave (some flee) that world for a new home where they are surrounded by people who do not know them, do not know their character, and do not have reasons to care for them. This movement from the familiar to the unfamiliar gives the transition to college an exciting but also terrifying quality for students. Students worry about fitting in, finding new friends, losing old ones, and balancing competing claims on their time and talents. Students' newfound freedom of being away from established structures and routines comes with the responsibility to form new relationships with other students, strange faculty, kind but overworked staff, and the occasional well-meaning administrator.

And it is precisely in this need to find fellowship with others that the value of the small liberal arts college becomes evident. Students thrown together almost randomly must learn to form communities among people who do not know one another. The small liberal arts college is "the place where persons connect with each other, find friends and companions, lay down strata of common experience shared by diverse spirits."[10] This is also, in a fundamental form, the practice of democratic life: strangers who are not tied to one another by kinship create a community united by a common purpose. Ideally, first-year college students learn to reconsider what they regard as familiar—not to reflexively reject their inherited customs or traditions but to develop their capacity to consciously choose the values and behaviors that define them. For some students (and instructors) this experience is unwelcome; some students may have to change practices they like, they may have to see themselves in an unflattering light, and they may be unwilling or unable to control behaviors that shape them. Teaching students involves working to give students the courage to challenge what is known, familiar, and stable without casting them adrift into a fashionable but childish nihilism. Done well, a liberal arts education simultaneously unsettles and affirms students' capacity to govern their own lives.

Persuading Educational Consumers of the Need to Think

Being able to govern one's own life is a capacity that is important personally, politically, *and* professionally. When colleges model themselves around the idea that education is a business that caters to demanding consumers, institutions reinforce the easy lie that students already know what they want from higher education, and do not challenge students to think through the hard questions and to think through those questions in conversation with others. I think of one pre-pharmacy student who, during a general education seminar on ethics, thought much of what I had to say was a waste of her time. I asked the pre-pharmacy students in this seminar class of twenty students what would you do if your community asked you, as the local pharmacist, not to carry or dispense the Plan B emergency contraception pill? How would you respond? What are your professional, personal, religious, and/or ethical obligations? How do you balance competing views? At the time, many students dismissed this exercise as "extreme" or "not realistic"— even in spite of the fact that I cited then-current examples of communities pressuring their local pharmacists. However, I received the following email from this student six months later:

> I used to think that the ethical topics you gave us were extremely controversial and difficult to pick a firm position on, but every discussion we had has proved applicable. In February, I went to [name redacted] University in [city name redacted] to interview for a spot in their pharmacy school. I had eight different interviews which were eight minutes each. I was given a topic or question on a note card, had two minutes to prepare, and then I had to discuss my viewpoint and solution with the interviewer quickly in six minutes. Every prompt had underlying ethical principles similar to those we had discussed in your class, and one of them was actually the Heinz dilemma.[11] I felt prepared because I had gone through similar discussions in your class, and the interviewers were surprised by my confidence in discussing the difficult topics.
>
> So I'm off to [name redacted] University in August, and I can't thank you enough for helping me get there. Thank you for never relenting when we complained in class that the topics you gave us were too crazy or debatable, because even if we

never came to one conclusion, we learned how to process every aspect of the discussion at hand and analyze each part carefully and logically. My interviewers said that I was one of the few who, instead of jumping to a conclusion, thought critically about every side of the question first. Sometimes, it's not really about your answer but more about what steps you take to try to get there. Thank you for teaching me such an important lesson![12]

One goal of small liberal arts colleges is to help students reach moral and ethical decisions, decisions that are relevant in all parts of their lives, in an informed and humane way. This is work that is often uncomfortable for students at first, work that does not initially seem "relevant."

The paradox of telling students to focus on developing individual professional skills is that they are told to do so in ways that disengage them from conversations with one another, conversations with other generations, and conversations with the professional communities many of them aspire to join. A well-conceived liberal arts college education is centered within such conversations. To presume that individual students know what course of study is best for them ignores the way educating a person involves changing preconceptions and revising "existing knowledge." At a fundamental level education challenges what David Foster Wallace called "your default settings." For Wallace, the "real world" does not encourage people to thoughtfully question how they live their lives:

> And the so-called real world will not discourage you from operating on your default settings, because the so-called real world of men and money and power hums merrily along in a pool of fear and anger and frustration and craving and worship of self. Our own present culture has harnessed these forces in ways that have yielded extraordinary wealth and comfort and personal freedom. The freedom all to be lords of our tiny skull-sized kingdoms, alone at the center of all creation.[13]

Many students come to us thinking they know more than they do, and they often expect learning new material to be easier than it is—easier because they assume *they* will not have to change their "default settings." Assuming that education now takes place by students teaching themselves with "the information at their fingertips" through the Internet is largely false. Such an autodidactic approach to education ignores the way education requires interaction between people who challenge one another's viewpoints. As Pamela Hieronymi describes, "Education is not the transmission of information or ideas. Education is the training needed to make use of information and ideas. As information breaks loose from bookstores and libraries and floods onto computers and mobile devices, that training becomes more important, not less."[14] The false assumption that students already know what they need to know ignores the critical role of human fellowship for educating college students.

A culture that preaches the consumer/student is always right fosters an instrumentalist attitude toward higher education where students already know what they need to learn in order to succeed in their programs of study. A culture of indifference and minimal effort—the culture of "Cs get degrees"—takes hold when students feel that their degrees are merely the gateway to a better financial future. Students will put in the minimum amount of effort to earn their degrees when they see no purpose to working harder. After all, why work or try harder? What would be the point? What more does a student receive for working harder? Absent a self-evident or compelling purpose to their education, students' default reaction is to narrowly focus on what they know, what is comfortable and safe.

This focus on the safe and the self is the dominant message students receive about higher education, their lives, and their future careers. As David Brooks once described, the recent tenor of college commencement addresses are speeches where college graduates "are sent off into this world with the whole baby-boomer theology ringing in their ears. . . . Follow *your* passion, chart *your* own course, march to the beat of *your* own drummer, follow *your* dreams and find *yourself*. This is the litany of expressive individualism, which is still the dominant note in American culture."[15] For Brooks, college graduates are "told to be independent minded and to express their inner spirit," but they are not taught "doing your job well often means suppressing yourself."[16] Too much of what shapes the outlook of undergraduates today is an uncritical celebration of self. The technology many students now consider second nature is a technology of self-promotion, a technology of ease and comfort that serves to insulate people from the costs and consequences of sharing a world with strangers over whom we exert little to no control; the communications technology today expands the reach of a self-referential world where people can ignore those closest to them and seek out like-minded people.

To this end, I try to meet first-year students where they *are* before attempting to move them toward a fuller and more expansive understanding of their experiences. If I am lucky, students will learn to appreciate the ennobling possibilities of their capacity to choose what they ought to do with their lives, and who and what they can become. Therefore my job is not to supplant my judgment, perspective, or viewpoint for theirs but to develop students' capacities to think, evaluate, and judge for themselves the worth of what they choose. As I see it, my job is to teach students that they can learn to become active citizens, not just passive consumers.

Helping Students Find a Purpose Worthy of Their Devotion

Though some students drift through college without a sense of purpose, that does not mean our students do not seek out such a purpose. Students come to college hungry, not just for self-discovery or vocational training but also for knowledge that will help them make sense of their lives. If we do not want to settle for the lackadaisical attitude whereby "Cs get degrees," then we have to commit ourselves to a model of teaching that is more interactive and face-to-face than the solutions of online courses offered by those critical of such an "expensive" way of teaching students, those who want to cut the costs of education with the promise of manufacturing graduates cheaper and quicker.

At its core, the small liberal arts college aims to teach students to work toward what is excellent. And it becomes the professor's job to distract and then captivate the passions of students to guide them toward both discovering and demanding the best that higher education has to offer. Students search for purposes worthy of their devotion. In a seminar discussing the origins, causes, and consequences of patriotism in political life, I ask my students to put themselves in the position of defending who and what they love; I ask my students to clarify, publicly, their obligations to others. I ask them who, or what, they are willing to sacrifice their lives for, and for whom or what are they prepared to take another person's life. This class is not easy. I demand that every student answer both questions. This is a question really asking students to weigh in on what they see as valuable, worthy of their love and sacrifice, what they regard as truly excellent. This is what David Foster Wallace may mean by finding something "to worship."

The focus on wealth as the touchstone of academic success provides students with a ready-made excuse to retreat from a concern for the broader social and political world. The outside world becomes someone else's problem as students worry only about improving their own material prosperity. If higher education focuses primarily on job training, preparing students for soon-to-be-obsolete jobs, then the colleges will produce students who regard the default narcissism of the adult world as healthy, and who see passive dependency on administrative despotism as benign. The small liberal arts and sciences college teaches against educational trends that celebrate an unapologetic tyranny of the self. And in doing so, the small liberal arts and sciences college "throw[s] its force against the mainstream."[17]

Part of a drive for excellence depends upon students believing that the best that civilization has to offer is rightly the property of all. That the moneyed and educated elites do not own or have claims by birth to the best human life has to offer. But this also demands that students acknowledge their responsibility to put forth their best effort and do the hard work of democracy—this cannot be assumed, it must be taught. Part of what the small liberal arts college teaches is that the best of the arts and sciences world is yours by right, indeed that every one of us is fully entitled to Plato or Machiavelli, to Beethoven or Shakespeare, to Virginia Woolf or Brontë (Emily not just Charlotte), to Curie or Tesla, to Galileo or Bohr, or Madison, or Ellison, or Rembrandt. It is in pursuit of what is best that we discover who we are, that we learn how to "find ourselves," to know ourselves, to become who we might be—all that by means of passionately dialectical encounters with other minds. Wallace captures the way in which this learning to think means being conscious of the choices we make in a world that does not encourage or reward such thoughtfulness. The liberal arts college tries to teach students how to think in a culture that does not value or reward thoughtfulness, a culture that gravitates to the easy answer, the comfortable response. For Wallace,

> Learning how to think really means learning how to exercise some control over how and what you think. It means being conscious and aware enough to choose what you pay attention to and to choose how you construct meaning from experience. Because if you cannot exercise this kind of choice in adult life, you will be totally hosed. Think of the old cliché about the mind being an excellent servant but a terrible master. . . . This, I submit, is the freedom of a real education, of learning how to be well-adjusted. You get to consciously decide what has meaning and what doesn't. You get to decide what to worship. . . . there are all different kinds of freedom, and the kind that is most precious you will not hear much talk about much in the great outside world of wanting and achieving and displaying. The really important kind of freedom involves attention and awareness and discipline, and being able truly to care about other people and to sacrifice for them over and over in myriad petty, unsexy ways every day.

As Wallace puts it, "That is real freedom. That is being educated, and understanding how to think. The alternative is unconsciousness, the default setting, the rat race, the constant gnawing sense of having had, and lost, some infinite thing."[18]

The Promise (and Hope) of a Liberal Arts Education

When it works, a liberal arts education prepares students to accept the obligations of democratic citizenship. And to be a citizen in a democracy is to seek to be worthy of *public* esteem and honor; it is to put one's faith in the American belief "that all men [and women] are equal in their claim to justice, that governments exist to give them that justice, and that their authority is for that reason just."[19] Teaching the liberal arts means teaching the value of liberty, not just the freedom to be left alone to horde as much personal wealth as possible but the responsibility of exercising liberty as a citizen, where freedom is measured by what you owe to others. To want to be a citizen is (and ought to be) a worthy goal; to be educated at a liberal arts and sciences college is to be educated to accept the responsibility for sharing a life with *other* people. Democratic citizenship demands that people come to value what David Brooks once called thanklessness: "the ability to keep serving even when there are no evident rewards—no fame, no admiration, no gratitude."[20] Citizenship asks that each of us stake a claim in being equals, in taking our part to realize the promise of moral equality that comes with self-government. As G. K. Chesterton describes, it is the belief that "no [one] must aspire to be anything more than a citizen, and that no [one] should endure to be anything less."[21] This is what the liberal arts colleges teach: an equality that values the contributions and ability of people to participate in the creation of shared public life.

Profit defines our age, which is why the assault on small liberal arts colleges is essentially an assault on democratic citizenship: the small liberal arts college is an organization that is not value extracting; we don't generate profits. A liberal arts education asks students to aspire for more than the leisure and happiness of hedonism, to want more from the world than the comfort of material self-indulgence. But in doing so, we have to make the rewards of liberty, fellowship, and democracy that come from a life lived among equals worthy of our students' devotion. As Christopher Lasch warns, if we are unable to "show that democracy embodies a demanding, morally elevating standard of conduct. If democracy means no more than a 'reduction of the work day,' . . . 'improved automatic techniques in production,' and 'abundance of commodities,' it is not worth defending. How can such a paltry vision, as William James said, inspire anything but contempt?"[22]

In *Invisible Man*, Ralph Ellison's protagonist declares toward the end of the book, "It's winner take nothing that is the great truth of our country or any country. Life is to be lived, not controlled; and humanity is won by continuing to play in the face of certain defeat."[23] This is not an easy lesson to teach students who are inexperienced in devoting themselves to pursuits that lack a clear payoff, but it is the most important lesson to teach our students if, as David Foster Wallace once hoped, our graduates are to live lives of "freedom that involves attention and awareness and discipline."

We have to understand that the communities we create at liberal arts colleges are primary; the "ends are secondary and derivative."[24] If we are willing to care for, possibly even love, each other generously, thoughtfully, and toughly enough, if we demand from each other the best that we can offer, then the ends, the values, the hopes we share and keep developing at liberal arts and sciences colleges are likely to be the right ones. "They might even be deep enough or strong enough in time to reconstruct our fractured, fearful, yet still somehow democratic republic."[25]

Notes

This essay was originally delivered as a talk to faculty colleagues for being awarded the Stephen E. Corson Award, which recognizes the distinguished teaching of first-year students at the University of the Pacific in Stockton, California. The award was created and funded by John and Sylvia Corson to memorialize and honor their late son Stephen. The award is intended to lift up the importance of the professors who teach first-year students by encouraging faculty to develop their teaching of first-year students. The Corsons believe that the influence of dedicated faculty in a student's first year of college could make a substantial difference in shaping a student's future.

1. The University of the Pacific consists of a liberal arts college, a law school, a dental school, a pharmacy school, a business school, a music conservatory, and an education school.

2. This line is from an anonymously submitted proposal to revise the residential colleges at UC Santa Cruz in 1991—titled "What Is a College For?"—known then as the "Bread and Roses" proposal. I can only speculate on its authorship, but to the best of my knowledge the author intentionally left the document orphaned. The history of the phrase "Bread and Roses" does have a lineage appropriate to the condition of higher education in the twenty-first century. See the 1912 Lawrence Textile Strike and the poem "Bread and Roses" by James Oppenheim, https://www.marxists.org/subject/women/poetry/bread.html (accessed July 2, 2014)

3. W. E. B. Du Bois, "On the Wings of Atalanta," *The Souls of Black Folk* (New York: Barnes and Noble Classics, 2003), 59–60.

4. See Marc Musick, "Analysis of Efficiency and Graduation Rates at the University of Texas at Austin and Other Public Research Universities in the United States," September 2011, http://www.utexas.edu/news/attach/2011/campus/analysis_efficiency.pdf (accessed July 2, 2014).

5. See http://www.dailyfinance.com/on/college-costs-tuition-rising-student-debt-infographic/ (accessed July 10, 2013).

6. John (Jack) Schaar posed this question to a History of Consciousness graduate seminar on postmodernism in the spring quarter of 1990 at the University of California, Santa Cruz.

7. See chapter 21 of Antoine de Saint-Exupéry, *The Little Prince* (New York: Harcourt Brace, 1971).

8. Aristotle, *The Politics* (Chicago: University of Chicago Press, 1984), book 1, chapter 2, 37.

9. "What Is a College For?" 3.

10. Ibid., 2.

11. The "Heinz dilemma" is an example of moral reasoning taken from Lawrence Kohlberg's *The Philosophy of Moral Development*. In his study of moral reasoning, Kohlberg asked children whether a man (Heinz) who cannot afford a drug to save his ailing wife should steal the drug from a pharmacist. See Lawrence Kohlberg, *The Philosophy of Moral Development* (San Francisco: Harper and Row, 1981).

12. Student email received on May 7, 2012.

13. David Foster Wallace, 2005 Kenyon Commencement Address, May 21, http://web.ics.purdue.edu/~drkelly/DFWKenyonAddress2005.pdf (accessed July 1, 2014).

14. Pamela Hieronymi, "Don't Confuse Technology with College Teaching," *Chronicle of Higher Education*, August 13, 2012, http://chronicle.com/article/Dont-Confuse-Technology-With/133551/.

15. David Brooks, "It's Not about You," *New York Times*, May 30, 2011. Emphasis in original.

16. Ibid.

17. "What Is a College For?" 2.

18. David Foster Wallace, 2005 Kenyon Commencement Address, May 21, http://web.ics.purdue.edu/~drkelly/DFWKenyonAddress2005.pdf.

19. G. K. Chesterton, "What I Saw in America," in *The Collected Works of G. K. Chesterton, Vol. 21* (San Francisco: Ignatius Press, 1990), 41.

20. David Brooks, "The Rugged Altruists," *New York Times*, August 23, 2011.

21. Chesterton, "What I Saw in America," 48.

22. Christopher Lasch, *The True and Only Heaven* (New York: W. W. Norton, 1991), 305.

23. Ralph Ellison, *Invisible Man* (New York: Knopf Doubleday, 1995), 577.

24. John H. Schaar and Wilson Carey McWilliams, "Uncle Sam Vanishes," *New University Thought* 1 (1961): 62.

25. These last lines are an adaptation, and a direct quote, from Bruce Payne's eulogy at Wilson Carey McWilliams's memorial service delivered on June 18, 2005. Bruce, who taught at Duke for thirty-five years, is now Distinguished Lecturer at Baruch College (CUNY).

PART FOUR

The Community

Unlearning Helplessness

The Liberal Arts and the Future of Education

Adam Kotsko

Adam Kotsko is Assistant Professor of Humanities at Shimer College in Chicago. He is the author of Why We Love Sociopaths: A Guide to Late Capitalist Television; Awkwardness; Politics of Redemption: The Social Logic of Salvation, *and* Žižek and Theology, *as well as the translator of several works of Giorgio Agamben. He is the founder and chief contributor to the blog* An und für sich *(itself.wordpress.com), which covers a wide range of issues in the humanities, and has written widely on pedagogy and the academic life for* Inside Higher Ed.

I was a teenager when personal computers were first becoming widespread. I had a reputation for being good with them, and so I was frequently called upon to help various friends and neighbors figure out how to use their mysterious machines. These early pedagogical experiences were almost uniformly discouraging. My "students" were impatient and inattentive, hoping for a quick fix, a rote formula—in short, "the right answer." I frequently heard the nervous chuckling of self-confessed "computer illiterates" who had convinced themselves that I must possess some kind of occult knowledge forever inaccessible to them.

By any realistic standard, however, I was a much "worse" computer user than they were. I had spent countless hours struggling to get my computer to work, facing error after inscrutable error—in one case, my PC was essentially nonfunctional for more than a week. Even worse, I had brought these errors on myself with my incessant poking around. There wasn't a dialogue box I hadn't clicked, a setting I hadn't tinkered with, a configuration file I hadn't fatally mangled. I had read the manuals, of course, and searched the help files, and gone through the self-guided tutorials, but that wasn't where I really learned my computer skills. My education came from the tedious, frustrating process of messing up over and over again until I'd finally hit upon the best way to get the thing to do what I wanted it to do.

I eventually left aside my endless computer tinkering for other pursuits, but all the great tech wizards started out in essentially the same place. They were mostly self-taught, and if they had a teacher, that person was less like a traditional pedagogue and more like a peer who's a few steps ahead, someone who could confirm their intuitions or keep them from pursuing a blind alley. While their inventions often wound up being amazingly profitable, that was seldom their first motivation. They just wanted to figure out what they could get a computer to do, in collaboration with others who were trying the same thing.

It's almost universally acknowledged that our society needs more people like that. Yet I don't think it's an accident that so many of those lauded figures dropped out of college. Our institutions of higher learning do not cultivate that kind of bold exploration. Indeed, I'd go so far as to say that they more often produce people like my hapless computer students—chuckling nervously over their own ignorance, impatient to be given an answer they believe they could never figure out themselves, too worried about the possibility of making a mistake to even consider experimenting for themselves.

Much of the contemporary education reform movement is driven by those creative techies who were failed by the formal education system, and it shows. Many of the reform proposals, for instance, amount to plopping kids in front of computers to explore for themselves. Further, many education reformers seem to have a dream of somehow creating a teaching profession made up of nothing but those "inspirational," "transformative" teachers who can turn students from passive recipients into self-motivated learners—even if the method they have settled upon to find such teachers, namely standardized tests, results in even more stultification than traditional education does.

There is a kernel of truth here, a genuine hope that education could cultivate creativity rather than squelch it, but the vision is too individualistic, too focused on finding the lone transformative genius. The hope is that if we somehow remove all that is constraining about traditional education as we know it, more creative individuals will somehow emerge—but hope is not a plan. Not everyone fiddling around with a computer is going to turn into a heroic entrepreneur, and there's no guarantee that if we fire an uninspiring teacher, Robin Williams's character from *Dead Poet's Society* will apply to fill the vacancy.

The problem here might be that the libertarian ideology of the tech industry is causing many of these reformers to overlook aspects of their own experience. What's missing in these plans to make everyone more like the self-taught visionaries are the *communities* of self-motivated learners, the collaborative work that made the great individual achievements possible.

Once we recognize the necessarily social character of learning, suddenly a space for planning and even institutionalization opens up. We can think of ways to bring groups of students together to try to figure various types of things out collaboratively—things like computers, but also things like interesting and puzzling books or unexpected natural phenomena. We can also give them space to explore individually once they find something that really captures their interest. In such a setting, teachers wouldn't need to be once-in-a-lifetime inspirational pedagogues but could serve as slightly more advanced peers who can confirm students' intuitions and help them steer clear of blind alleys.

At their best, small liberal arts colleges are precisely those kinds of places. I know because I've spent much of my adult life in liberal arts colleges, first as a student and then as a professor. (In the meantime, I did my graduate work at a small institution that offered me the kind of intellectual freedom I'd come to expect from my liberal arts education.) For the purposes of this essay, I want to focus on my present institution, Shimer College, a very small liberal arts college in Chicago. I choose Shimer not only because I am most familiar with its approach, but because I believe its program and pedagogy are in many ways exemplary of the ways a liberal arts program can help students to overcome their learned helplessness and become more creative and self-motivated.

First, though, I think it would be helpful to think about why other educational models might, contrary to all their good intentions, cultivate the kind of learned helplessness that I confronted in my career as a failed computer tutor. The advent of online education and MOOCs has led to a great deal of debate about "distance learning," but I believe there's an important sense in which traditional pedagogical methods were *always* "distance learning." Everywhere the student turns, there's something between her and authentic knowledge. One always needs more background, more introductory material, more explanation and exposition—knowledge itself is always elsewhere, always just out of the student's reach. When the student does gain access to a primary source or an actual experiment, that only exacerbates the gap. How could I have ever gotten from this baffling philosophical text to the crystal-clear explanation my professor provided? How could I have ever figured out how to use all this lab equipment without the step-by-step instructions? An elect few somehow penetrate behind the veil to be inducted into the sphere of experts—everyone else is a spectator, confirming through their fulfillment of various pedagogical rituals that they were once in the general vicinity of knowledge.

Shimer's approach is just the opposite. In our classes, we continually confront our students with the primary source or experiment and set them to work figuring it out. All the layers of explanation and introduction and background separating them from the object of knowledge are absent, and our discussion-based pedagogy ensures that they have to rely primarily on their own efforts rather than on an expert who supposedly already knows everything. The source of knowledge and authority in the classroom is no longer the professor but the thing itself, the shared object of inquiry that everyone is trying to figure out. Knowledge isn't elsewhere—it's right here in front of us.

This focus on primary sources stems from Shimer's history as a school in the "Great Books" tradition associated with Robert Hutchins, who served as president of the University of Chicago from 1929 to 1945 and also helped to develop the famous *Encyclopaedia Britannica* Great Books series. Those unwieldy volumes could be viewed as something like the MOOC of their day, trying to make the benefits of an elite education available to a broader public—the intention was not that they would be attractive reference volumes, but that they could be used for personal edification and self-guided discussion groups.

There is much in the theory guiding the selection of these texts that appears questionable today, and so Shimer has not felt constrained by Hutchins's original curriculum. While we focus on long-established classics, our curriculum has also found considerable room for contemporary sources. The standard is not whether a given text is Great-with-a-capital-G or whether it somehow represents "the best" of Western civilization—but whether the text is *discussable*. Will the text capture the students' attention, and will it reward *sustained* attention? Will it "keep giving" after the basic concepts have been grasped? Will it appear new and strange again when approached from a different angle?

Similar questions arise when developing a course or curricular sequence. Yes, we want texts to build on each other, to provide "background" for each other, but more than that, we want them to leave space for students to make unexpected connections. Our curriculum is from one perspective highly structured—two-thirds of a student's credits typically come from a defined sequence of required core courses—but from another point of view, each group of students builds it anew each time. In addition to their coursework, students must take two comprehensive exams, which do not test their knowledge of the subject matter they have studied so much as their ability to apply the skills they have learned to new questions and problems.

Alongside the shared work of class discussion, students have individual work to do. This of course includes essays for each particular class, and our curriculum is structured in such a way as to allow students to gradually develop their writing skills across a variety of disciplines. They also undertake a series of self-chosen semester projects, during what at most institutions would be "finals week." Students try their hand at creative writing or artwork, they read books that aren't on our reading list and report back, they undertake scientific experiments or dissections—anything that takes a full week of work and is somehow related to their coursework is fair game. Finally, in their senior year, they write a thesis on a topic of their choice.

Our collaborative, democratic pedagogy carries over into the way the school itself is run. A significant part of Shimer's governance structure is the Assembly, which is a kind of "committee of the whole" where all community members—faculty, administrators, board members and students alike—have an equal vote. The Assembly elects committees relating to various aspects of the college's community life, and all committees include significant student representation. For instance, students help to organize college social events, participate in the admissions and financial aid process, and are even involved in decisions on hiring and retaining faculty members. In short, we try to help students to become active participants in as many aspects of their education as possible.

Shimer students continually astonish me with their creativity and motivation. I am constantly learning new things in class, even about texts that I know well. My students very frequently achieve things that I wouldn't even think to try. Perhaps most important in today's economy, where precarity is increasingly the rule, my students are adept at finding unanticipated opportunities and even creating their own. The college supports this process by providing funding to help students arrange summer internships for themselves, and students have taken advantage of this to explore everything from Chicago politics to micro-lending in Haiti, from beekeeping to running a bed and breakfast in Costa Rica.

In short, if the goal is to actively cultivate creative people who can do unexpected, transformative things, I believe that Shimer provides a workable model. This shouldn't come as a surprise, of course, because Shimer is practicing what basically all credible education research shows to be best practices—small classes, discussion-centered pedagogy, active learning.

There's just one problem, though: the Shimer model doesn't "scale." If the classes got much bigger, the experience would no longer be the same. It's the same with the faculty-student ratio—it wouldn't take much of a shift for the fundamental character of the institution to change. This is simply an unavoidable fact. If you want to cultivate the kind of person Shimer helps to cultivate, you need to invest deeply in people.

In an era where education costs are rapidly rising and seemingly every trend in higher education is pushing toward ever-larger class sizes, this might make the Shimer model seem far too unaffordable to be realistic. This perception is puzzling, however, because there's nothing inherently expensive about what Shimer does. All you really need aside from faculty members is some classrooms, tables and chairs, chalkboards, some basic lab equipment, and—to oversimplify somewhat—a bunch of Penguin Classics. There are administrative and recruiting costs as well, but compared to most institutions we have very little administrative overhead (probably too little!).

I suspect that academics have been a little bit too inclined to chuckle nervously when confronted with money talk, too inclined to take the self-appointed experts' word for it. Hiding behind the veil of what's "affordable" in the abstract is a series of important questions about priorities. Yes, it's expensive to pay professors a decent salary to teach small classes, but it's also expensive to have an ever-expanding administrative apparatus and money-pit athletic programs and fancy new buildings for donors to put their name on. If we can "afford" one, we can "afford" the other.

More broadly, though, we need to shed the habits of austerity, where the first impulse is always to "cut" and "the budget" rules over everyone like some kind of cruel god. In reality, we can "afford" a great deal. Never before in human history has there been a nation as abundantly wealthy as America is. Never before has there been such a large population of people with a graduate education, and never before have books been so widely and cheaply available. We can collectively "afford" to give everyone access to the education that liberal arts institutions like Shimer offer. It's just a matter of having the creativity and openness to exploration necessary to make it happen.

Liberal Arts Colleges

..•———•..

The Mothers of (Re)Invention

Jay Barth

Jay Barth is M. E. and Ima Graves Peace Distinguished Professor of Politics and Director of Civic Engagement Projects at Hendrix College. He was named 2007 Arkansas Professor of the Year by the Carnegie Foundation for the Advancement of Teaching and the Council for Advancement and Support of Education (CASE) and is a five-time winner of the Hendrix College Faculty Appreciation Award presented by the senior class to the faculty member who has shown "excellence in instruction and concern for the welfare of Hendrix students." Barth's academic work includes research on the politics of Arkansas and the South, LGBT politics, state governors, campaign advertising (especially radio advertising), and education policy. He is a member of the Arkansas State Board of Education.

ঌ

"What draws you to seek a position at a liberal arts college?" That's a typical icebreaker question during job candidate cattle calls of job candidates in a large hotel ballroom at the American Political Science Association's annual meeting across my two decades as a professor at a small liberal arts college. Regularly the answers begin something like this: "I'm really excited about the possibility of teaching small classes." While those of us who teach in liberal arts settings understand the many benefits of relatively small classes, when we hear the "small class size" answer, we know that the interview is likely a dead end no matter how impressive the young person's promise as a scholar because it betrays a shallowness of understanding about liberal arts institutions.

Job candidates with a limited understanding of liberal arts colleges also are prone to note their commitment to working with students in their development as writers, analysts, and critical thinkers. With this answer, the job applicant is clearly getting warmer, as aiding students in the honing of such skills is at the heart of the liberal arts.[1] Even then, this answer comes up short. Interviewers aren't convinced that the job candidate has a fundamental understanding of what it is to be a part of a liberal arts *community*. That is because the joys of working in a liberal arts setting involve much more than the centrality of teaching and the learning of lifelong skills.

How might these intensive communities provide ongoing relevance into the twenty-first century? Having spent more than half my life on a liberal arts campus, I've come to see that such colleges are fundamentally reinventors—of their students, of their faculty members, and, increasingly, of themselves. The innovation at the core of liberal arts colleges makes them a uniquely exciting higher education experiment. It is also what prepares their students for life and work in an ever-changing world. Moreover, in a higher education world in which changing market dynamics are a permanent reality, ongoing innovation will allow these institutions to survive so that they can serve to develop the thinkers, workers, and entrepreneurs of the future.

Commencement at Hendrix begins with all graduates walking through a human corridor of faculty. Although I've now been part of such events for twenty years, the emotional impact of this simple ceremonial act catches me off guard every year. By the time graduation occurs, I've developed personal bonds with any number of individuals. Commencement marks a separation from daily interaction with them, but the overriding emotion I feel during commencement is not sadness but joy at recognizing the personal transformations that have occurred in so many students. No matter the frustrations I've felt with the institution across the year that just ended, at that moment I'm always thankful to have the opportunity to be a faculty member at an institution that operates on a scale where regular interactions with a significant number of students allows awareness of those personal reinventions.

Many of these transformations are fundamentally academic in nature. (The enthusiastic learner who arrives with a writing style so overly flowery that his good ideas are lost and then leaves with a crisp writing style that maintains his personality as a writer. The smart kid who arrives with a vague interest in education comes to hone a skill and love for the analysis of education policy through courses and a senior thesis.) Of course, reinventions are not brought about just by what happens inside the classroom or through course-related work like undergraduate research or internships. Students' work outside the classroom (in student organizations and on playing fields) or even away from campus is just as often the source for change. (The young man who arrives wandering spiritually finds his ministerial vocation through work with a faith-based healthcare provider. The woman with a passion for reproductive justice develops leadership skills by organizing the first state-wide rally on the topic.) And, perhaps most important, small liberal arts colleges create safe zones for some of the most difficult of reinventions. (The gay kid from rural Arkansas who arrives on campus grappling with his newly discovered sexuality leaves confident in himself and on his way to happiness in love and life.) Watching students transform over a four-year period is, indeed, the greatest gift of being a professor at a small liberal arts college.

This is not to deny that scores of students have their lives changed each year through educational experiences in the array of other higher education institutions. I see it personally in my work with a nonprofit that provides scholarships for single parents; their newly gained skills fundamentally change the economic futures of themselves and their children. However, liberal arts colleges are unique in their commitment to thinking about the "whole student" in the growth that occurs during the undergraduate years and, just as important, in thinking about preparation of students for a life-time of growth. In that last area, I increasingly see my Hendrix students becoming aware that graduation from college is not a culminating event but instead only one key moment in a lifetime of unexpected personal innovations. In short, liberal arts colleges "change lives" (in the words of longtime observer of American higher education Loren Pope). But, more importantly, they prepare students for lives of change.

Liberal arts colleges are not just places with a propensity to change their students' lives. Liberal arts communities also provide a rare (indeed, almost unique) environment in higher education for faculty lives to be changed because of the freedom provided to those faculty members to take real chances intellectually and professionally. While ongoing professional development is a centerpiece of the evaluation process for faculty at any top-flight liberal arts institution, there remains decided flexibility at these colleges when professional work is construed as more than peer-reviewed research. Both explicitly and implicitly (particularly after tenure), faculty are therefore encouraged to take chances rather than playing it safe in the interest of publication for publication's sake.

Such liberation leads to some intellectual transformations, often driven by the interests of students. Among my faculty colleagues, I have witnessed classicists become children's literature experts, British literature scholars become specialists in African literature, and American political institutions researchers become scholars of Hannah Arendt. Moreover, the shifts have not been dilettantish but profound—deep investments of brain-power and time in new subject matter that provides outstanding models of lifelong learning and personal reinvention for students.

While I admit I'm something of an intellectual party hopper, for me it's been crucial that I've been able to pursue research veering from the politics of the South, to attitudes toward gay and lesbian Americans, to radio advertising in campaigns, to state immigration policymaking. Such variety has also significantly enhanced my teaching in helping students make connections across my diverse subfield of American politics. If my college required that I produce a certain number of publications for my annual performance report, without doubt I would have played it safer, investing more deeply in niche research. Both my students and I would have been poorer as a result.

Even more distinctively, from running for office to service on the state Board of Education, I have had the freedom to engage in the public arena as a component of my professional development. Involvement in politics and public service drove my desire to become a teacher and researcher of American politics; it quickly became clear to me that separating myself from that work would, therefore, be cutting off the fuel for my interest in my academic subject. I have found that a merger of academic analysis and hands-on political work can undergird a truly effective teaching phi-losophy in the field of politics. As I move back and forth between *teaching* American politics and *engaging in* American politics, I attempt to model this equilibrium for my students. Since I wear two hats—one as a political scientist, and another as a committed practitioner of politics—I use that opportunity to help students learn the appropriate occasion for wearing each. Such intellectual, professional, political, and personal freedom—all intermixed—can be uniquely showcased at a liberal arts institution, and I think all parties benefit from an integrative, as opposed to compartmental-ized, approach to education.

Because of the need for rapid adaptability facing all of higher educa-tion, this spirit of reinvention that inspires those who live and work at lib-eral arts colleges must now extend to the institutions themselves. And there is evidence that small liberal arts colleges are indeed well situated to engage in the pragmatic experimentation at the root of successful innovation.

I've seen this reinvention at my own institution. In 2004, in the midst of a market challenge that required change that went beyond mere market-ing, Hendrix launched an innovative engaged-learning initiative called Your Hendrix Odyssey: Engaging in Active Learning. The Odyssey program built upon the college's historical encouragement of engaged-learning endeav-ors, such as undergraduate research, which enhance, expand, and frame the knowledge and questions they encounter inside the classroom. In the

Odyssey program, all Hendrix students are required to participate in at least three engaged-learning projects drawn from three of the following six categories: Artistic Creativity, Global Awareness, Professional and Leadership Development, Service to the World, Undergraduate Research, and Special Projects. To increase the breadth of engaged-learning experiences, students must complete their three required Odyssey experiences in separate project categories. While engaged learning was common at Hendrix, it did not exist campus-wide, and when it came to such challenges as revamping graduation requirements, some faculty members were wary of reform. Yet, the faculty did move forward with this reinvention of the institution. Payoff has come not only in the form of greater attraction in the marketplace for new students but also in meaningfully deepening the educational experience for those students who came to Hendrix.

Why are small liberal arts colleges advantaged when reinvention is needed?

First, this is a place where size does matter. It's clearly easier to steer a smaller vessel in a new direction. Second, when fostered by the institution's leaders, a sense of community provides social trust that allows those who are part of that community to take risks, together. Third, it's easiest to innovate when an institution has confidence in its core tenets; healthy liberal arts institutions understand their mission in terms of the academic and holistic preparation they seek to instill in students. The best innovations in an institution do not involve wholesale change but rather decided tweaks that allow it to perform more ably.

While it is important not to overstate the ease with which such reinventions will happen at liberal arts institutions, the rapid change in higher education during the first decades of this century should convince us that reinvention is going to be crucial for their survival. Liberal arts institutions that lack the internal community of a shared mission will be unable to transform and may well die, or else be forced to shift completely away from their identity with the liberal arts. Those vast, conference hotel ballrooms with their institutionalized sameness may be a necessity of the academic job search, but they also connote a rigid dullness at odds with the viability of higher education. The liberal arts model of openness to change offers a fresh alternative: a space within American higher education where students and faculty alike can continue to practice the joy of reinvention.

Note

1. Skills that match those most desired by employers as shown in "How Should Colleges Prepare Students to Succeed in Today's Global Economy?" a national poll by Peter D. Hart Research Associates commissioned by American Association of Colleges and Universities in 2007.

The Best Kind of College

Spelman College

DONNA AKIBA SULLIVAN HARPER

An internationally recognized Langston Hughes scholar, Donna Akiba Sullivan Harper has taught English at Spelman College since 1987 and served as Dean of Undergraduate Studies at Spelman from January of 2003 to December of 2004. She is currently the Fuller E. Callaway Professor of English, teaching composition and African American literature. She is a member of the executive committee of the College Language Association (as English Area Representative) and will become President of the CLA in 2018. A founding member and past president of the Langston Hughes Society, she is the author of the only book-length study of Hughes's celebrated Jesse B. Semple stories, Not So Simple: The "Simple" Stories by Langston Hughes *(1995). She has also edited four volumes of short fiction by Hughes. A Phi Beta Kappa graduate of Oberlin College, she earned her MA and PhD from Emory University as a Danforth Graduate Fellow. Her awards and recognition include the Faculty Award in African American Literature, 1999, in recognition of exemplary scholarship and dedication to excellence at Spelman College; the Langston Hughes Prize for Excellence in Literature and Vision, 1998; the Spelman College 1995 Presidential Faculty Award for Scholarly Achievement; and the 1991 Distinguished Teacher Award, funded by the Sears-Roebuck Foundation Teaching Excellence and Campus Leadership Award Program.*

Having attended a small liberal arts college (Oberlin), I've happily devoted my life to teaching in one. Even after nearly forty years, I remain in touch with my own college professors, and via social networking, I am in touch with hundreds of Spelman College graduates. Thus, the genuine and enduring human interactions that can occur at the small college strike me as being superlative. Since we do not have graduate students, we teach our own classes. We also have longevity, so our alumnae can return to Spelman for their fifteenth and twentieth reunions and often find some of their professors still actively engaged in teaching. We are delighted to keep informed about the accomplishments of our graduates, whether they are finding true love, having children, earning advanced degrees, or working executive positions in corporate America. We often invite our alumnae to return to campus as convocation speakers or participants in programs, because they know and love their Spelman sisters and are eager to inspire them. In the spring of 2014, for example, JaDawnya Butler, Spelman class of 2001, the 2012 president of the Georgia Association of Black Women Attorneys, gave the keynote address for the convocation to celebrate students who had earned honors during the 2013–2014 year. JaDawnya used lines from the Spelman hymn to encourage current students to face with courage any challenges that might lie ahead in their quest for a law degree, a medical degree, a graduate degree, or a job.

Not surprisingly, however, these enduring interactions between professors and students (or former students) are often focused on ideas. The small liberal arts classroom insists upon dialogue and interaction. The lecture format is nearly alien in our literature program. The faculty members are well published, and we deliver exciting lectures at national and international conferences, but in the classroom, we invite the voices of our students. Likewise, students' essays are actually read and evaluated by their professors, not by graduate assistants. We challenge and praise not just the writing but the ideas. Thus, even years after graduation, professors and former students find themselves debating and analyzing the latest news, the latest films, the latest books, and the latest speeches. We boast a desire to instill lifelong learning, and many of our students really catch the fever! Recently, as I posted my comments to Maya Angelou's life and legacy on Facebook, Tiffany Reese posted this comment to my enthusiasm for memorizing poetry: "Dr. Harper, I have been out of school almost 20 years and you are still my favorite professor. You continue to educate me."

Spelman College is special even among the rest of the small liberal arts colleges, because Spelman is one of only two colleges in the United States devoted to the education of young women of African descent. Curricular decisions always include a deliberate examination of the roles and contributions of women—especially black women. We require of all our students a course called African Diaspora and the World, which covers many of the topics that would be investigated in a more typical World Civilization course but with an intentional centering upon the lives of women—especially women of African descent. Many impressive black women have been highlighted convocation speakers and have been awarded honorary degrees, thereby giving them the spotlight. Some of these honorees are celebrities, such as Oprah Winfrey, and national icons such as First Lady Michelle Obama. However, we also bring to the center of the stage international female leaders, such as Ellen Johnson Sirleaf, the twenty-fourth and current president of Liberia. We invite women leaders in all arenas—mathematics, medicine, and literature. Faculty members often incorporate these visits into the curricular activities of the classes we teach. When Spelman hosted the symposium Reading Toni Morrison Reading *Home*: Male Kin and Family Matters, leading scholars from all over the United States and a couple of international scholars convened in the Cosby Academic Center. Some of us rearranged our syllabi so that our students had completed a reading of Toni Morrison prior to the February 16, 2013, symposium. Students who attended were thrilled to engage personally with these leading scholars, and the experience literally influenced a couple of them to decide to pursue a PhD so that they could follow the path of these inspiring literary experts.

Extracurricular activities are also designed to identify the talents of our students. At Spelman, of course, all the many organizations are led by women. The environment, as we often describe it to our potential students, "was created just for you." Thus, whether the group is designing and competing internationally with Spel-bots (robotic dogs that play soccer) or traveling the nation to sing in the nationally acclaimed Spelman College Glee Club or traveling internationally to participate in the Model UN, the participants at Spelman are women.

Small liberal arts colleges can offer genuine human interactions, exciting intellectual exchanges, and an environment that nurtures leadership and recognizes talents of individual students with names—not just student identification numbers. I loved that environment when I was an undergraduate, and I cherish the opportunity to contribute to this environment as a professor.

Athletics in the Liberal Arts

———•———

JENNIFER SHEA LANE

Jennifer Shea Lane is an Adjunct Professor of Physical Education and the Head Softball Coach at Wesleyan University. Hired in 2001, Lane has led the Cardinals' softball team to the New England Small College Athletic Conference (NESCAC) championship game three times, winning the title in 2010 and advancing to the NCAA tournament. For her team's success, Jennifer was voted NESCAC Coach of the Year by her peers in 2010. She was also honored as Co-Coach of the Year in 2008 when the Cardinals hosted the NESCAC tournament and finished as Runners-Up. During her tenure, the Cardinals have also won the coveted "Little Three" title in 2008 and 2013. In 2012, Lane wrote an article titled "Know the Process and Don't Overlook Division III" about the recruiting process for prospective Division III student-athletes that was published in the National Fastpitch Coaches' Association's Fastpitch Delivery. Lane received a BA in American studies from Amherst College and an MS in exercise and sports studies from Smith College. As an undergraduate, Jennifer captained both the softball (1997 and 1998) and field hockey (1997) teams. As a pitcher, she helped lead the Lord Jeffs to finish sixteenth in the country her senior year and was named to the New England Regional All-Tournament Team. A sweeper in field hockey, Jennifer was selected to play in the Division III North-South Senior All-Star game in 1997. Originally from Hatfield, Massachusetts, Jennifer now resides in Middletown, Connecticut, with her husband, James Lane Jr., and their four children—Julia, Andrew, William, and Olivia.

∾

Why are small liberal arts colleges so important to higher education in the United States? When asking this question, it's important to not only look in the classroom but also to look outside of it. While the "traditional" learning occurs inside the classroom, outside of the classroom is where students learn so much more without even realizing it. Conversations with professors over lunch and discussions with other students in the dormitories help students express their passions and learn about others' points of view. The playing field is another venue where this occurs. Athletics and the small liberal arts experience go hand-in-hand. Much of what is valuable about a small liberal arts college is also what is taught, and therefore learned, in the athletic arena. To me, the value of the liberal arts education is about pursuing your passion while discovering new ones. It is about interacting with others, face-to-face, and learning social skills in a world that is centered on technology and social media. It is about dealing with failures and learning from your mistakes. It is about pushing yourself outside of your comfort zone to learn what motivates you and what it's going to take to reach your potential. Not only are those characteristics of the small liberal arts college, but they are also the characteristics of athletics.

I'm biased: I have been involved with small liberal arts colleges for over half of my life. My first experience with a small liberal arts college was during the summers of high school when I worked doing landscaping at Amherst College, where my father was, and still is, the head of the Grounds Department. As my high school career was coming to an end and I started to look at colleges, I did not fully realize or understand the value of a liberal arts education, even though I had worked at one for several summers. I looked at many schools in New England and ended up at the last one I toured, although I already knew it well: Amherst College.

I feel very fortunate to have attended a small liberal arts school, and Amherst in particular. When I entered college, I thought I was going to major in mathematics or computer science and go on to become an engineer. However, after freshman year, those interests changed. I had taken courses in both of those disciplines and done well in them but felt my true passion was elsewhere. Besides being at a top-notch academic institution, I also had the privilege of continuing my athletic career in not one but two sports—field hockey and softball. It was not until I was a student at

Amherst and was working for the sports information director that I began to realize that maybe my passion for athletics could lead me to a career in sports. I thoroughly enjoyed working for the sports information director and thought maybe I would go into sports journalism. However, after a summer internship at local paper in the sports department, I realized I did not want to be covering the games; I wanted to be on the field coaching them. And being at a small liberal arts college afforded me that opportunity. I brought my passion for athletics into the classroom as well, writing my senior American studies thesis on the history of women's physical education and athletics. Being a student at a small liberal arts college opened doors that I never knew were available to me. Because I was able to change my major to something completely different from what I had originally planned, I followed an unintended path to where I am today.

The opportunity to follow your own passion in a small learning environment is second to none at these schools. Being from a *very* small public high school (graduating class of twenty-nine), I thought of Amherst, with an enrollment of approximately 1,600, as being big at first. But the discussion classes were the perfect size. What I liked most about the classes was that they were composed of students from four different class years who brought different experiences and vast knowledge to the table. The professors did not stand in the front of the room and lecture; they were engaging and wanted the students to voice their opinions and give their interpretations of the book or topic being discussed.

On the athletic fields, the benefits of the small liberal arts college continued. On walks out to practice, my teammates and I would talk about our classes, assignments we had pending or tests we had just taken. On the field, we worked hard, learning to be one cohesive unit competing together to defeat our opponent. In the classroom at a liberal arts school, you are taught how to think and how to translate those thoughts into a paper; on the playing field at a liberal arts school, you are also taught how to think and how to utilize your skills to perform your sport to the best of your ability. Again, the small liberal arts school and athletics go hand in hand, with one reinforcing the principles of the other.

After graduation from Amherst, I began my coaching career at my alma mater while pursuing my master's degree at another small liberal arts school, Smith College. Exercise and sports studies is a two-year program with about a dozen students in the major. To learn the discipline of coaching in the classroom of a small liberal arts college is a rarity. Our classes combined theory and science, with much of the learning coming from being an on-the-field assistant coach as well as from conversations with other graduate students in the program. Again, the smallness of the classes and the availability of the professors (and coaches) to discuss topics outside of class made the experience invaluable.

From Smith, I moved on to Wesleyan University where, for the past thirteen years, I have been the head softball coach and an adjunct professor of physical education. I have met and worked with many amazing people, both colleagues and students. The physical education and athletics department at Wesleyan is a microcosm of the small liberal arts college. The faculty coaches share ideas and apply principles from one sport to another. We are constantly talking about ways to make our programs better by finding new methods of motivation, team building, or leadership development. We learn from each other's successes as well as mistakes and failures to help our student-athletes become not only better at their sport but also better people.

My favorite part of working at a small liberal arts college is getting to know the students—both the players on my team as well as the other students at the university. As a professor of physical education, I teach the class Swimming for Fitness. I try to get to know my students—where they are from, what brought them to Wesleyan, what they want to do upon graduation. Wesleyan is such an exciting place in that it draws students from all over the country and all over the world. To know the composition of the university makes me a better coach. I may only know the students in my class for half a semester, but one of the special things about the small liberal arts college is that the students are more than just a number. It is important to me, as a professor, to get to know the students so they can have the best experience possible during their four years at the university.

Of course, I enjoy my student-athletes. Coaching is like a puzzle; I have to put together a group of students who will excel both academically and on the softball diamond, while making sure that Wesleyan is the correct fit for them and that they are the right fit for Wesleyan. The essence of a liberal arts school is to take students from different backgrounds—socioeconomic, geographical, racial, among others—and bring them together to learn on the same campus. The same is true in athletics. I had a student-athlete many years ago tell me that the one common theme that brought her together with her friends was softball. Without it, they may have never become friends. And now as alumnae, they stay in touch and are friends for life.

Not only have I gotten to know my student-athletes as softball players, but I have also gotten to know them off the field. The important thing about many student-athletes at liberal arts colleges is that they are not just students or just athletes. They pursue many interests. I have seen my players act in plays, sing in concerts, and perform in dance recitals. I have heard them speak on panels and attended their art shows. I have supported their endeavors to start tutoring programs in the local schools. I have let them borrow my own children to create music videos for final projects. To me, coaching at a liberal arts school is more than just about what happens on the field. It's about helping to prepare the women on the softball team for the real world as best I can.

Another advantage to being a student-athlete at a small liberal arts school is the capacity to network with alumni. At Wesleyan, we have the A+ Program, which connects current student-athletes with alumni in the career field they want to pursue. While often the connections are made within the same sport, we also have instances where connections are made with a current student-athlete in one sport to an alumnus in another sport. The opportunity for job shadowing and firsthand experience in a field that the student-athlete wants to pursue is priceless.

I have seen the small liberal arts college from many different views—as an employee, as a student, as a coach, and as a professor. The education one receives at these institutions is second to none. The opportunity to work one-on-one with professors, to participate in small discussion classes, and the prospect of connecting with alumni for future endeavors and employment possibilities is unique. The ability to pursue different disciplines to find one's true passion helps make students care more about what they are studying and take ownership of their course of study. The capacity to be able to "think outside the box" is the groundwork of the liberal arts education, and without it, the world would not be as innovative as it is today.

Going Elsewhere, Coming Home

Yolanda P. Cruz

Yolanda P. Cruz teaches developmental biology and epigenetics at Oberlin College. In 2012, she was included in The Princeton's Review's Best 300 Professors. *A few months after writing this essay, she won a Fulbright scholarship to return to her college campus, the University of the Philippines at Los Baños, to teach developmental genetics.*

Attending university was never a question in the home where my siblings and I grew up. Educational attainment was more a matter of what to specialize in when the time came. Our parents were academics; Father was a professor and Mother was the principal—more like a headmistress, really—at the local private grade school. We lived practically on the campus of Father's university, two minutes' stroll from the main library, a kilometer's walk from the gym and tennis courts. Mother's school was *on* campus, having begun its life as a school for faculty children. My brother, sister, and I all went to Mother's school, most of our classmates the children of Father and Mother's colleagues. We were an academic family living in a small college town.

My grade school and high school years were spent with more or less the same classmates each year. We learned arithmetic and geometry together, mastered the periodic table, studied history, did home economics (or shop if you were of the other sex), memorized poems, read classical poems and avant-garde novels, dissected frogs, went on annual school trips to museums and zoos, and learned all those intricately clever knots in Girl Scouts. In high school, one of my English teachers was Father's landlady when he was a university student; my biology teacher, one of his former students. I knew the families of nearly all my classmates. On weekends we hiked in a national park adjacent to our town, swam in the local hot springs, snuck out to the local cinemas, went to the same barn dances and jam sessions, dressed up for the proms, shared meals in one another's houses. We forged friendships that have lasted five decades.

At sixteen I was ready for college. Big-city university campuses had their cosmopolitan appeal, but the academics at the university campus in our backyard persuaded my family and me that it was the best place for me. My friends' parents pretty much felt the same way about their children's education. And so I went to college with friends I had known since kindergarten. This resulted in the unsurprising comfort of a familiar milieu for all of us, and not just because practically all our professors were each other's parents, but also because attending classes with friends made our college experience seem like an endless summer of learning new things about the natural sciences, literature, history, art, politics, philosophy, judo, calculus, and swimming. All this in a small, familiar, cozy, comfortable setting where the professors, storekeepers, and janitors knew us by name—mainly because their kids were my classmates. We took neighborhood safety for granted—most homeowners never thought to lock their front or back doors. Children came and went into neighbors' yards, had unchaperoned play dates and dragonfly-snaring excursions to the small brook that ran through the back of our neighborhood. There were mom-and-pop shops in town that let me purchase snacks on an eat-now-pay-later plan, because the store clerk knew that Father or Mother would likely be in at some point and merely had to be informed that I had had an ice cream bar or boiled ear of corn earlier in the day but did not have my wallet with me. I remember unknowingly leaving this same wallet in one of the public minibuses that served campus, only to discover the bus driver at our front door the next day—he had come to return my wallet, apologizing that he hadn't come the evening before, knowing I would miss my wallet, but that he had some chores that kept him from doing so.

The Arcadian nature of life in our small campus and town marched to the rhythm of the academic year, for the university dominated the culture and most aspects of everyone's existence. The economic welfare of the town was inextricably combined with the well-being of the university's employees and students. The notion of personal space graded seamlessly into our idea of the common weal: weddings and funerals were everyone's affairs, as much as growing vegetable gardens and pruning hedges were neighborhood enterprises. Elections and church functions were as effective as family reunions or birthdays for eliciting block parties and Saturday picnics. Father undertook house remodeling in my junior year, and the carpenters and masons who helped him realize this project were word-of-mouth referrals from his Scrabble friends. When Mother had a gardener prune our crotons and bougainvilleas, the cuttings were part of his day's earnings. Ours was a cozy world.

My sense of living in a fishbowl or acting a bit part in a school operetta took a while to shift from spellbinding to overwhelming. Thinking back now to establish just when this transformation occurred, I suspect it crept up slowly but steadily on me. At first it was the adolescent yearning for more drama in my life then, somewhat later, the feeling that my future lay before me, not an uncharted adventure with surprises and pitfalls at every other turn but rather a familiar landscape gradually heaving into view. Surely I would follow in Father's academic footsteps, not perhaps in his chosen field of economics but in whatever field of knowledge I fancied. This unfolding vista was never articulated at home at dinnertime or at any other time, but it lay in wait, ready to be considered and pursued.

It's of course entirely possible that I imagined this, that an expectation was somehow an unbreakable edict. I loved learning, was good at it; I could not then (or now) imagine a more engaging and satisfying career to pursue. And yet the patness, the inevitability of it all, troubled me. I was convinced that there had to be other possible futures, other probable lives. After all, *most* people were not professors. *Most* people neither grew up nor spent their lives in small, sheltered, and secure college towns.

By age twenty I had completed my college degree and obtained a teaching position at my (and Father's) university. It chagrined me to continue to be thought of as my father's daughter, even by my former professors who were now my colleagues. Sensibly enchanted, however, by the idea that I could take courses toward a master's degree at a discounted rate while teaching full-time, I signed up to do so. This enabled me to take the few university courses I had not yet taken but wanted to, and more. Unfortunately, it also showed me that I was boxing myself ever more certainly into a university career on the very same campus on which I had grown up. Gradually, the comfortable familiarity of living a circumscribed life with my family and friends in our small college town first lost its appeal, then started to wear on me. Soon I noticed the stirrings of a growing disdain for the predictability of the academic career I somehow unthinkingly managed to embark upon. Was that all there is? I began to feel like the kid watching the tail end of a parade, sun setting, trampled confetti on the ground, waning sound of the brass band slowly marching off into the distance.

My master's degree emboldened me to venture forth and assert myself in another country. With equal measures of excitement and anxiety, I left the campus I had grown up and been educated in, determined to embark on a life that offered more daring undertakings, beckoned with friends yet to be made, invited adventure, promised a welcome contrast to the small-college-town existence I had every eagerness to leave behind. It was the mid-seventies, the end of the Vietnam War, the dawning of the Age of Aquarius, ending the decade that saw the Free Speech Movement, the Green Revolution, Neil Armstrong on the moon, and women's lib. Haile Selassie and Salvador Allende had been overthrown, the war in Angola had begun, the Khmer Rouge had taken over Cambodia, East Pakistan was turning into Bangladesh, Richard Nixon had resigned, Cyclone Tracy had devastated the city of Darwin, Cesar Milstein and Georges Kohler had figured out how to make monoclonal antibodies, Noam Chomsky had written *The Logical Nature of Linguistic Theory*. It was, to say the least, an extraordinary time.

Extraordinary times stir up extraordinary ideas. My dream was to finish the PhD degree in large part to fulfill the filial duties of a loyal daughter and be done with family obligations, later eschew the looming inevitability of a respectable but insipid academic existence, never again settle for life in a small college town, become a citizen of the world, reside in a different country every few years, and live happily ever after. The bit about the PhD was straightforward, requiring only hard work made worthwhile by the intellectual rewards inherent in the exercise itself. But the rest of that idyllic tableau was trickier to realize. Coming to grips with "going elsewhere" proved more daunting than I had anticipated. What had presented itself as an intoxicating array of enchanting experiences to be had, cool people to meet, and revolutionary ideas to put to work became frighteningly confusing and, later, simply overwhelming. Instead of the kid enjoying the parade, I became the tot dumbfounded by the blare of a brass band, stupefied by the unfamiliar sights and sounds of a world that was rapidly turning out to be more intimidating than exciting.

By age thirty, I had worked myself into a midlife crisis. It became excruciatingly difficult to choose between the bleakness of a safe, prosaic, milquetoast academic existence and the mesmerizing but daunting, inhospitable realm of the henceforward. I felt myself floating in a sea of indecision. Enervated and depressed, I considered going home, back to my old job, but with my PhD unfinished; doing so would have been seen as a disgrace, a dismal failure, certainly loss of face in Father's and Mother's social and professional circles. At about this time, John Lennon crooned, "Life is what happens to you while you're busy making other plans." This struck even greater fear into my already addled mind: I wasn't even *making plans*! I felt stuck. I needed to plot my life's trajectory, to part the water and swim purposefully *toward* some shore of my choosing and not merely *away from* familiar waters I had already explored. I *was* swimming, but in the dark of a moonless night, the shore was hard to even make out, much less aim for.

By some miracle, however, my studies suffered little. After a bad semester, I got back into a good groove, coasting on what I now believe must have been sheer momentum from those long-ago days in the college town where I grew up. In just a few years I found myself reluctantly declining job offers in two of the largest, hippest metropolitan areas in the country, accepting instead a tenure-track appointment at a small liberal arts college in an equally small, quiet Midwestern town. I'd had a déjà vu moment during my job interview: the campus felt oddly familiar; the quiet, tree-lined streets safe and reassuring. I even remember thinking, as I crossed the campus quad, how I could see myself walking home from work, some thirty years into the future.

The irony of this decision did not occur to me until just a few years ago, a full twenty-five years after I moved to and settled in what is now my hometown. I live in a house just a few minutes' walk from my office. Each time I return to our street, from a long day at work or several weeks abroad, I feel the sort of serenity and calm that tells me I have come home. Several of my neighbors are, like me, professors at the college. I am as likely to see them at faculty meetings as at the grocery store in town. I know the names of their grown sons and daughters as well as those of the children who live on our street, just as I knew the names of the children (and their parents) my daughter played with when she was in the local grade school. The post office clerk greets me by name, as does the receptionist at the gym. A gardener friend alerts me when this year's plant sale will be held at our favorite local nursery; another never fails to invite me over when her grandchildren visit from Oregon. I keep an album of wedding invitations and birthday cards I regularly receive from former students. Several of them have become research colleagues in other institutions here and abroad. Two of them are on the same college faculty as I, right here in town. Two others have alerted me that their daughters would be in next year's incoming class. When I started here, I was too young for my students to see me as a mother; today I am nearly old enough to be grandmother to some of them, although I rarely volunteer that information.

The years have been good to me. I look forward to each semester with the same mixture of excitement and dread at the thought of lectures to be written, exam papers to be marked, term papers to be read and reread. On most nights, I repair to my bed exhausted from thinking about the reports and reviews due next week, the grant proposal awaiting resubmission, and the lab experiments that seem unworkable, only to be buoyed up by the thought of my early-morning workout at the gym in winter or weeding our flower beds in summer. Faculty colleagues keep me on my intellectual toes to about the same extent that my students do. I will admit that, over the years, both colleagues and students have sometimes been more vexing than necessary—but in each case, I have learned something useful about my career or myself, frequently both. I love my job. Every one or two years I have managed to travel—on business or on vacation—to places I dreamed about in grade school all those years ago. One year it was Cappadocia and its fairy chimneys; another, it was Kilimanjaro; yet another, it was Uluru. Not too long ago it was the Routeburn Track; a few years ago, Aconcagua. Last year it was Baalbek, this year it was Halong Bay and Mayon Volcano. My work has taken me to universities on four continents, numerous conferences to places even I never dreamed of. Best of all, I feel content and at peace with how, as my retirement looms in the distant horizon, my career has turned out. The fact that I have lined up a few more projects for the next few years is quiet reassurance that I have finally learned, with intent and focus, to *swim toward* a destination on the shore, moonless night notwithstanding.

On Not Lamenting Our Virginity

Jane F. Crosthwaite

Jane F. Crosthwaite, Professor of Religion at Mount Holyoke College, teaches courses in ethics and American religious history, with advanced seminars in feminist theologies and the American Shakers. In 2011, The Princeton Review named her as one of 300 Outstanding Professors in America.

ॐ

We dedicate this day to all the heroes and heroines in this country and the rest of the world who sacrificed in many ways and surrendered their lives so that we could be free.

Their dreams have become reality. Freedom is their reward.

We are both humbled and elevated by the honour and privilege that you, the people of South Africa, have bestowed on us, as the first President of a united, democratic, non-racial and non-sexist government.

We understand it still that there is no easy road to freedom.

We know it well that none of us acting alone can achieve success.

We must therefore act together as a united people, for national reconciliation, for nation building, for the birth of a new world.

Let there be justice for all.

Let there be peace for all.

Let there be work, bread, water and salt for all.

Let each know that for each body, the mind and the soul have been freed to fulfill themselves.

—Excerpt from Nelson Mandela's 1994 Inaugural Speech

Italo Calvino said, in a lecture at Mount Holyoke College in the mid-eighties, that to consider the universe, one could best begin with the top button of an overcoat, examining the texture, dimensions, and function of the single button. I have recounted this story hundreds of times to students seeking to capture fleeting ideas in a single paragraph, to situate a semicolon, or to anchor a footnote. In the small, intimate advising moments at small liberal arts colleges, buttons become the occasion for global discussions. And as a professor at a small liberal arts college for women, I have worked to uncover the universal and timeless lessons embedded in gender-specific stories. In this Baccalaureate Address delivered some sixteen years ago, I hoped to remind students that old stories, like small buttons, require reexamination, creative enlargement, and attentive, passionate work.

Madame President, Assembled Parents, Guests, and Members of the Class of 1999: I am pleased—and frightened—to address you on this auspicious occasion. I am especially distressed because, as those of you who know me can testify, I have conflicted responses to your graduation. Though I may be proud of you and wish you well, I am miffed at your eagerness to leave Mount Holyoke College. I thought we were getting along fairly well. I thought you were happy here. I thought you had finally learned how to document a quotation and not to split an infinitive. They say that you now want to "get on with your life" and that you want to move off into the world of work.

All right, then, let us talk a little bit about work—about that world you are heading into. Leaving aside the quibbles about whether or not you have been working all along, or whether what I do is "work," we have before us several texts, a few pieces of common knowledge, and some old ideas to string together. We are going to talk about the dangers of lost dreams and the bliss found in the hot pursuit of dreams. While Langston Hughes dared us to think of what happens to a dream deferred, imprisoned, or sacrificed, others have pointed to the pleasure of the eureka moment in scientific discovery—those moments where heart, head, and hands come together. The American Shakers, for instance, imagined that one could put hands to work and hearts to God. Tibetan Buddhists call followers to seek the "erotic, ecstatic oneness with reality." So, if we are going to talk about work, we are going to have to do a little bit of work.

I want to turn our attention to a difficult, dense, and, indeed, a terrifying story to draw out a complicated agenda. During this semester, some of you have read the biblical story of Jephthah's daughter with me. Others have worked and reworked this story in a liturgical setting on campus. Most of you know it anyway. It is a simple and brief story found in Judges

11:28–40 in the Hebrew Bible, but it is a story that, all too often, crosses cultures and histories. Jephthah volunteered to help his people against their enemies.[1] As an extra fillip of public relations, superstition, and desperation, he vowed to sacrifice the first thing he saw upon a victorious return. His dancing daughter greeted him; seeing her, he tore his clothes and said she had brought him low; she said if you must fulfill your vow, give me two months with my companions; she and her friends retreated to lament and bewail her virginity; she returned; her father sacrificed her; Israel was ordered to mark the event annually.

Perhaps it is all too clear why the instruction to memorialize the daughter of Jephthah has not been followed; rather the story and its possible lessons have been forgotten, ignored, avoided. But to forget this story, especially as women who have been on a mountain—on a four-year educational retreat together—would be to compound the daughter's loss. Some stories have been solemnly recorded with the intent that those events are *not* to be repeated. They are the lessons in what *not* to do. This is one of those stories. Jephthah is not praised. Indeed, he is distraught. He is part of a deadly system in which he has benefited—until now. Now he sees that this system—or his allegiance to it—requires that he sacrifice his daughter. How long he has been blinded to the fact that this patriarchal system has also required the sacrifice of the nation's sons, as well, is something of a mystery. How many were lost in the so-called victorious battle? How desirable is a system that gives big rewards to a few, yet costs so much? Normally, it would seem to me that this is a story told primarily to fathers, a story told to remind them of what they already know—even when there is profit in the denial—that there is much to change, that even apparently good systems can harm the girls and the boys, the young men and the young women. For our purposes here in this setting, particularly, the story reminds us that fathers can thrive only if their daughters thrive.

Let us pursue this story in a different direction now and look at some of the lessons the daughter learned in her retreat on the holy mountain with her women friends. We need to examine the questions of what Jephthah's daughter is supposed to have lamented. What does it mean that she is to bewail her virginity? Here I propose that we have oversexualized the story. Had the daughter sought sex or a fling with a beloved, she could have found that pleasure in her mountain retreat. No, I propose she lamented the loss of her full flowering, the loss of the work she could have done in the world. Virginity is not just, only, or mostly about sex. It is the wellspring of our creativity, the source of hope against all odds, the creative capital that one can draw on throughout one's life. Virginity is not a package to be auctioned off to one's spouse so that he can track his paternity. Neither is it to be squandered in vain and superficial escapism. Virginity is the innocent expectation that systems can change, and it is the mature choice to continue to work toward that change against all odds. Virginity was the belief that Nelson Mandela could leave prison and become president of South Africa.[2]

As a young person and as a woman, Jephthah's daughter had the additional and peculiar understanding that belongs only to the oppressed, only to the minorities, only to the expendable. She must have been biding her time during the war, drawing up schemes for a better world, plans to address hunger, poverty, and ignorance. She must have danced forth with timbrels to welcome her father, in order to share with him her plans for improvements now that peace was possible. Her dreams and her enthusiasm and her passion were quickly stifled. It was, finally, their failure to mature that she would have to lament.

The poet Audre Lorde has written an essay that many of you have read and some of you have had to read very carefully.[3] Audre Lorde shocks her readers by calling us to find and treasure "the erotic" source within us. Then she shocks us further by spending *no* time talking about sex and *much* time talking about work. Lorde chose defiant language to give a charge to her message that meaningful and creative work is rooted in passion. She warns us against trivializing our feelings and says that we have an "internal requirement toward excellence" that we ignore only at great cost. She asks us not to bury our dreams, not to deny our abilities, not to submit to passing sensations, but to trust and feed and educate the best that we know about ourselves. Thus, virginal possibilities can blossom into creative work. Do not throw your dreams away. Do not let others take them from you.

At the same time, dreams must be shared. Virginity and the erotic seek union with others. Dreams fuel our desires for friendship, for love, for community.

Nelson Mandela's speech makes this important connection when he promises that our light, our work, has direct possibilities for others. And if you thought that the hope, the beauty, the power, the erotic in you was only about you alone, then you are sadly mistaken. Jephthah's daughter did not go to the mount alone for an internal, purely private moment. She went with her sisters, and they all came back with lessons that were to be shared and enacted. They learned, as you have been learning for four yours, that you are not alone in this world. You become yourself only in direct relation to others you encounter.

You know who you are only by the work of your mind and heart and hands. The virginity to lament is that of the isolated, the frightened. The virginity to lament is the virginity that has not found the loving power to reach out to others in passionate and meaningful work.

One thing further we know about Jephthah's daughter. She did not have a name. Like nameless other women and men who populate our world, she remains identified by her relationship, especially with her father. In this case, let us not lament in the wrong direction. With a name, her story can change; with an education, there is power and possibility for the future. Her sacrifice can mark an ending and a beginning. This way she can assume any name. She is Rachel and Lisa and Mary and Carmen and Kristin. She is Elizabeth and Crystal and Maria and Erika and Megan. She is each name who will be called at graduation tomorrow. She is the woman in the mirror; she is the next woman you meet.

The last task is not just to name her but to let her name us. Let her teach us that love is more important than sex, that facts mean nothing without values, that bread and roses must be united. The extravagance of violence can be identified, can be resisted, can be opposed by clear thinking, by simple acts of kindness, and by passionate work. Let the Daughters of Mount Holyoke do the creative and passionate work that the Daughter of Jephthah could not do. Let us be well educated about the dangers, the needs, the limits and the possibilities: and so let us now go forth with timbrels and dancing to the work before us. It is time to go forward and join the creation.

Notes

1. See also Phyllis Trible, *Texts of Terror: Literary-Feminist Readings of Biblical Narratives* (Philadelphia: Fortress Press, 1984).

2. See the epigraph to this chapter, Nelson Mandela, *In His Own Words: From Freedom to the Future: Tributes and Speeches*, ed. Kader Asmal, David Chidester, Wilmot James (London: Little, Brown, 2003), 68–70.

3. Audre Lorde, "Uses of the Erotic: The Erotic as Power," *Sister Outsider: Essays and Speeches* (Trumansburg, NY: Crossing Press, 1984), 53–59. Interestingly, this essay was first read at Mount Holyoke College, August 25, 1978, at the Fourth Berkshire Conference on the History of Women.

PART FIVE

The College

Departures

K. E. Brashier

K. E. Brashier received his BA from Oxford as a Rhodes Scholar, his MA from Harvard, and his PhD from Cambridge, after which he began teaching Chinese religions and humanities at Reed in 1998. Author of Ancestral Memory in Early China *and* Public Memory in Early China, *he is currently studying the idea of purgatory in late imperial China. In 2006, he was recognized as the national Outstanding Baccalaureate Colleges Professor of the Year by the CASE/Carnegie Foundation, but his chief goal in life remains a futile attempt to get his two cats to respect him.*

John F. Kennedy International Airport, January 8, 2012

I am sitting on the floor of the Delta departure lounge waiting for my return flight to the West Coast, surrounded by piles of blog printouts, press releases, and glossy strategic planning reports. They were my homework before conducting initial interviews of a few possible candidates for the Reed College presidency. There's also a program to the Broadway musical *Spiderman: Turn Off the Dark* lying next to me, although out of embarrassment I quietly tuck it under one of the piles. (Our search committee's executive assistant, married to a New Yorker, had recommended *The Cherry Orchard*—Chekhov's last play—but I opted for shallow spectacle over thoughtful content.)

Conducted at a posh law firm just behind Grand Central Terminal, the interviews had gone well, and my colleagues and I—in total two teachers and three trustees—thought there was at least one potential candidate to consider for the next round. Despite my internet preparations which, in one case, went so far as to net the name of the candidate's spaniel, I always began with the same introduction to everyone: "My name is Ken Brashier, and I teach Chinese religion and Chinese humanities at Reed, where my goal is to put China on the radars of our students." And before my tailored questions, I then led with my assigned (and perhaps predictable) query on justifying the liberal arts: "When I'm sitting down with my students' parents, how do I justify their investment in an expensive liberal arts education in today's world?"

Their answers (perhaps just as predictably) fell into two camps. The first camp focused on the question's "in today's world." One college dean explained how business leaders and alumni recognize that critical thinking, clear communication, and ethical judgment (alongside literacies in both scientific and cultural paradigms) are needed in the modern economic climate. Another highlighted how the internet age is no longer a jobs-for-life world, everyone changing careers at least once, and that the basic skills honed at liberal arts colleges are readily transferable to different circumstances.

The second camp contended that developing the interior life of the mind is an eternal human goal, regardless of era and circumstance. One sitting president highlighted how the centuries-old mission of *artes liberalis* was to "free" the human being (Latin *liber* meaning "free"), even though that freedom is largely unquantifiable. Another potential candidate argued how the liberal arts could lead to the moral reasoning of an ethical citizen who is then able to evaluate what is *ipso facto* good (as opposed to what is good for strictly utilitarian reasons). A third suggested that we must habituate people into becoming lifelong learners to understand the stories that we tell about others and about ourselves.

What I didn't hear was whether these two camps of worldly circumstance and interior life should actually be merged into one. That is, there was always a distinct assumption that the outer, profane world of economic and social realities contrasted with an inner, sacred life of the mind. No one contended that the new outer world should somehow *dictate* our new habits of thought. Indeed, our own twenty-two-page "Invitation to apply for the position of the president" firmly wedged outer and inner apart:

> In an age when science, technology, and industry dominated the public imagination, [the founders of Reed College] sought to breathe renewed life into the traditional liberal arts education. They believed that a rigorous education in the liberal arts and sciences

would endow Reed graduates with the ability to lead productive and examined lives in the fast-changing world in which they lived.

Here, the examined life is juxtaposed with the circumstances of the age, the former to eclipse the latter as it renews an earlier tradition.

Perhaps the greatest educationalist to come out of New York was John Dewey, who taught at Columbia for twenty-six years; he recognized this perceived juxtaposition as a remnant of an older European age. In the past, truth was viewed as a static, transcendent ideal, and the pursuit of that truth was considered an elitist, even aristocratic privilege. That is, the template for the examined life was from somewhere else, from a higher plain, as religion and philosophy elevated it above the map of our profane lives. But in the democratic United States of Dewey's 1930s, we were no longer aristocrats, and in the industrial and scientific revolution of the twentieth century, we now saw ourselves as part of nature and cosmos rather than beneath them. A European traditionalist might condemn these new American values as nothing but wretched corporateness and shallowness, and Dewey largely agreed. The new age's quantification, mechanization, and standardization had indeed led to homogenization of thought and emotion, to an unchallenging entertainment industry and to the mass susceptibility brought on by advertising. In sum, we were the victims of a new mental and moral corporateness.

Yet in the pursuit of a "theory of life," Dewey said we shouldn't renew those old European ideals generated by a very different set of circumstances. We should instead examine our new world brought on by democracy, science, and mass culture; we should cut through the veneer of shallow corporateness by learning how to enjoy the delights of thinking and inquiry; and we should then evolve habits of thought from our own circumstances. "In reality, a machine age is a challenge to generate new conceptions of the ideal and the spiritual," he wrote in his *Individualism Old and New*.[1] "Individuals will refind themselves only as their ideas and ideals are brought into harmony with the realities of the age in which they act."[2]

To Dewey, there was no longer a truth floating out there above our map; in his new world of democracy and science, everything was here, existing together within a common frame of reference. We should not resurrect an older liberal arts tradition as an antidote to a public imagination dominated by science, technology, and industry; we should instead build our life of the mind on *our* foundations. Liberal arts is neither about getting by in the exterior circumstances of the world nor fostering the interior life of the good mind; it's about figuring out how our exterior circumstances can create a good interior life if we learn how to delight in thinking about the connection.

With my *Spiderman* program hiding amid these internet downloads, I suspect Dewey would rightly see me as not yet getting past the veneer of shallow corporateness, including its unchallenging entertainment industry. Regardless, this New Yorker thoroughly complicates my own attempt at an examined life while starting the search for a new president.

Chicago O'Hare International Airport, January 21, 2012

I am standing at the map to Concourse L, trying to decide whether I should go straight to the Alaska Airlines departure lounge or have time to detour into Starbucks. What I find most intriguing about this map is that I've just walked from the airport's own Hilton—where today's interviews took place—to this concourse without actually leaving the building. I've avoided the effects of the snowstorm so far, but my luck might change if I get grounded. I wonder if I'll see some of the potential candidates stuck here as well.

My set question for them today was whether they had noticed a change in incoming students over the past ten years, which is how long it's been since we've conducted a presidential search. The short answer was "yes" but in different ways. One college dean highlighted how more than a quarter of freshmen now complained of feeling overwhelmed in their senior years of high school by all the testing it took to get into good universities, and he lamented how this competitive culture was taking the joy out of learning. Another said that, once the new students arrive, they now expect more active teachers who don't simply lecture but instead foster more student engagement. To monitor these changes in students, she had in fact set up a program asking every student to specify his or her own learning goals. A third recognized that new students could feel a bit more lost in less-structured curricula than had once been the case, his college responding, not with more structure but with more undergraduate advising programs that crystallized goals and outcomes rather than established requirements and minimum standards.

Perhaps because my own area of study makes me prone to existential musings, I've often wondered if there's an even bigger difference in our incoming students. Take this concourse map where I'm standing. Its edges encompass the whole of the airport, and there's a handy "You are here" pointer—the technical term being an "ideo locator"—marking my spot at the end of Concourse L. Yet these maps are now a bit old-fashioned as my iPhone will walk me through the terminal directly to my departure lounge.

Old maps were centered on the heart of a culture, whether it be Jerusalem or China, and even if they lacked a sacred center, they still located your position relative to the big, bordered, static picture. Now the center of the map is you, and the big picture only measures about three inches and changes with you. The map itself can even be tailored to your personal likes, highlighting the coffee shops you pass en route, and so the map I see isn't the one you will ever see. According to *New Scientist*, small-screen, smartphone-based maps centered on you may be affecting how we build maps in our minds, affecting spatial cognition and losing contextual markers, and it goes so far as to suggest we might become "duller, less questioning and more unadventurous" because of our increasing reliance on these curated, virtually mediated spatializations.[3]

But we're not just the new centers of space. When I get home to Portland, I can check my iPhone to see when my particular bus will leave the airport to take me home; I need not resort to cumbersome, all-inclusive time schedules. Each bus and train in Portland is now tracked via GPS, and as it happens, my partner designed an app called "PDX Bus" used all over the city that allows commuters to dispense with approximate universal schedules and see the actual location and progress of only the bus they themselves would use. With bookmarks and alarms, the app then tailors each commuter's trip to his or her own needs. Just as you are today the center of your spatial map, you are also the center of your temporal schedule without resorting to the big picture (or to the big time, as the case may be).

Our incoming students are now habituated to this kind of world, and surveys show how they rely on technological aids for other personal locators such as birthdays and even their *own* phone numbers, their memories not as well developed as that of their parents.[4] When it comes to their education, we're all familiar with the arguments about how the Internet is changing our students' thinking processes as knowledge, for good or ill, is currently navigated at great speed.

Dewey in the 1930s recognized how the new world of science and technology had taken his own generation unaware, thereby resulting in a corporate shallowness without any self-reflective "new habit of mind and sentiment" evolving yet. He also recognized that the essence of such an examined life is the "integrated individual": "Human nature is self-possessed only as it has objects to which it can attach itself."[5] We all possess ties to the things in the world around us, but in the unexamined life, we take them for granted and never think them through, he contended.

I wonder if our current habits of mind are the next logical step of what Dewey observed eighty years ago as the integrated individual becomes the internetted individual. That is, Dewey maintained his generation was moving away from transcendent truths as science and democracy positioned everything within a common frame of reference. His generation was losing its sacred, dualistic reference points that once hovered above the maps of their profane lives. Now, we're losing the map as well. Focus shifts from a bordered big picture within which the self was located via an ideo locator, to the self-as-center navigating its own way across the terrain—and even the notion of "center" here becomes meaningless because it implies a static, shared, relativizing context. I really wonder if my students see themselves in their world the way I see myself in mine, and of course I then wonder how much it should matter to me when I am their teacher.

For now, I check the concourse map one last time and head for my gate, turning off my iPhone as I get ready to board.

San Francisco International Airport, February 12, 2012

I am standing beneath the ceiling-mounted televisions in the Alaska Airlines departure lounge, having just returned from the gift shop to buy my partner an apology for yet another lost weekend during this search. The only trinket I could find that didn't seem too tacky was a wine bottle stopper with an uninspiring picture of a trolley car on it. Above me, CNN coverage is entirely focused on the death of Whitney Houston, which was indeed news to me as I'd been sequestered with still more potential candidates for the Reed presidency all weekend. Glancing around the crowded lounge, I see various travelers with their heads down, gazing at their own screens and tablets, not really interacting with the people around them.

This weekend I had the chance to ask various educational leaders about how technology affected the liberal arts beyond offering new tools in the classroom, and one of the more upbeat answers rather surprised me. A college vice president observed that the Internet has led to an explosion of reading and writing, adding that several scholars have likened the proliferation of email, blogs, and discussion groups to a new Republic of Letters. Another potential candidate of course gave the flipside because quantity isn't quality. Always in search of the link button, students using the Internet are more cursory and limited in the attention they devote to onscreen readings, not marking them up or writing out marginal notes.[6] Yet even she was upbeat because we will eventually habituate ourselves to using this new medium well and won't just hide behind our screens.[7]

I suspect the internetted world is affecting not just students but also their teachers in unforeseen ways. Liberal arts colleges have long boasted how teaching and not research is paramount, and our own "Invitation" asserts that "Reed is fundamentally a teaching institution. It never succumbed to the siren song of research primacy." In fact, the dedication to my first book reads "To the students of Reed College without whose help this book would have been finished ten years ago." Yet I worry that liberal arts colleges might potentially change in nature because younger faculty are more habituated to being connected with their colleagues at other institutions via the Internet than are the older faculty. Increasingly, they are comparing their own efforts and accomplishments with those of their same-aged colleagues who happened to have found themselves at research universities. That is, they now measure themselves against their publication-producing colleagues more so than before, and naturally they don't want to be left behind. I don't think it's a coincidence that the younger faculty at Reed are much more focused on getting out books and articles—the more concrete measures of personal progress in their fields—than are the stalwarts of "Old Reed." As the younger faculty become the older faculty, the nature of a liberal arts college may duly change, and it all starts with how the Internet forms new kinds of communities.

Even this presidential search is not immune to the Internet's snares. Ten years ago in our last search, we brought the finalists to campus and held open forums so that all the students and faculty could see and react to them. Now presidential final rounds are almost universally held behind closed doors, usually with only the search committee meeting the candidates. Otherwise, word of one's candidacy would inevitably leak out almost immediately via social media, and as college deans and sitting presidents are often involved in fundraising campaigns, news of their "jumping ship" could have expensive consequences.[8] Other colleges who had recently conducted searches as well as our retained executive search firm are all warning us that an open search might halve our pool, even removing the best candidates who are both heavily engaged in fundraising and firmly present on the Internet. Because I am personally orchestrating the final round at a college that values transparency, I've already had more than one tense faculty meeting (including rude jeers of "That's not how we do things at Reed!") even though as many as sixty-five faculty, staff, and students, who all must sign confidentiality statements, will be meeting our finalists.[9] As in the case with new faculty, the Internet has collapsed the old frames of reference; it has torn up the earlier maps with their safe, fixed borders, leaving a messier reality behind.

When Dewey was formulating his belief that an examined life must manifest the inherent qualities of its own era and not others, he of course had education in mind because schools were "the formal agencies for producing those mental attitudes, those modes of feeling and thinking, which are the essence of a distinctive culture."[10] Yet he felt the educationalists of his day were clinging to an earlier, outmoded vision because intellectuals and "literary folk" in pursuit of pure truth and uncontaminated beauty were looking—just as their European forebears had done—for something transcendent, some kind of otherness that was off the map. That dualism split theory from practice, intellectual from worker. In contrast, the integrated individual now found his or her reference points closer to home, not necessarily idealizing industrialization but figuring out how to make the new underlying paradigm meaningful in the quest to be a good integrated individual.

Hence Dewey would have education change from creating the individual with transcendent reference points to creating the integrated individual, in which all reference points were on the same map he shared with others. If we then move from that mapped individual to the internetted individual who is relatively unmapped—that is, even less tied to external reference points as that individual becomes "self-centered" (which here does not necessarily mean "selfish" or "egotistical" in the negative sense)—should education also change in the hope of generating a new examined life?

One way to go about answering this question might be to look back at a college's contrasting efforts to put all its students together on a common map on one hand and to encourage individuality on the other. In many ways, the history of Reed (as we portray it in our "Invitation") could be read as a tension between these two positions. Starting with the latter, historically Reed has exhibited a "principled neglect of student support outside the classroom." That is, "students were meant to respond to the highly intense intellectual regimen, but to take responsibility, largely independently of the college for their personal lives." At one time, students mostly lived off campus, and even today the structures around which student communities often form—fraternities, sororities, sports teams, and religious organizations—remain generally absent at Reed. In much of its history, Reed students have had less opportunity to locate themselves within defined communities set out on preexisting maps drawn by others.

Much has changed. Student support has grown immensely over the past decade, and our "Invitation" seeks a new president who will carry forward that momentum because "helping individual students attain their highest potential must be a more integrated, community-wide effort." On-campus residency has climbed to 70 percent. The old "principled neglect" has gone, and the retention and graduation rates reflect the new safety nets and corporateness. In 1982, about 28 percent graduated in four years (54 percent in six); as for 2007's incoming class, 70 percent graduated in four years (a projected 80 percent in six).

Yet there's another curious and probably unrelated statistic coexisting with the aforementioned. In its history, thirty-one students left Reed to study at Oxford as Rhodes Scholars, ranking it second highest among liberal arts colleges. (The "Invitation" proudly includes this achievement in a list of five distinctions that set Reed apart.) What is not mentioned is that only two of the thirty-one were elected in the past thirty-four years. There's probably no connection in trends because correlation is not causation, and Reed does well in other types of scholarships such as National

Science Foundation fellowships. Yet it does make me wonder about a bigger theoretical issue: Is it possible that, when we move away from a tradition that vaunts student independence (unmapped and messy as it is) to one that stretches out safety nets to keep everyone together on the same map, we also potentially decrease the number of truly exceptional individuals leaving a college? That's not necessarily a bad thing because it's better to stop mining for a few rare diamonds and instead dig for lots of good-quality coal that, in real terms (excepting environmental impact), is much more essential to the world we live in.

Here I must emphasize that a declining number of Rhodes Scholars may indicate nothing at all; it's hardly the canary in that mine—diamond, coal, or otherwise. But—confession time—I myself am a biased beneficiary of the Rhodes Trust and hence these questions get raised in my own mind, even if they must ultimately be answered by other means. Just what does it mean to lead an examined life of an internetted individual? Does that life have an analogue within a liberal arts education? And are we moving toward or away from it?

Reed College Front Lawn, September 21, 2012

There's a strange trick of fate that, while I and others literally traveled from coast to coast and in between to interview potential candidates for the Reed presidency, the eventual winner was from just down the road in Portland itself. And so here I now sit, bedecked in my ornate British academicals, in the audience at the formal inauguration of our fifteenth president. While my travels didn't directly produce the next college president, they gave me ample opportunity to meet many educationalists and to think about what the liberal arts college is doing here and now, in the United States of the twenty-first century.

Reed College's first president was a product of John Dewey's Teachers College at Columbia University, and its second was a Rhodes Scholar who introduced our small group, discussion-oriented pedagogy at Reed because of his experiences at Oxford. Perhaps it shouldn't be surprising that Reed began with an emphasis on individualism rather than corporateness. Yet Dewey never offered an exact goal or definition of what his new individualism should embrace if one wanted to pursue an examined life in the 1930s. He couldn't. If the integrated individual must manifest his or her changing environment (rather than define the self as relative to a fixed, transcendent, eternal truth), then the ideal itself must drift with the times. "In such a situation, fixed and comprehensive goals are but irrelevant dreams."[11] Instead, we as products of the new science-permeated age should employ the scientific method as *our* tool for pursuing that examined life. We should not assume any absolutes, but we can test and question our progress, living contingently and relatively in a way that tolerates and even enjoys self-skepticism. Dewey's incorporation of scientific method into individual disposition is in my opinion the best part of his argument and is even more relevant today for the internetted individual of the 2010s than it was for the integrated individual of the 1930s:

> Scientific method would teach us to break up, to inquire definitely and with particularity, to seek solutions in terms of concrete problems as they arise. . . . The first move in recovery of an integrated individual is accordingly with the individual himself. In whatever occupation he finds himself and whatever interest concerns him, he is himself and no other, and he lives in situations that are in some respect flexible and plastic.[12]

That plasticity—and the logical adoption of the scientific method as the means of negotiating it—well characterizes our own circumstances in which we each now spin out our own individual and unique webs from the center rather than rely on set reference points at the side or even above the map.

In my opinion, the new examined life means it's best to see no fixed reference points at all, including my "self" in the center (as "center" assumes fixed map thinking). Instead I am a knot on a relationship net; I am the sum of my ties to those around me rather than a discrete, static unit. My examined life is then to always be cognizant of my relationship between myself and my nearest knots because, if I get tugged up or down, they can rise or fall but just not quite as much. And then I must look at how my surrounding knots affect *their* surrounding knots and so on in an ongoing ripple effect.

Does this breed of selfishness preclude my caring about a knot in distant Mexico or my showing concern about big issues such as the environment? Absolutely not—and in fact just the opposite. If, for example, I were to buy drugs coming up the I-5 corridor, I've chosen to interconnect into that network that stretches down to Mexico and, because a knot ties to the next knot, which in turn ties to the next, I may now be 0.003 percent *personally* responsible for a particular drug cartel death in Tijuana. If today I drive to work instead of bike, I may now be 0.06 percent *personally* responsible for the localized air quality that in itself is cumulative and has further effects. In fact, current discussions of individual carbon footprints already reflect this kind of internetted individualism, and so this application of Dewey's thinking is perhaps saying nothing new. Accurate calculations on how much the knots interact are of course excruciatingly complicated, but that's precisely why we need education, not just to habituate ourselves and our students into always thinking this way about all things, but also to provide the tools of science and humanities to measure this ripple ethics as accurately as possible so that we make good decisions.

Logistically, I believe the small liberal arts college is in a better position to foster this new kind of examined life than are larger institutions. Small, interactive classes where the center of gravity is the evolving individual are better than larger corporate settings where more-or-less static pronouncements must be made by the sage on the stage. "Individuality is inexpugnable because it is a manner of distinctive sensitivity, selection, choice, response and utilization of conditions," Dewey explained. "For this reason, if for no other, it is impossible to develop integrated individuality by any all-embracing system or program."[13]

One way Reed in particular takes this a step further is by not routinely circulating grades to its students. Papers come back with comments but not grades; semesters end without students knowing whether they got an A or a C. Studying no longer consists of individually cramming for the A (and for the next A, and for the next A . . .); it instead becomes a preparation for the communal conversation, both inside the classroom and inside their heads. That is, if I happen to be walking the corridors and courtyards after having just returned papers, I often find students perched on benches or hidden in niches slowly reading through their comments, trying to make sense of how their prose meshes with my reactions and trying to thereby ascertain my general evaluation from that. A simple, unambiguous grade posted above the person's name on the first page would threaten to deny that internal conversation. Like most other institutions, Reed still assigns grades to all work done, but those grades only go to the Registrar's Office. Students can access those grades by asking their academic advisor, but the general tradition is *not* to ask.[14] And in my opinion, this is a further removal of external reference points. Doing well is not to be pegged on a grade map relative to others; doing well is readying the self to navigate future uncharted waters in later classes and later life. Not relying on a grade map makes a huge difference to the college's academic atmosphere both inside and outside the classroom.

And while the Internet has been a major force responsible for our new circumstances, it does not itself necessarily supply the solution. Our "Invitation" from ten years ago already warned against distance learning because "students continue the process of learning in discussions with each other in their residence halls and over meals." Our retiring president also worried about how the Internet-based information technology revolution would play out at Reed, and he saw signs of it bubbling up in the curriculum via pilot projects, workshops, and the individual efforts of faculty members. And our new president seems to be just as concerned, expressing as much in tonight's inaugural address:

> Look, technology is our friend and technology can do amazing things in the classroom. . . . But we should not make any mistake: education is not passive. Perhaps if your model of education is 700 or 800 students sitting in a lecture hall listening, you might believe that education can be delivered over the Internet. But education, for me, is interactive. Education, for me, happens in the conference when students are talking amongst themselves. Education happens when people after class are getting together to talk about the ideas that really inspire them. These are things that the Internet cannot deliver. And one thing I think we have to do in the coming years is more forcefully articulate our vision of education as a human and social endeavor, one that can't simply be reduced to a business model that labels efficiency as its highest goal.[15]

Hence the Internet is part of the circumstances creating the new individual, but it's not by itself capable of leading to the examined life of that new internetted individual. Dewey similarly recognized that science and democracy had provided the new circumstantial paradigm of his own day, but the integrated individual had to first get beyond the homogenization of thought and emotion created by 1930s corporateness.

Conclusion: The Author's Backyard, June 28, 2013

I am sitting in my garden on what promises to be a hot day for Portland as the temperature approaches ninety degrees. During the academic year, Portland is a relatively rainy place to live (which is also why it's so green), and we customarily identify the beginning of our summer as July 4, when we enjoy three months of warm, sunny weather. It appears our summer has begun just a bit early this year. Yet I'm sitting out here not to enjoy the sun but because carpenters have taken over my house and exiled me here. I needed a quiet place to think back through the year of looking for a college president as well as my personal conclusions about the liberal arts that had developed along the way.[16]

I admire carpenters because they get to see the product of their work take shape right before their eyes. I suspect scholars at research universities are a bit like carpenters because they too regularly get to witness their aspirations taking shape in front of them in the form of new books, successful experiments, and worthy art installations. They are rewarded by directly seeing their constructed products at hand. Teachers at liberal arts colleges often don't get a chance to see the ultimate product of their best work. We're more like brick makers and are instead focused on making the bricks to hand to our students who will then build their own things later in life somewhere off campus.

But if I can extend an overstretched image a bit further, perhaps what I most want to be is a brick maker giving his bricks to students who will one day use them to build their own kilns and in turn make bricks for others to build kilns. That's how in these new, unmapped circumstances I would spin out my own ideal web without tying it to external reference points. As a teacher, I must enable enabling; I must figure out concrete pedagogical structures that teach the knots around me how to teach the knots around them. That to me is the logical extension of Dewey's vision of the integrated individual who navigates his or her world without fixed, external reference points. Precisely how I might accomplish that pedagogy within my own field is best left to later musings, but for now, it's time to go inside and admire some new cabinetry.

Notes

1. John Dewey, *Individualism Old and New* (Amherst: Prometheus Books, 1999), 73.

2. Ibid., 35.

3. Kat Austen, "Where in the World . . . ?" *New Scientist* (January 19, 2013): 44–47.

4. Ben Quinn, "Mobile Phones 'Dumbing Down Brain Power,'" http://www.telegraph.co.uk/news/uknews/1557293/Mobile-phones-dumbing-down-brain-power.html.

5. Dewey, *Individualism Old and New*, 30.

6. For a discussion on how online reading and learning is different from that of books, see Nicholas Carr's *The Shallows: What the Internet Is Doing to Our Brains* (New York: W.W. Norton, 2011). Reed College created one of the country's first information technology infrastructures and continues to engage in many experiments on how technology can improve the student's learning experience. Yet I've personally struggled with the medium. For example, I have the world's largest website devoted to Chinese hell scrolls, an immense site with more than a hundred scrolls as well as translations, explanations, essays, and links to relevant materials that is used at several colleges and universities teaching Chinese religion. Yet when I recommend that my students spend three to four hours of preparation working through this database to prepare for a class—thereby giving it as much attention as they would any other resource—I afterward learn from Google Analytics that the average was closer to twenty minutes. I also sense a decreased retention and thoughtfulness about texts read online rather than as hardcopies that can be highlighted and annotated.

7. Some of my Reed colleagues require all texts to be printed out and forbid laptops in the classroom entirely. Others allow laptops as long as the screens are fully extended, flat against the table, so that no one is hiding behind an electronic wall during a classroom discussion.

8. I have of course refrained from identifying any candidates or institutions here, and while the various details of this account are true—even down to the exact dates I was in each departure lounge—I am intentionally blurring where certain matters were discussed and even sometimes changing the genders and positions of the unnamed candidates. (I've even changed the breed of the candidate's dog whose name I discovered in my internet preparations.)

9. Now writing from the summer of 2013, I can report that the final round was logistically a success with happy finalists and no breaches in confidentiality. Yet even though it was logistically a success, the controlled search left a feeling of ill will (although fortunately not directed at the new president) among a vocal minority of faculty. Because of my uncomfortable experience, I would advise other colleges in search of presidents to sort out secrecy and confidentiality matters long *before* any search committee is formed so that the searchers are not also being held responsible for contentious search procedures.

10. Dewey, *Individualism Old and New*, 62.

11. Ibid., 73.

12. Ibid., 80.

13. Ibid., 81.

14. Students suffering from low grades (a C- or below) are still flagged and informed of developing problems, but there is no open stratification of the student body via grades. I strongly advocate this system, and it has also kept grade inflation at bay.

15. John Kroger, "Inaugural Address," September 21, 2012. See www.reed.edu/president/speeches/inauguration.html.

16. I feel that I should stress the fact that I'm not fictionalizing here. I really have been exiled to my garden, and the carpenters are putting the final touches to my new kitchen as I type this.

What Matters Most?

Liberal Arts Colleges in Perilous Times

JOHN K. ROTH

John K. Roth is the Edward J. Sexton Professor Emeritus of Philosophy and the Founding Director of the Center for the Study of the Holocaust, Genocide, and Human Rights (now the Mgrublian Center for Human Rights) at Claremont McKenna College, where he taught from 1966 through 2006. In 2007–2008, he served as the Robert and Carolyn Frederick Distinguished Visiting Professor of Ethics at DePauw University. In addition to service on the United States Holocaust Memorial Council and on the editorial board for the journal Holocaust and Genocide Studies, *he has published hundreds of articles and reviews and authored, co-authored, or edited more than forty-five books, including* Approaches to Auschwitz, Ethics During and After the Holocaust, The Oxford Handbook of Holocaust Studies, Rape: Weapon of War and Genocide, *and* Encountering the Stranger: A Jewish-Christian-Muslim Trialogue. *Roth has been Visiting Professor of Holocaust Studies at the University of Haifa, Israel, and his Holocaust-related research appointments have included a Koerner Visiting Fellowship at the Oxford Centre for Hebrew and Jewish Studies in England as well as an appointment as the Ina Levine Invitational Scholar at the Center for Advanced Holocaust Studies, United States Holocaust Memorial Museum. In addition, he has chaired the national board of the Federation of State Humanities Councils. The recipient of several honorary degrees, Roth was named the 1988 U.S. National Professor of the Year by the Council for Advancement and Support of Education and the Carnegie Foundation for the Advancement of Teaching, and in 2012 he received the Holocaust Educational Foundation's Distinguished Achievement Award for Holocaust Studies and Research.*

♪♪

The world is a beautiful place / to be born into / . . . if you don't mind a touch of hell / now and then . . .

—Lawrence Ferlinghetti, *Pictures of the Gone World*

Not for the first time, but in particular ways that presently press hard upon liberal arts colleges, the tasks of teaching and doing research in liberal arts settings take place in perilous times. In that situation, and specifically in the middle of the twenty-first century's second decade, when debates about MOOCs (massive open online courses), "flipped" classrooms, and the future of the humanities are often center stage, the question "What matters most?" looms large. Reflecting on themes related to those propositions, considering in particular how perilous times ought to affect teaching practices, especially in liberal arts colleges, I will draw mainly on two sources: (1) the insights of some poets who have been meaningful guides for me in the latter stages of my career as a teacher-scholar, and (2) thoughts not only related to those insights but also prompted by lifelong engagement with liberal arts colleges and the education they need to foster. Figuratively as well as literally, my reflections have much to do with rivers, dark times and places, and ordinary but immensely valuable particularities of the earth in which human life is planted and spent.

Privileges and Responsibilities

Counting my undergraduate education at Pomona College, I have spent more than fifty years in close affiliation with small, residential liberal arts colleges. Born in 1940, eventually trained in philosophy, I began my college teaching career in 1966. My life has coincided with perilous times: World War II and the Holocaust; the ravages of colonialism, civil rights struggles, and nuclear threats; Vietnam and Watergate; ethnic cleansing in the former Yugoslavia; genocide in Rwanda and Darfur; carnage in Iraq, Afghanistan, and Syria; militant religious fundamentalism; the Palestinian-Israeli conflict; natural disasters and economic upheavals of one kind or another; global warming and climate change—that's the short list. Nothing suggests that the disaster count will shrink any time soon, let alone that it will end. All the while, I have been privileged, really privileged, to be a liberal arts college professor. What have I done with that advantage? In the life that is left to me, what will I do with the privileged existence that continues to be mine in perilous times? As the twenty-first century unfolds, what should liberal arts colleges do in their fraught circumstances?

In the summer of 2001, I gave a beginning-of-the-year talk to first-year students as they entered Claremont McKenna College (CMC), the liberal arts college that was my academic home for more than forty years. My remarks contained a poem from Lawrence Ferlinghetti's *Pictures of the Gone World*. Its opening lines, the epigraph for this essay, move like this: "The world is a beautiful place / to be born into / if you don't mind happiness / not always being / so very much fun / if you don't mind a touch of hell / now and then / just when everything is fine."[1] Using Ferlinghetti's poem as a point of departure, my theme for the new liberal arts students at CMC on that late summer evening was that *we should take nothing good for granted.*

My talk ended. Everyone left. The students went their ways. I headed home. When I got up the next morning, I found myself watching hijacked-planes-turned-into-al-Qaeda-missiles as their attack on the World Trade Center changed twenty-first-century life decisively. I hope and trust that nothing resembling 9/11 will take place the morning after these words are read, but Ferlinghetti's observations about the fragile and even problematic beauty of the world and the reminder to take nothing good for granted are among the themes that are worth revisiting, particularly as liberal arts colleges and, in particular, we liberal arts college professors consider privileges and responsibilities.

One further preliminary word: With the discipline of philosophy at its base, my liberal arts college teaching and writing have concentrated on the Holocaust, genocide, and other mass atrocity crimes, including sexual violence in conflict situations, as well as on various American studies topics. The latter emphasis produced a focus on that tantalizing, ambiguous, fraught, clichéd but persistent idea of the American Dream. That work has taken me into the fields of history and literature, religion, politics, and more. Among other things, it keeps me looking for American poets who may help me. So, with the company of Ferlinghetti and three more American poets, consider what might happen as a result of thinking about what matters most with special reference to liberal arts colleges and the education they need to provide in perilous times.

The Niagara River

One of North America's breathtaking sights is the Niagara River as it becomes Niagara Falls. One can scarcely watch that transformation without feeling terror as well as awe. For the beauty of the place can be chilling as it makes one consider the fate to be met by whatever is swept over the escarpment, plunged into the mist, and dashed on the rocks below.

These days I think about the Niagara River not because I have recently been to Niagara Falls but because of the California poet Kay Ryan. By now poet laureate of the United States, MacArthur Fellow, Pulitzer Prize winner, recipient of the National Humanities Medal, and more, she was a stranger to me until I heard her interviewed one summer evening in 2006 and listened to her read some of her poetry on what was then the *MacNeil/Lehrer Report*, the PBS newscast that features American poets from time to time. I was hooked by a poem that spoke about the ways in which a person's life "should leave deep tracks" but, for one reason or another, usually doesn't. Ryan calls that poem, "Things Shouldn't Be So Hard," which is also the line with which it ends.[2]

Ryan's poem and especially its conclusion are about important things. A liberal arts college could be governed, a whole liberal arts education could emerge, by unpacking the elements embedded in them. I will come back to that claim momentarily, but when I learned that the source of the poem—about hard things that shouldn't be—was a collection titled *The Niagara River*, my interest grew. When I got the book, I found it full of poetic provocations that include the title poem, which Ryan also read that night on PBS. It envisions people floating on the Niagara River, calmly conversing, picnicking, and observing the shoreline as they go with the river's flow. They do know, the poem says, that they are on the Niagara River, but, Ryan warns in closing, "it is hard to remember / what that means."[3]

What about liberal arts colleges, the education they offer, and the professors who are responsible for both? Are we on the Niagara River? What would such location mean? Why are things—remembering among them—so hard? In their deceptively simple noticing and imagery, Kay Ryan's poems are loaded not only with senses of peril and loss but also with questions that weave their way through them, questions that make us think about what matters most. They—the poems and the questions—can make one inquire in significant ways. So while the first main point that I want to make about liberal arts colleges in perilous times is that they should teach us to take nothing good for granted, the second can be put in this way: Liberal arts education is not primarily about a core curriculum or a textual canon. It is not mainly about information that every so-called educated person needs to know. At least in my experience, *liberal arts education is fundamentally about questions, about the inquiry they invite and the thoughtfulness they inspire.* The questions I have in mind are ancient but also fresh and new. By no means is Kay Ryan's poetry the only source that evokes and invokes them. Far from it, for the questions are embedded in our living, in history, in events and experiments, in art and music as well as in words. They can even be found in silence and in wonder, which Plato thought was the experience that led to philosophy.

Many questions belong in and to the liberal arts, questions that need to be at the heart of the liberal arts college, but none are more important than those that pertain to ethics. High on my list are the following examples: What should we do? What is right? Am I doing my best? How should we live given the context of our times? What must we do to keep atrocity at bay? At its core and at their best, liberal arts colleges highlight persistent and systematic inquiry governed by such questions and the data that inform such inquiry if it is to be pursued responsibly and well. The goal of such education is not so much to teach people what to think, although that work has its place, but rather to show why sound inquiry is important and what it entails, to promote respect for evidence, and to explore how feeling and emotion as well as dispassionate research can best instruct and guide us. The dispositions that characterize my understanding of the liberal arts do not settle what should be unsettled and unsettling, but instead they open minds and hearts to foster learning so that evidence for and against positions and policies can be assessed in ways that encourage wisdom about the common good. This work ranks high on the list of things that matter most. It does so because, in one way or another, we are on the Niagara River. As Kay Ryan reminds us, it is not enough just to know this; we also need to remember what that means. Otherwise, things will be harder than they should be—indeed, to such an extent that they may just be over.

This Failure

Paul Hunter, another contemporary American poet, lives and works in Seattle, Washington, where he also is a self-described "grassroots arts activist" and "shade-tree mechanic."[4] Hunter spent formative years on farms, Kentucky fields among them. "It's the lens through which I see the world," I heard him say on another of those PBS evening news poetry spots. Hunter's diverse interests and talents include repairing things, often things that have been thrown away because, apparently, they have no value. He says,

> For most of my adult life now, I've been finding broken instruments or people give me broken instruments, and I fix them, and they get another life. There's a part of me that's so cheered

by that, and it may be part of the same thing that happens with words, with language, that you take a phrase, you take a phrase, you take a set of phrases that are shopworn, that people have had around them and not recognized, and take them and put them into a context that gives them a sharpened meaning of freshness.[5]

This combination of experiences and the moods attending them finds expression in poetry by Hunter that concentrates on failures, on mendings of the shopworn that can approach miraculous, and on what he calls "ripening," which is also the title of one of his poetry books. Two samples of Hunter's perspectives can further focus what's most important about and for liberal arts colleges in perilous times. First, in a poem called "This Failure," Hunter concentrates on the ground on which we stand, which, in its way, can be akin to Kay Ryan's Niagara River. Hunter takes his reader into a farm field that won't yield a crop this year. Too much rain or not enough has fallen. The sun has been too hot or the temperature has dipped too low. Bugs and blights have wreaked their havoc. Cultivation hasn't worked, and what's to be made of this loss? If it is not to be the end, "if there is to be another crop," writes Hunter, someone must "clear away or turn under / mow rake and burn off this failure."[6]

If liberal arts education, the mission of liberal arts colleges, and the responsibility of liberal arts professors are fundamentally about questions, especially ethical ones that drive inquiry about what is most important, then experiences of the kind that Hunter's poem ponders are of utmost significance as well. Absent failure, discouragement, and despair, things would not be so hard, but it is scarcely possible to imagine life without them—and even worse. The philosopher G. W. F. Hegel was right when he referred to history as "this slaughter-bench, upon which the happiness of nations, the wisdom of states, and the virtues of individuals were sacrificed."[7] Even while we consider why things take those turns and how they get and seem to stay that way, the issue persists: So long as liberal arts colleges endure, their question-oriented work remains to be done if, as Hunter says, "there is to be another crop," a different and better one perhaps. So a third theme that greatly matters in and for liberal arts education and the colleges and professors entrusted to advance it in perilous times is that *the future, scarred though it is and stripped of illusions as it must be, still awaits determination.*

The outlook of a second Paul Hunter poem, one called "For the Miracle," enriches that theme.[8] This time Hunter envisions not a barren field but a cluttered workshop. The partners of its grease-stained bench and its well-worn but ever-ready vice jaws are old coffee cans filled with assorted nails and screws, mixed nuts and bolts, waiting to be of use. On the floor are broken, shopworn things, odd parts of this and that, stuff that has gotten in the way but been consigned to this place by someone, sometime, for who knows what. Hunter sees these elements—maybe trash, good for nothing, to some—as raw materials waiting "for the miracle," the caring, imaginative, and creative human touch that could redesign and reconfigure, recreate and relate them to be of service anew.

This "ripening" of Hunter's suggests that what is fragmented, what has been ripped apart, what has been let go, broken, heaved, tossed aside, and dumped may yet have new life, can still "serve in turn," can be "of use once again." Hunter should not be misunderstood. This repairer-of-brokenness is not saying that everything will turn out well. He's not saying everything can be fixed and made whole again. His poetry is not a theodicy that finds everything happening for reasons that are ultimately sufficient. Hunter himself puts it this way:

> For a long time, I thought I had only one note, the elegiac—speaking well at funerals, barefoot in the rubble of the past. But then I realized that was a stall, a dodge, and getting on with one's life entails savoring the present moment while squishing one's toes in the muck of history, smacking one's lips over the memorable meal, praising what the cook forgot to season, singing even on an empty stomach. And further, piling crib and love-nest and sickbed with music and jokes and stories and edible tidbits—all of which go into making good poems, that together might conjure the world to come, the world lost.[9]

Hunter knows "the muck of history," the sadness, melancholy, and grief that swirl through it. But he's about "getting on with one's life," doing the best one can to defy the odds that would wear the world—and us—down and out. Liberal arts education isn't worth much fuss, liberal arts colleges and professors aren't worth supporting, unless through and through they really help us to do just that kind of "getting on with one's life." Such striving uplifts a fourth point that seems worth driving home as we think about the liberal arts college in perilous times: In the shops of liberal arts education, on the work-scarred planks of its benches, where, as Hunter says, "grease meets paint meets sawtooth chisel," *a premium belongs on honest appraisal of the human predicament.* That appraisal must not be general or abstract but needs to bear down with lucidity about the particularities of our predicament, sorting them, in Hunter's words, "by size wingnut from locknut / from wood screw machine screw," and with emphasis on figuring out how things in their brokenness may be mended and restored and, at least to that extent, "finished and praised."[10]

The Darkness around Us Is Deep

The year 2004–2005, a sabbatical year—one of the special privileges that liberal arts professors enjoy from time to time—took me to the Center for Advanced Holocaust Studies at the United States Holocaust Memorial Museum in Washington, D.C. Walking to the museum each day, I passed the red brick, next-door building that housed the United States Forest Service. As I went by the Forest Service headquarters, which at the time included a special exhibit about the history of Smokey the Bear, I also thought about the great—sometimes burning—forests of the American Northwest and the town called Winthrop where my granddaughter lives and, now, so do I.

Winthrop is about as far from Auschwitz as one can get. It sits small in the Methow Valley, a place of spectacular beauty on the eastern slope of the majestic Cascade Range, far north in the state of Washington. Native Americans knew that valley and its glistening rivers long before it became one of the last places in the American West to be settled by white men and women.

While visiting the Methow Valley during the Christmas holidays in December 2005, I noticed that my daughter had given my son-in-law a small book called *Even in Quiet Places*. It contains poems by William Stafford. Born in Kansas in 1914, Stafford died in 1993. After taking the unpopular stance of conscientious objector during World War II, he taught for many years at Lewis and Clark College, a liberal arts college near Portland, Oregon. He won many awards for his poetry, which gripped me as I read *Even in Quiet Places*.

My further reading of his poetry and about his life turned up the fact that two forest rangers, Curtis Edwards and Sheela McLean, had contacted William Stafford one day. They had an unusual request: Would he help them create some "poetry road signs" for the North Cascades Highway? Stafford accepted their invitation, which led to his writing some twenty poems that form a collection now called "The Methow River Poems." Several of these were selected for the poetry road signs that can be found at various places along or adjacent to that magnificent mountain road.

Stafford's poems often focus on the natural world and frequently on our abuse of it. Also drenched in history, his verse laments the carnage we human beings inflict and encourages resistance against it. Although the Holocaust was not Stafford's theme, he knew plenty about war and genocide. In a short poem called "Meditation," for example, he conjures up weapons "loaded with darkness" and suggests that while God holds still, that darkness threatens, if it does not engulf, the world "again, / and again and again."[11]

Stafford also had a keen sense for the difficult, painful choices that life puts before us. These choices are ones where we know that none of the options are very good, but where we have to make a decision and take a stand. In "Traveling through the Dark," arguably his best-known poem, Stafford drew on an episode in his own experience to explore that dilemma and the responsibilities it confers. One night he came across a deer struck to death by a preceding car on the narrow Wilson River road. Realizing the danger that other drivers might encounter, Stafford stopped and dragged the deer to the side of the road, seeing as he did so that "she was large in the belly" because this doe's fawn, still alive, was waiting to be born. Stafford hesitated: What to do? "I thought hard for us all—my only swerving," he says, "then pushed her over the edge into the river."[12]

Stafford's poem does not say what he thought about when he mentions that he "hesitated" and "thought hard for us all" before he pushed the doe "over the edge into the river." It seems dubious that his mind turned to salvation for the fawn "alive, still, never to be born." He was too realistic for that. More likely, Stafford was in agreement with Kay Ryan that "things shouldn't be so hard." But this time that's the way they were, and the decision Stafford made—steeped in regret and sadness and irony that continued to haunt him, for the poem came sometime after the actual episode—was for the sake of life-saving. Here the fifth insight I want to drive home is not an assertion but a question: *Can liberal arts education, colleges, and professors equip people to live like that in perilous times?* Their value, it seems to me, is dependent on the extent to which the answer to that question can be *yes*. In large measure, whether that possibility is remote or near at hand depends, in turn, on the commitment and determination of teacher-scholars who are privileged to do their work in liberal arts colleges.

Reading, as much of it as possible, is crucial for that work. Liberal arts colleges have to be places that persistently emphasize careful reading, an ongoing activity that needs to take place interactively as well as individually. "A Ritual to Read to Each Other," another of William Stafford's poems, augments and amplifies those propositions. The reading that Stafford seems to have in mind depends upon but is not confined to books and articles, poems and stories. Moving through and beyond them, especially in the experience of sharing them together, inside and outside of classrooms, an expansion of understanding can be found. That understanding can keep our "mutual life" from getting "lost in the dark," because it includes both knowing one another better and, crucially, uprooting what Stafford calls "the root of all cruelty": namely, "to know what occurs but not recognize the fact." I think I see what Stafford is underscoring, for it was through reading that I found my teaching, writing, indeed my life, changing as I learned more about the history and ongoing reality of atrocity and found it to be a fact—not a relativistic value judgment—that such things are wrong, that I must not be indifferent to them, and that I needed to do what I could to change my liberal arts college, my academic fields, and myself accordingly. Stafford helped me to see what I believe liberal arts college professors especially should know and enact. Not only is it crucial that "awake people be awake," but also his poem about reading to each other emphasizes that "the signals we give—yes, or no, or maybe— / should be clear: the darkness around us is deep."[13]

In perilous times, *one more thing that matters most is that we do not get lost in the dark.* Liberal arts colleges grounded in questions that keep us awake, tempered by spirits of resistance against despair, steeped in commitments to mend and repair so that what is broken can yet be of good use—these are capacities that together, in Paul Hunter's words, "might conjure the world to come, the world lost."

Teaching Practices

To advance the aims that I take to be at the heart of the matter for liberal arts colleges, I have found that two specific teaching practices—essay writing and tutorials—can be especially helpful in encouraging such movement. Both are so integral to liberal arts education and so congenial to the mission of liberal arts colleges that these institutions cannot be at their best if those practices are slighted. The two practices, moreover, are far removed from the MOOCs that have occupied much of the academic limelight of late. MOOCs may have their place in the liberal arts college, a possibility I leave to others to defend, but they can never be a substitute for the practices I have in mind. Furthermore, if my recommended practices get the attention they deserve, especially but not only in liberal arts colleges, the perceived significance of the humanities will grow. As traditional as they are important, essay writing and tutorials underscore the importance of questions; both maximize opportunity for considering what is most important and for helping people to avoid getting lost in the dark by taking good things for granted. Liberal arts colleges should always excel in emphasizing writing. Rooted in that tradition, I have long believed that one of my chief responsibilities as a liberal arts professor has been to urge my students and myself to write, rewrite, and write some more. For in the silent grappling with questions that writing requires, insight emerges as it can in no other way.

At their best, liberal arts colleges teach students that they can and need to write in different ways to advance robust thinking and thoughtful action. To enhance such writing, liberal arts colleges must have professors who practice well the very writing they need to teach. Again and again, my teaching introduced students to the discipline of writing short reflective essays. In a less-is-more approach, these essay-writing opportunities encouraged students to gain mastery and perspective on the substantial reading that accompanied the writing assignments, to explore their own angles of vision, and to see that every answer leads to other questions, which is a discovery that, among other things, can teach people to take nothing good for granted.

In each of my courses, but especially in those on the Holocaust, genocide, and other mass atrocity crimes, I typically planned a sequence of question-based topics that formed the parameters for the students' reflection. Each topic began with a quotation from the reading we had done together. Then it posed questions for the students to ponder as they thought best. The essays needed to be compact. No more than four or five double-spaced pages, I would tell the students, nudging them to make every word count, for much can be learned—as poets show—in discerning what can be done with a handful of words. That discipline creates its own instructive tensions between speech and silence, between what can and cannot be said.

My intentions did not control what the students said or how they expressed themselves. Instead, I hoped that the topics would lead to lines of thought that incrementally deepened both the students' understanding and their senses of wonder. As I read and evaluated what the students wrote, I found that such results took place not only for them but also for me.

The liberal arts college provides the context and the privilege that can allow these developments to flourish. Relatively small classes, opportunities for close interaction between teachers and students—these are central among the favorable conditions that liberal arts colleges provide like no others. Seizing them to the fullest advantage with regard to the irreplaceable educational benefits that come with persistent and well-supervised writing is both the privilege and the responsibility of liberal arts professors, especially, but not only, those in the humanities.

Whenever possible, I found it helpful to intensify my courses and their writing inquiry by the ritual of reading to each other that is classically embodied in the tutorial, a time-honored way of learning that creatively toppled lecture-driven and test-governed relations between teachers and students long before the buzz gave "flipped" education cutting-edge status. Neither a class nor a seminar—and certainly not a MOOC—but complementary to all three, tutorials can be defined and organized in various ways. They can be developed in the sciences as well as in the humanities, but whatever their precise format may be, these intensive, interactive encounters between teachers and students epitomize what liberal arts education and liberal arts colleges must reemphasize if they are to be true to their best traditions and to make their most distinctive contributions.

In my teaching, the following plan had good results. Students in a class of mine were paired to meet with me for an hour or more. The day before our meeting, the two students exchanged the papers they had written and gave me copies as well. The students and I read the essays and prepared written comments about them before the tutorial took place. The tutorial itself would begin with one student's oral response to the other's essay. The aim of this succinct response—indeed the aim of the entire tutorial process—would be less to criticize and more to encourage the writer to explain, expand, and defend the main points that she or he wanted to make. As the writer responded and conversation between the two students ensued, I mostly listened, intervening mainly to question, clarify, and coach. Midway through the tutorial, the students reversed their roles, and we explored some more.

At the tutorial's conclusion, the written comments prepared earlier would be shared. Subsequently, the students revised their essays in light of the tutorial discussion and the written comments. I responded to those revisions with further written commentary. Circumstances permitting, the next time the students had a tutorial with me, their partners would be different. As this process continued throughout a semester, progress would be made on the full range of comprehension envisioned in Stafford's poem "A Ritual to Read to Each Other."

In perilous times, liberal arts colleges are on the Niagara River. Among the most important meanings of that condition is that liberal arts colleges need to ramp up, revitalize, and double down on the teaching practices that are predominant within them when such colleges are in their prime. Abundant and careful reading together among students and teachers, intensive and frequent essay writing, the close contact between students and teachers afforded by tutorials (every liberal arts college student should regularly experience them in one form or another)—these are hallmarks of the liberal arts college at its best. The darkness around us is deep. Therefore, one of the things that shouldn't be so hard is the rededication of liberal arts colleges to accent and advance the practices of essay writing and tutorials. Absent that rededication, "the muck of history" is more likely to engulf us.

Epilogue

One of William Stafford's "Methow River Poems" is called "Being a Person." It invites a reader/observer to contemplate the Methow River as its clear, cold water rushes to the Columbia River and then to the Pacific Ocean. In perilous times, that poem's ending makes a good conclusion for this stock-taking about liberal arts colleges, the education they should encourage, and the professors who are privileged to teach in those special places.

Stafford invites his reader to "stand by the river." That place might be along the Niagara as well as the Methow or the Columbia. It might be where floods of tears are shed amid the cruelty of mass atrocity crimes. Or the standpoint might be closer to the insistent hope of the biblical prophet Amos: "Let justice roll down like waters, and righteousness like an ever-flowing stream" (Am 5:24). In any case, Stafford's urging is to "be a person here. . . . How you stand here is important. How you / listen for the next things to happen. How you breathe."[14]

Whatever else it may be, liberal arts education in perilous times is about those things: what we hear as we listen for what is happening, how we breathe, how we stand. Nothing could matter more for liberal arts colleges and professors as we keep remembering what is hard, namely, that nothing human, natural, or divine guarantees respect for what is good and right, beautiful and true, but nothing is more important than our commitment to honor and defend those things, for they remain as fundamental as they are fragile, as precious as they are endangered.

Notes

1. Lawrence Ferlinghetti, *Pictures of the Gone World* (San Francisco: City Lights, 1995 [1955]). The poem is number 25. No page numbers are provided.

2. Kay Ryan, *The Niagara River* (New York: Grove Press, 2005), 40–41.

3. Ibid., 1.

4. See the biographical information about Hunter on the website for the Silverfish Review Press: http://www.silverfishreviewpress.com/?page=books&bookID=19.

5. See Hunter's interview with Gwen Ifill at the PBS website: http://www.pbs.org/newshour/bb/entertainment/july-dec07/ripening_07-09.html.

6. Paul Hunter, *Ripening* (Eugene: Silverfish Review Press, 2007), 37.

7. G. W. F. Hegel, *Introduction to the Philosophy of History*, trans. Leo Rauch (Indianapolis: Hackett, 1988), 24.

8. The poem can be found at the PBS website containing Hunter's interview with Gwen Ifill: http://www.pbs.org/newshour/bb/entertainment/july-dec07/ripening_07-09.html.

9. Hunter, *Ripening*, 83.

10. See "For the Miracle," which can be found at the PBS website referenced in note 8.

11. William Stafford, "Meditation," in *The Darkness Around Us Is Deep: Selected Poems of William Stafford*, ed. Robert Bly (New York: HarperCollins, 1993), 123.

12. William Stafford, "Traveling through the Dark," in *The Way It Is: New & Selected Poems* (St. Paul: Graywolf Press, 1998), 77.

13. William Stafford, "A Ritual to Read to Each Other," in *The Way It Is: New & Selected Poems* (St. Paul: Graywolf Press, 1998), 75–76.

14. William Stafford, "Being a Person," in *Even in Quiet Places: Poems by William Stafford* (Lewiston: Confluence Press, 1996), 89.

Importing the American Liberal Arts College?

·•——•·

KRISTINE MITCHELL AND COTTEN SEILER

Kristine Mitchell has a joint appointment in the Political Science and International Studies departments at Dickinson College. Her research focuses on the intersection between international relations and comparative politics and investigates the impact of European integration on individuals, groups, and institutions in the various EU member states. She has collaborated extensively with students in her recent research on the relationship between study abroad and political identity and co-authored an article on the subject with a Dickinson student. A product of the liberal arts, she completed her BA (in European studies) at Oberlin College before earning her MA and PhD (in political science) at Princeton University. She has been a visiting researcher at Northwestern University, Science Po (Paris), New York University, and University of California, Berkeley.

Cotten Seiler is Associate Professor of American Studies at Dickinson College. His teaching and research interests include US cultural and intellectual history, popular culture, and social and political theory. His work on automobility and US history has appeared in a number of international journals and in his book Republic of Drivers: A Cultural History of Automobility in America *(2008). He also serves as book review editor at* American Quarterly.

ॐ

The liberal arts model of higher education is simultaneously under attack in the United States—the place where it is most entrenched—and being embraced, at least in part, elsewhere in the world. In this essay, we look at the utilitarian concerns that motivate these domestic and international shifts, paying special attention to what Chinese experiments with liberal arts education might mean for future developments in that country.

"Irrelevant"? The Attack on the Liberal Arts Model in the United States

In recent years, there have been a number of high-profile challenges to the funding of liberal arts disciplines in American public universities. A number of prominent and vocal critics portray allocation of public funds to these fields as wasteful and decadent. Florida governor Rick Scott, for example, said in a 2011 interview that he wanted to shift funds away from programs like anthropology (his daughter's major!) and instead "spend our money getting people science, technology, engineering and math degrees. That's what our kids need to focus all of their time and attention on: Those type of degrees that, when they get out of school, they can get a job [sic]."[1] The idea was echoed more recently by North Carolina governor Pat McCrory, who, in a 2013 radio show, belittled gender studies and foreign language programs, asking, "What are we teaching these courses for if they are not going to help get a job?"[2]

Liberal arts education is often caricatured as a foolish, irrelevant diversion of an out-of-touch elite, not something to be pursued by anyone interested in employability. As Scott told his audience, anthropology is "a great degree if people want to get it, but we don't need them here [in Florida]." McCrory remarked, "If you want to take gender studies that's fine. Go to a private school, and take it. But I don't want to subsidize that if that's not going to get someone a job."

Scott and McCrory ignore, however, the good reasons—discussed here—to believe that the liberal arts model is excellent preparation not just for a life of philosophical contemplation but for a substantive career in any number of fields. But the idea that the purpose of higher education is to slot graduates directly into currently popular professional niches has become pervasive, leading some to advocate cutting public funding for higher education, or as a 2012 article in *Forbes* magazine suggested, "eliminating the departments that offer majors that employers do not value."[3]

The comments of Scott and McCrory (and others) are representative of the most recent attack on liberal arts institutions and curricula; but targeting liberal arts institutions is far from new. In fact, the critique of liberal arts education in America is nearly as old as the institutions that provide it. The most influential historiography of US higher education puts the heyday of the liberal arts college at around 1820, before the advent of Jacksonian democracy and the Industrial Revolution. Denominational, insular, and resolutely elitist, these eighteenth-century institutions prepared propertied, white male students for leadership in local and regional political-religious communities, and in the larger civic life of the nation. The curriculum combined the classical with the ecclesiastical, the intellectual with the ethical, to produce the types of virtuous citizens the new republican form of government required. In the historian Richard Hofstadter's recounting of the emergence of academic freedom, the replacement of the tradition-bound "old-time college" by the dynamic, progressive university based on the German model in the latter decades of the nineteenth century was the best thing to have happened for the sake of American knowledge, industry, and democracy.[4] As the university emerged as a force in US higher education, it portrayed itself in opposition to the liberal arts college, which university officials cast, in the words of one Stanford president, as "antiquated, belated, arrested, starved."[5] The university, by contrast, was said to foster industrial growth and social change, by providing students with a more applied and diverse curriculum, severing most ecclesiastical ties, and revising the hidebound policies of most liberal arts colleges that excluded women and people of color.

Driving most of these changes were the two phases of the Industrial Revolution that transformed the US economy and society in the nineteenth and early twentieth centuries: the first phase saw the emergence of industrial manufacturing and the market economy; the second, the expansion of and intensification of control over the productive process by means of technology and "scientific management" of labor. These developments created the need for the university and shaped its mission of generating practical and specialized knowledge and training effective technicians and professional managers for the new corporate economy. The early twentieth century saw an intensification of the disdain with which the universities and their supporters regarded the liberal arts college, with its curriculum of subjects irrelevant to these technocratic and bureaucratic ends. Progressive reformers, too, saw universities as the key sites of activist scholarship, mostly in new social sciences such as sociology, geared toward the amelioration of the social problems generated by industrial capitalism.

There were (and are) real differences between the university and the liberal arts college, but the nineteenth-century critiques of the liberal arts colleges were misleading. The elitism charge also applied to universities, which despite their rhetoric of democratization tended to be sites of reproduction of elite power and privilege. And the liberal arts college changed significantly during the Progressive Era. Pressed to respond both to the university's critique and the political and economic upheavals and ethical dilemmas of the nineteenth century, the majority of surviving liberal arts colleges evolved into more ecumenical places. Led by pioneering progressive institutions like Oberlin, Middlebury, and Spelman, liberal arts colleges began to educate both women and African Americans in increasing numbers. Even the more religious colleges shed much of their asceticism as they responded to these pressures, and as the sects that they served took up more of a worldly mission themselves.

Moreover, despite characterizing the liberal arts as outdated, by the first decade of the twentieth century, many universities had begun to incorporate or emulate liberal arts colleges and to praise their merits as feeders to and partners with the universities. Harvard president A. Lawrence Lowell, speaking at his 1909 inauguration, called for a resuscitation of the liberal arts college, which he described as giving "a freedom of thought, a breadth of outlook, a training for citizenship, which neither the secondary nor the professional school in this country can equal."[6] Indeed, a number of educators and intellectuals in the Progressive Era and the interwar period rebelled against what they saw as an increasing instrumental higher educational system. This system might have been producing effective "professionals," but it was failing at a more profound educational mission, which, in the words of Antioch College president Arthur Morgan, speaking at a 1931 conference, was "to orient and to integrate personality, to develop the entire mind of the student."[7] On the eve of World War II the liberal arts college had emerged as the institutional locus of experimental pedagogy within US higher education, drawing inspiration from the theories of John Dewey and others that stressed creativity, autonomy, and a democratic ethos in the transmission and acquisition of knowledge. The Deweyan insistence on experiential rather than received learning, and on the student's intellectual self-discovery, continues to animate most liberal arts colleges to the present day.

In recent decades, however, the tide of public sentiment has again turned against the liberal arts. Today, well-intentioned parents and guidance counselors often advise students that—especially in a tough economy—it's "safer" to pursue a degree in a professional field like health or business rather than indulge in the "luxury" of a liberal arts major like biology, American studies, or politics. Numbers of liberal arts majors have declined, and demand for professional and technical degrees increased, even at institutions that claim to offer a liberal arts education.[8]

It's not just the larger public institutions that are backing away from the liberal arts model. The private liberal arts colleges that are nearly unique to the United States have increasingly adopted the pre-professional model of higher education, either alongside or in place of the traditional liberal arts model. And where pre-professional programs have been adopted, they have often taken over. One researcher found that, by the 1990s, two-thirds of institutions claiming to offer a liberal arts education were, in fact, dominated by students studying in professional programs.[9]

In 1990, the economist David W. Breneman posed the question "Are We Losing Our Liberal Arts Colleges?" in a controversial article of the same title in *The College Board Review*. Breneman answered in the affirmative, finding that of the approximately 600 institutions the Carnegie Foundation for the Advancement of Teaching listed as liberal arts colleges, only 212 could be defined as such under the more rigorous criteria he used. According to Breneman, liberal arts colleges were "distinguished by a mission of providing four-year baccalaureate education exclusively, in a setting that emphasizes and rewards good teaching above all else," by "offering a curriculum that does not cater to current student concerns with the job market," by their small enrollments, and by their lack or dearth of professional programs. Breneman argued that the nearly 400 institutions he excluded had veered from the liberal arts model in response to economic pressures, becoming, "for want of a better term—small professional colleges."[10] A 2012 study reapplied Breneman's criteria to the remaining 212 liberal arts institutions and reaffirmed that the liberal arts had become increasingly decentered as a result of expanding professional programs at approximately 70 of them. The researchers found that despite the "liberal arts" moniker, many of these institutions no longer distinguished themselves by "a curriculum based primarily in arts and science fields; small classes and close student-faculty relationships; full-time study and student residence on campus; and little emphasis on vocational preparation or study in professional fields."[11]

What Makes a Liberal Arts Education Unique?

While there is often disagreement over precisely what the term "liberal arts" refers to in higher education, we submit—on the basis of our reading of literature on the subject and our personal experiences with the liberal arts model—that there are four characteristics that distinguish the liberal arts model from the alternatives.

First, a liberal arts education has a particular objective, namely, to *educate* individuals for a life of learning and intellectual growth rather than to *train* them in preparation for a certain type of career. Liberal arts education is not about offering certification or credentials, although to be sure, the BA functions as such as surely as an MBA or a JD. While reasonable people may disagree about whether this major or that is "really" a liberal arts discipline (computer science springs to mind, but at our institution, international business and management is even more hotly contested), to our minds, what is more important is the institutional objective for teaching a subject, and—relatedly—the approach to teaching it. When a subject is taught with the aim of imparting marketable skills that will attract employers after graduation, it enters into the territory of vocational training—whether the skills in question are the ability to speak Mandarin, perform econometric analysis, write computer programs, or take blood samples. Because the objective is skills transfer, training rarely moves beyond the mechanical "how-to" level. This is not to imply that such training is in any sense basic; on the contrary, the topic may become quite advanced and the techniques extremely sophisticated. Yet so long as the primary objective is the development of a set of practical skills, this is best characterized as vocational training. In the Middle Ages, such training was referred to as the *artes mechanicae*—the mechanical or practical arts.

Now, to be clear, such training is the prerequisite of all education, regardless of discipline or educational objective. At the most fundamental level, one must be trained to read. Beyond that, classicists have to learn the mechanics of Latin and Ancient Greek, historians have to learn names and dates—there's no way around it. The question is really about whether the training has a utilitarian objective (this will get me a better job) or whether it is intended to serve as a stepping-stone toward further intellectual inquiry and growth. For when these skills are learned, not as an *end* in themselves but as the *means* to investigate the world around us—well, now we are in the realm of the liberal arts. When students learn, not only the foundational knowledge or the mechanics of a subject but also how to be critical of those foundations, how to challenge the conventional wisdom, and how to use insights from other disciplines to pose new questions and answer old ones, then they are learning within the tradition of the *artes liberales*—the liberal arts—whether the subject is computer science, classics, or anthropology. For the primary objective of a liberal arts education is to teach students to think for themselves.

The second characteristic of liberal arts education is its distinctive curriculum, which privileges academic breadth. In contrast with the dominant model in global higher education, where students specialize early (often prior to arrival at the university) and pursue a single course of study throughout their degree, a liberal arts education hinges on the idea that students with knowledge of multiple disciplines are able to translate insights from one field to others, to think creatively about problems, and to find connections that specialists in only one area might otherwise miss. The American Association of Colleges and Universities (AACU) defines a liberal education as one that "provides students with broad knowledge of the wider world (e.g., science, culture, and society) as well as in-depth study in a specific area of interest."[12] What this means is that students not only complete a major in their chosen field but also complete a core curriculum or satisfy distribution requirements that expose them to the humanities, social sciences, and natural sciences. In short, while students complete a major that aims to provide academic depth in a single subject, exposure to other fields of study and areas of inquiry *complements* this specialization.

A third distinctive element of a liberal arts education is its pedagogy, which is premised on the idea that there is a synergy between academic research and teaching, and that the best source of knowledge about a subject is the scholars who actually shape that discipline. Contemporary liberal arts college faculty are neither exclusively teachers nor "mainly" researchers who also spend a few hours every week lecturing to undergraduates. They overwhelmingly tend to be contributors to their field who equally prize the opportunity to share their knowledge about their fields—or perhaps more accurately, to join with students in a process of inquiry. Because liberal arts pedagogy is animated by this spirit of joint inquiry, it requires engagement on the part of both students and faculty. Students are expected to be more than vessels into which knowledge is poured; they are expected to take responsibility for their own learning. Faculty are expected to be not just the talking head at the front of the classroom but facilitators who assist each student to navigate his or her way through the complexity of the subject at hand and to see connections between phenomena that may, at first glance, seem disparate. The liberal arts classroom is a place of two-way exchange between students and faculty rather than a one-way transmission belt from faculty to students. Cultivating this type of relationship between students and faculty means that large lecture halls must (for the most part) be traded for small classes where interaction can actually occur, where—on a daily basis—students contribute, and where faculty monitor students' progress, modifying the course as necessary to account for students' responses.

Finally, the fourth distinctive trait of a liberal arts education is its commitment to educating the whole person, both inside and outside of the classroom. The residential college, where students live together on campus, provides numerous opportunities for students' intellectual and personal development: student clubs for virtually any conceivable interest (some of which have faculty participation as well); cultural opportunities; extracurricular speakers; all manner of sports, athletic, and fitness activities. The whole point of the residential experience is to foster a sense of community and place, where students are free to develop their intellect and discover (or create) who they are going to be as adults. This is not considered to be peripheral to the liberal arts mission but central to it. Indeed, what happens outside the classroom can have as profound an effect on a student's intellectual growth as what happens inside.

Surely this emphasis on educating the entire individual stems from the rootedness of the liberal arts model in the Christian tradition. In the medieval European universities—the first liberal arts colleges—the entire intellectual endeavor was geared toward better understanding God and humans' relationship with the divine. And the small independent liberal arts colleges that sprang up in North America in the seventeenth, eighteenth, and nineteenth centuries were most often tied to specific confessional groups or sects. But though the liberal arts model has been almost completely secularized, the ideal of cultivating the entire person has endured.

The four characteristics that make a liberal arts education distinctive— eschewal of expressly professional objectives, broad curriculum, pedagogical commitment to faculty-student exchange, and promotion of extracurricular development of the whole individual—together comprise a liberal arts ideal. But does that ideal matter? Why should we care if the liberal arts model flourishes?

There are two characteristic defenses of the liberal arts model, a civic one and a utilitarian one. The civic rationale is predicated on the idea that a liberal arts education produces good citizens. The notion that liberal education is the cornerstone of citizenship goes back to ancient Greece and persisted through the Middle Ages, the Renaissance, the Enlightenment, and into the Modern Era. We believe it is still relevant today. Liberal arts students have the tools to become full signatories to the social contract: they are educated to be historically astute, confident about human potential but leery of hubris, simultaneously loyal to the nation and attuned to an egalitarian justice that transcends national borders. Let's call these claims the Jeffersonian defense of the liberal arts, as Jefferson envisioned a republic composed of citizens educated to practice public virtue.

This Jeffersonian rationale has been eclipsed of late by what we might call an instrumentalist defense of the liberal arts. According to this com- paratively recent line of reasoning, those trained in the liberal arts are particularly well poised to rise to prominence in their professional lives, precisely because their education enables them to recognize patterns, con- nections, and unfilled niches, to think creatively about problems, and to argue persuasively—to investors, customers, and courts—in promotion of their particular enterprises. In contrast to the pessimism of Rick Scott, Pat McCrory, and others regarding the unemployability of liberal arts graduates, the instrumentalist defense of liberal arts education asserts that the disposi- tions of resourcefulness, versatility, and autonomy stressed in a liberal arts education sustain and advantage graduates as they navigate the job market.

Supporters of the liberal arts like to say that a liberal arts education prepares students for jobs that haven't even been invented yet. Indeed, a liberal arts education can provide students with intellectual flexibility and an ability to think both critically and creatively. Whether they seek it out or not, students in a liberal arts program are exposed to different intellectual norms and different methods of asking and answering questions. They learn to grapple with clashing opinions and contradictory points of view. They are confronted with the fact that what constitutes evidence, an effective argument, and proof varies widely from one context to another.[13] Ideally, this results in intellectual agility, as students learn to navigate such disparate areas of inquiry. Learning foreign languages (even Swahili, so derided by Governor McCrory) can provide a window into other cultures and provide fresh insights into the assumptions of one's own culture. Responding to Governor Scott's derision of anthropology, Michael Crow, the president of Arizona State University, wrote in *Slate* that, if we want students capable of technical accomplishment, "we need all of the skill sets from anthropology to zoology as well as transdisciplinary perspectives. . . . Inspired engineering, in other words, could come as a consequence of familiarity with the development of counterpoint in Baroque music or cell biology. Or even the construction methods of indigenous tribes." The goal of education, he continues, "should not be to produce predetermined numbers of particular types of majors but, rather, to focus on how to produce individuals who are capable of learning anything over the course of their lifetimes."[14]

It is one thing for college and university presidents to tout the instrumental value of a liberal arts education, but recent surveys indicate that employers also recognize the importance of liberal arts training. A 2013 survey of American employers conducted by the AACU finds that employers view graduates with both broad and field-specific knowledge and skills more favorably than those who are more narrowly specialized. Indeed, 80 percent of employers reported that every college student, regardless of major, should acquire broad knowledge in the liberal arts and sciences, and 74 percent said they would recommend liberal arts education as the best way to prepare for success in today's global economy.[15] Furthermore, as we discuss later, the liberal arts model has been making inroads in China, Japan, and Korea, where "employers have complain[ed] about the inflexibility of a workforce educated without a focus on creativity or problem solving."[16] According to an education professor at the University of Hong Kong, "These countries realize that, in order to become a global leader, you need a creative class."[17]

It is fascinating that, at the same time that liberal arts education is pilloried in the United States, it has received increasing attention elsewhere. What is even more fascinating is that, while the liberal arts are too often dismissed in the United States as professionally irrelevant, the rise of the liberal arts abroad is driven precisely by utilitarian concerns. (This is in marked contrast to the civic and religious motivations that drove the creation of liberal arts colleges in the United States in the eighteenth and nineteenth centuries.) Among the recently developed international liberal arts programs with which we are familiar, the instrumentalist rationale is central for all but one (the exception being Quest University Canada).

Liberal Arts à la Carte

In the past fifteen years, there has been a growing international trend toward promoting the liberal arts as a means of promoting employability and driving economic development. Around the world, a number of new liberal arts programs have been created that are consciously modeled on the American liberal arts college. Sometimes these programs arise within existing universities; sometimes they motivate the creation of new institutions. But despite their common roots in the American liberal arts college model, these new programs have pursued a variety of paths, opting for certain elements of the liberal arts model while foregoing others.

At one extreme are institutions that adopt all four of the distinctive characteristics of the liberal arts model: the deferral of the professional objective, the curricular breadth, the centrality of pedagogy, and the extracurricular emphasis on community and development of the whole person. For example, at Quest University Canada, established in British Columbia in 2002, 425 students live on campus, where they spend half of their degree completing a core curriculum that ranges widely across the arts and sciences and then design their own inquiry for the second half. (Canada, it must be noted, also has at least two liberal arts colleges founded in the mid-nineteenth century, Saint Francis Xavier University and Mount Allison University.) In the Netherlands, a host of so-called university colleges have been established since 1998. These honors colleges, which are appended to venerable universities in Amsterdam, Leiden, Maastricht, Middelburg, Rotterdam, Twente, and Utrecht, enroll some six hundred to seven hundred undergraduate students, who live together and take courses in the humanities and social and natural sciences. The residential component is less central at Campion College, a Catholic institution founded in Sydney, Australia, in 2006, but establishing an intellectual community and providing for the education of the whole person are nevertheless clearly central to its mission. Campion bills itself as the "first Liberal Arts College in Australia" and offers a core liberal arts curriculum that includes Latin, literature, history, philosophy, theology, mathematics, and science.

However, the "whole package" of the liberal arts model is only rarely adopted. There are rather more examples of existing institutions that adopt certain liberal arts characteristics while leaving others aside. For example, a number of established European universities have seized, in particular, on the principle of academic breadth, while foregoing the other elements of the liberal arts model. New undergraduate degrees in liberal arts or liberal studies are now offered alongside the traditional, more specialized, disciplines at more than two dozen European universities, including Charles University (Czech Republic), Jacobs University Bremen (Germany), Warsaw University (Poland), Gotland University (Sweden), and University College London (UK). The introduction of liberal arts degrees is a fairly radical departure from the "Continental" model of higher education, which has traditionally emphasized specialized study within a single discipline and, often, an early differentiation between academic and professional education.[18] In Germany, for example, the separation of educational tracks into academic and vocational begins already at the late-primary level, while in France and Sweden certain types of vocational training begin at the secondary level.

If existing universities are experimenting with the adoption of a liberal arts curriculum, there is also a trend of establishing new institutions that are influenced by aspects of the liberal arts model, even when vocational training remains the major focus of undergraduate education. For example, Ashesi University, founded in 2002 in Accra, Ghana, offers its six hundred students degrees in business administration, computer science, or management information systems—disciplines intended to be vocational. But its founder, a Ghanaian alumnus of Swarthmore College and former engineer at Microsoft, insists the required core curriculum in the liberal arts "nurtures ethical thinking and fosters critical thinking" and will eventually help to "educate a new generation of ethical, entrepreneurial leaders in Africa [and] to cultivate within [its] students the critical thinking skills, the concern for others, and the courage it will take to transform a continent."[19] Beaconhouse National University, founded in 2003 in Lahore, calls itself the "first liberal arts university of Pakistan." In reality, its School of Liberal Arts comprises only one of nine faculties (the rest being professionally oriented). But its policies promote the curricular breadth, pedagogical style, and extracurricular development of the whole individual that are characteristic of the liberal arts model. For example, Beaconhouse offers credit for coursework done outside students' own degree programs; it fosters the creative and performing arts; and it emphasizes small, interactive classes, faculty mentorship of students, and the use of frequent written assignments rather than comprehensive exams as the basis for student evaluation. Certainly its claim that "students are encouraged to question assumptions, listen to diverse opinions and challenge convention" cleaves to the liberal arts tradition.[20]

China represents a particularly interesting example of the selective application of liberal arts principles to an existing system of higher education. As in the other cases, the move to incorporate the liberal arts into Chinese higher education is motivated by the utilitarian impetus of what we characterized as the instrumental defense of the model. As discussed earlier, that rationale asserts that material benefits accrue to those individuals, and by extension to companies and nations, trained to see and think broadly, to navigate and process complex and disparate knowledges, to foresee and adapt to change, and to communicate effectively and persuasively.

Over the past decade, Chinese educational leaders have signaled their recognition of the economic utility of the liberal arts education. Looking to models in US liberal arts institutions—which, like many US universities, have experienced a recent surge in matriculation of Chinese students—Chinese educators have taken to partnering with those institutions to create hybrid programs, creating their own standalone liberal arts colleges, and introducing liberal arts curricula into the traditional professional and technical universities. Experimental institutions such as Yuanjing Academy in Chongqing, Bo Ya College at Guangzhou's Sun Yat-Sen University, Yuanpei College at Beijing's Peking University, and Zhuhai's United International College are state-sanctioned alternatives to the Soviet model that has predominated in China since 1949. That model trains students in highly specialized fields oriented to industrial advance and military strength, and in the collectivist political philosophy of the state under Maoism. Its success in achieving for China the type of modernization its twentieth-century leaders sought cannot be denied.

Many educational authorities in China today, however, argue that for the current phase of national transformation, the Soviet model has limited utility. As envisioned by the now somewhat ironically named Chinese Communist Party (CCP), which has retained its grip on the state and economy despite the transformational turn away from Maoist doctrine and toward state capitalism that began with Deng Xiaoping's reforms in the 1980s, the China-to-come will not merely participate in global modernity but shape it, setting templates rather than following them. Its economy—robustly capitalist, though tightly regulated by the state—will not merely serve a supporting manufactory role to the West's creative lead. The liberal arts institutions that have sprung up recently testify to the perceived need among elites for a means of fostering the type of Chinese citizens that will effect this transformation. The mission of these institutions appears to be one of familiarizing students with more eclectic and multidisciplinary forms of knowledge, instilling in them a salutary cosmopolitanism, and enhancing the imaginative faculties that will drive productive innovation and the generation of intellectual property. In presenting themselves to the world in their online materials, the colleges largely use the rhetoric of developing China's human capital, with a secondary focus on crafting of citizens and "critical thinkers" that animates virtually every US liberal arts college's mission statement.

The minimal purchase in China (as elsewhere) of what we've called the Jeffersonian defense of the liberal arts, and the prevalence of the instrumental defense, conveys something important about the caution with which the CCP contemplates broadening the liberal arts college experiment. There is very likely a tension between the instrumentalist and Jeffersonian logics. Even as the civic values of liberal arts education are eclipsed by utilitarian objectives, the humanist values that a liberal arts education is likely to engender may ultimately clash with future (potential) opposition to the dispositions of market capitalism, and perhaps to other authoritative social structures and political regimes. Though the connection between a liberal arts education and American-style representative democracy may be exaggerated, it is apparent that liberal arts colleges in the United States have been, since their "heyday" in the mid-nineteenth century, sites of resistance to policies and laws perceived as unjust, and to social and economic inequalities. Moreover, a recent study of political orientation among higher education faculty in the United States found that professors at liberal arts colleges identify more strongly with antiauthoritarian and egalitarian politics than their colleagues at other types of institutions.[21] Another study has found "a modest global effect of attendance at a liberal arts college on the development of liberal political views" by students.[22]

The specter of the 1989 student protests at Tiananmen Square, and the repression that followed, still haunts the CCP, which watches the Chinese liberal arts experiment closely, wary that it could produce not only, in the words of Beijing's Yuanpei College website, "qualified graduates who impress schoolmates in graduate studies with their creativity and colleagues in corporations with their adaptability and leadership potential" but a formidable class of dissidents as well. The challenge faced by the CCP in the growth of liberal arts education in China is one of preventing the innovative and liberating ideas students are likely to develop from spilling over into the political arena; it seeks no revolutions there. From the CCP's perspective, no promises of growth and transformation of the Chinese economy are worth the risk of social and political upheaval. Hence the Yuanpei College website assures the visitor that, in addition to inculcating creativity, freedom, and critical thinking, the college "simultaneously . . . administrates the students' four-year in-college life and study, political theory education and party-league activities."[23]

Neither Jeffersonian nor instrumentalist, the Chinese argument for the more centripetal component of a liberal arts education may be more properly described as *communitarian*, retaining the collectivist emphases of Chinese education and society more generally. Liberal and capitalist dispositions have the potential to corrode China's social contract, one already compromised by several generations' rigidly disciplinary education and indoctrination in Maoism, a doctrine that, though still officially powerful, has lost much of its credibility and vitality in everyday life. Perhaps the liberal arts can address a tendency, described here by a vice president of Fudan University in Shanghai, of "highly specialized education to often ignore ethical, cultural and moral values. Along with a lack of humanity, some students are missing a sense of social responsibility."[24] Shoring up this sense is another component of preserving national harmony in a changing China, and of crafting a more flexible and socially conscious citizenry. Hence Zhuhai's United International College's "Whole Person Education" curriculum that includes modules in "emotional intelligence" and "experiential development" and summer opportunities for students to "serve in backward regions of Western China."[25]

As with the growing consumer and car cultures in contemporary China, the liberal arts educational experiment has been heralded in the US and Western media as evidence of a more general "liberalization" there. Such triumphalism is wrongheaded. As has been done elsewhere, China will borrow from the US liberal arts tradition not wholesale but selectively, developing a distinctive liberal arts ethos with, as Deng Xiaoping famously described his nation's system of socialism, "Chinese characteristics."

Notes

1. Quoted in Adam Weinstein, "Rick Scott to Liberal Arts Majors: Drop Dead," *Mother Jones*, October 11, 2011, http://www.motherjones.com/mojo/2011/10/rick-scott-liberal-arts-majors-drop-dead-anthropology.

2. Tyler Kingkade, "Pat McCrory Lashes Out against 'Educational Elite' and Liberal Arts College Courses," *Huffington Post*, February 2, 2013, http://www.huffingtonpost.com/2013/02/03/pat-mccrory-college_n_2600579.html.

3. Peter Cohan, "To Boost Post-College Prospects, Cut Humanities Departments," *Forbes*, May 29, 2012, http://www.forbes.com/sites/petercohan/2012/05/29/to-boost-post-college-prospects-cut-humanities-departments.

4. Richard A. Hofstadter, *The Development of Academic Freedom in the United States* (New York: Columbia University Press, 1955).

5. Quoted in Hugh Hawkins, "The University Builders Observe the Colleges," *History of Education Quarterly* 11.4 (Winter 1971): 355.

6. Quoted in Hawkins, "University Builders," 359–360.

7. Quoted in Katherine C. Reynolds, "Progressive Ideals and Experimental Higher Education: The Example of John Dewey and Black Mountain College," *Education and Culture* 14.1 (Spring 1997): 2.

8. Professional degrees have outnumbered liberal arts degrees by two to one at least since the 1970s (U.S. Department of Education, "Digest of Education Statistics" 2011, http://nces.ed.gov/programs/digest/d11/tables/dt11_286.asp?referrer=report) and possibly since the 1940s. See Steven G. Brint, Mark Riddle, Lori Turk-Bicakci, Charles S. Levy, "From the Liberal to the Practical Arts in American Colleges and Universities: Organizational Analysis and Curricular Change," *Journal of Higher Education* 76.2 (March/April 2005): 151–180.

9. Michael Delucci, "'Liberal Arts' Colleges and the Myth of Uniqueness," *Journal of Higher Education* 68.4 (July–August 1997): 414–426.

10. David W. Breneman, "Are We Losing Our Liberal Arts Colleges?" *AAHE Bulletin* 43.2 (October 1990): 3–5. Originally published in *The College Board Review* 156 (Summer 1990).

11. Vicki L. Baker, Roger G. Baldwin, and Sumedha Makker, "Where Are They Now? Revisiting Breneman's Study of Liberal Arts Colleges," *Liberal Education* 98.3 (Summer 2012): 1.

12. See http://www.aacu.org/leap/what-is-a-liberal-education.

13. See, for example, the former president of Smith College on this topic: Carol T. Christ, "Myth: A Liberal Arts Education Is Becoming Irrelevant," http://www.smith.edu/docs/president/Spring2012Christ.pdf (accessed July 16, 2013).

14. Michael M. Crow, "America Needs Broadly Educated Citizens, Even Anthropologists," *Slate*, October 21, 2011, http://www.slate.com/articles/news_and_politics/politics/2011/10/michael_m_crow_president_of_arizona_state_university_explains_wh.html (accessed July 25, 2013).

15. Association of American Colleges and Universities, "It Takes More than a Major: Employer Priorities for College Learning and Student Success," April 10, 2013, http://www.aacu.org/leap/documents/2013_EmployerSurvey.pdf (accessed July 20, 2013).

16. Quoted in Christ, "Myth: A Liberal Arts Education Is Becoming Irrelevant."

17. Quoted in Karen Fischer, "Bucking Cultural Norms, Asia Tries Liberal Arts," *Chronicle of Higher Education*, February 10, 2012.

18. Brint et al., "From the Liberal to the Practical Arts in American Colleges and Universities," 152.

19. See http://www.ashesi.edu.gh/about/mission-and-vision.html (accessed July 19, 2013).

20. See http://www.bnu.edu.pk/index.php?option=com_content&view=article&id=47&Itemid=56 (accessed July 19, 2013).

21. See http://www.insidehighered.com/news/2007/10/08/politics (accessed July 21, 2013).

22. Jana M. Hanson, Dustin D. Weeden, Ernest T. Pascarella, and Charles Blaich, "Do Liberal Arts Colleges Make Students More Liberal? Some Initial Evidence," *Higher Education* 64 (2012): 366.

23. See http://yuanpei.pku.edu.cn/cate_en.php?cid=33 (accessed July 22, 2013).

24. Lu Fang, vice president of Fudan University in Shanghai, quoted in Austin Ramzy, "A New School of Thought in China," *Time*, October 12, 2012, http://www.time.com/time/magazine/article/0,9171,2124984,00.html (accessed July 30, 2013).

25. See http://uic.edu.hk/en/wpe (accessed August 4, 2013).

Nationalism and the Liberal Arts College

·•————•·

W<small>ILL</small> B<small>ARNDT</small>

Will Barndt is Assistant Professor of Political Studies at Pitzer College in Claremont, California. Previously, he taught politics at Princeton University, Pomona College, the University of Redlands, the New Jersey Governors' School for Public Issues, and the University of California–Riverside, where he won the Professor of the Year Award in 2010. He is a graduate of Colby College.

๑

I recently had the very good fortune of joining the faculty of Pitzer College, a small residential liberal arts college in Claremont, California. Since I accepted the position, a dozen or so people at the college have told me that Pitzer is now (or is becoming) a "national liberal arts college." This set me wondering: What exactly is a national liberal arts college? What is in the assertion that a liberal arts college is "national"? What does it mean?

In pursuing these questions, this little essay runs through some larger considerations of nationalism, professionalism, subversiveness, and the aspirations of higher education. But it ends up at home, where I believe our residential liberal arts colleges continue to lead us. Thank goodness.

Nationalism

To call a liberal arts college "national" is to claim that is worthy of consideration by the nation. But why might this be so?

One interpretation is that national liberal arts colleges actually bring the nation together. For example, national liberal arts colleges do go out of their way to assert regional diversity: a student from (almost) every state! Still, nearly all end up with an "over" representation of students from the region where they are located. To take just a few examples: More than 40 percent of the Swarthmore student body is from the Mid-Atlantic; more than 40 percent of the Bowdoin student body is from New England; more than 40 percent of the Claremont McKenna and Pitzer student bodies are from California. Even at mighty Amherst and Williams the student body is about 20 percent New Englander.[1] The faculties of many of these institutions also seem to follow this pattern, with a plurality of professors at most schools having attended college in the same region.[2] Other forms of national diversity are also, as is well known, unevenly represented at almost all national liberal arts colleges.

This is not just going round the world to count cats in Zanzibar. If liberal arts colleges are, in fact, national, one might expect them to be nationally representative, in one sense or another. Yet while these colleges are certainly bringing in folk from across the country, they are not exactly national microcosms. Even if an aspiration of these colleges is to represent the nation—and it may or may not be—I think something else is in the claim.

A clue can be found in the popular *U.S. News & World Report* rankings. A little-commented-upon peculiarity of the rankings is that the magazine compiles separate lists of what it calls "national liberal arts colleges" and what it calls "regional colleges." National liberal arts colleges "emphasize undergraduate education and award at least half of their degrees in the liberal arts fields of study."[3] Regional colleges also focus on undergraduate education but grant fewer than half their degrees in the liberal arts.

Which is to say the following: to be a college focused on the liberal arts is, for *US News*, to be a *national* college.

This is so strange as to merit further examination. Why in the world would "national" and "liberal arts" *necessarily* go together? Why would focusing on the liberal arts in and of itself make a college national? If this were just a quirk of that silly magazine, we might leave it at that. But it is not: liberal arts colleges—not just my own[4]—are using this language to describe themselves. And while the language of nationalism of course conveys some naked status-seeking, it seems odd that the status being sought is "national" rather than (or in addition to) "selective" or "excellent" or even "really good." So, again, what is in the claim?

I want to suggest here that the claim of nationalism is most importantly about what "national" liberal arts colleges think they are imparting to their students. By preparing their students in the liberal arts, these colleges are carefully if informally training their students to belong to a *national* culture and a *national* labor market. Another way to say this is that national liberal arts colleges are educating their students in ways that, among many other things, seek to free them from the constraints of any particular place. To nationalize them.

Let me begin with a relatively benign example from my alma mater, Colby College, where a running line had it that we were all developing "the NESCAC accent." This was shorthand for the flattening of not only our regional dialects (I exchanged 'ra-dē-,ā-tər for 'rā-dē-,ā-tər) but also our regional cultures (I was made to understand that applesauce was not the invention of the Pennsylvania Dutch). I now know that the line was not Colby-specific: students at other national liberal arts colleges associated with the New England Small College Athletic Conference heard and said it as well. Together we gradually, and to greater or lesser degrees, adopted an accent devoid of the particular places we were from.

But this acculturation to placelessness was about more than lengthening vowels and obliterating local culinary myths. It is at the crux of a "national" liberal arts education: an education that readies students to do *anything anywhere*. Note that this is precisely what we promise our students: "You can do whatever you want with a liberal arts degree!" You can become lawyers in Colorado, or staffers on Capitol Hill, or community organizers in Houston, or editors in San Francisco, or doctors outside Atlanta, or non-profiteers in Philadelphia, or biotech researchers in Madison, or teachers in Vermont, or financial analysts in New York.

Notice also that there are two parts to this promise. First: students will be able to do *anything*, by which is generally (though not exclusively) meant anything that is or seems or counts as professional class. That is, liberal arts colleges endow their students with the capacity to join any of the liberal professions—or at least to act as if they were of those professions. Second, students will be able to do this *anywhere*: the training they receive to join these liberal professions will serve them equally well wherever the liberal professions thrive. Going to Colby consigned me neither to New England nor to any particular vocation.

This is a critical point, as it sheds light on the condition that underlies the existence of "national" liberal arts colleges. A promise to students that they can do whatever they want, wherever they want, assumes the existence of a world into which a degree from a national liberal arts college can serve as a passport. It assumes there is some nationwide culture out there that national liberal arts colleges can prepare their students to join. And there is: America's national professional culture, a culture in which we all say 'rā-dē-ˌā-tər and know that applesauce is an import from the Old World.

Of course, this orientation toward a national professional culture is not just something that students at national liberal arts colleges get through osmosis. We faculty are ourselves training students to write and to speak and to think in ways that allow them to inhabit this national culture. Indeed, it is one of the things we are paid to do: it is considered part and parcel of the social mobility used to justify our endeavors. As they have historically, these endeavors continue to center on cultivating in students the broad arts of reading, writing, debate, and Socratic conversation. Yet the nationalization of our liberal arts colleges has not left these arts unchanged.

As nationalization has rolled on, we faculty have also become more oriented toward our own national professions. The extent to which this orientation has increased over time is subject to some debate, but few would deny an increase in "professionalization" of liberal arts faculty in recent decades. For example, more liberal arts faculty today are more oriented toward national organizations—like the American Political Science Association, the American Historical Association, the American Geophysical Union, and the Modern Language Association—than in previous generations. We ourselves are increasingly nationalized.

As the orientation of faculty toward the nationalized version of our own professional discipline increases, so too does our inclination to teach our students to read and to write and to think (to act, really) in accordance with the standards of that national profession. An example: I recently had a conversation with a director of a writing program at one of the best national liberal arts colleges in the country. Writing is evidently a critical part of a liberal arts education. This director told me, insisted to me, that when evaluating writing we are always evaluating through the lens of our own discipline. That we are reading student writing as if it were written for political scientists, as if it were written for historians, as if it were written for chemists.

By this account, we faculty inhabit our own national professional sub-cultures—then teach our students to inhabit them. We endeavor to cultivate in our students the arts of reading, writing, debate, and other forms of Socratic conversation *within the boundaries of our own specific professions*. As liberal arts professors, however, we avow that this teaching is not intended to turn our students into political scientists, historians, or chemists. It is not vocational training. So why would we do this?

I want to return to this question later, but for now let me say that I think the most generous interpretation is that it provides further instruction in national professionalism. As our students take classes across the disciplines, they not only learn to read, write, and think as liberal arts students should—but also receive exposure to what it looks like to adapt one's broad training in national professional culture to a specific profession. The intention is not that students become professional political scientists, historians, or chemists themselves, but that they understand *what it means* to join a specific profession.[5] If one wanted to be painfully blunt, in this regard one might describe national liberal arts colleges as finishing schools for the American professional class.

And so what is a national liberal arts college? To this point, I have argued that it is a liberal arts college where students learn to become national professionals. As part of this process, nationally oriented professors increasingly train students in the liberal arts within the confines of their own professions' national standards. In the process students become (literally) acculturated to national professionalism: they are readied to do anything anywhere. Every liberal arts graduate a clerk.

Home

Yet if my argument ended there, my conclusion would have to be that national liberal arts colleges are, in fact, not unique. For our colleges are not alone in in their goal of having nationally oriented faculty prepare students in the national professional culture. The best national universities also do this, and do it quite well. If this were all these colleges did, then the best national liberal arts college would be nothing more than a miniaturized Stanford.

Fortunately, I do not believe this is the case. What is special about liberal arts colleges is not that they effectively instill a national professional culture in their students: it is that they *simultaneously subvert that culture*. This tension is inherent in the liberal arts college. And it is this tension, this self-subversiveness, that makes liberal arts colleges special, and perhaps deserving of our affection.

National liberal arts colleges do not just prepare their students to join a national professional culture anywhere—they do so on the little campuses that provide students, for the better part of four years, with a place to live. Residential liberal arts colleges, unlike large universities, are not small cities. They are tiny valleys. On such campuses, as any liberal arts student knows, most faces quickly become familiar; local reputations emerge; and local cultures are adopted, adapted, and passed on between generations.

In other words: the odd twist of national liberal arts colleges is that their students are nationalized while navigating extremely local cultures. Liberal arts students often complain that they live in a "bubble." The way they mean it, the phrase suggests an impossible isolation. But it unintentionally captures more than this: it captures how students experience the localness of life at a liberal arts college—and it captures the fragile beauty of that life.

Now there are particular cultures associated with *all* institutions of higher education. Yet there is an important difference between the culture of a university and the culture of a liberal arts college—or at least of a residential liberal arts college. It is a difference inherent in scale, and in the face-to-face character of our colleges. Imagine chance meetings of alumni who graduated from the same college the same year but had never before met: one pair from Berkeley, the other pair from Bates.[6] Berkeley and Bates both train their students to join the national professional culture, but at Bates those students also accumulate an intimate knowledge of the lives of their co-students. They came to know and understood the local world that they, and other past and future alumni, occupy and constitute. The shared knowledge—of common friends, acquaintances, and particular events—is exponentially greater for Bates alumni than for Berkeley alumni.

No doubt this knowledge also accounts for the ironic way that students at liberal arts colleges often throw around the word "community." Our students spend remarkable amounts of time talking about—and hearing about—living in a community. (Indeed, national liberal arts colleges incessantly market this aspect of their experiences.) But for liberal arts students, the rhetoric of community quickly runs up against the actual experience of living together in the same place. Over four years, students end up knowing what community really entails, warts and all. Romanticism encounters reality.

And here we come to the crux of my argument: there is something good about learning to navigate a national professional culture while actually living the local culture of a small residential liberal arts college. The experience reinforces in students the knowledge of what it means to live *in place* while propelling those students into national placelessness. This tension is at the heart of the experience of the national liberal arts college.

The placeless professional graduates of our national liberal arts colleges thus have the experience of knowing what it was like to become placelessly professional *in place*. This is haunting knowledge for many of them. They are haunted while they practice law in Colorado, or staff a congresswoman on Capitol Hill, or organize in Houston, or edit in San Francisco, or heal people outside Atlanta, or raise money in Philadelphia, or research biotechnology in Madison, or teach in Vermont, or analyze finance in New York. Yet this haunting is not just some ghostly nostalgia: it suggests to graduates that there is something missing and something amiss in the national placeless culture of American professionalism they have come to inhabit. It suggests to them what more they ought to demand of themselves—and of their nation.

This is what is subversive about a national liberal arts education and what differentiates it from an education at the best universities. National liberal arts colleges simultaneously uproot their students and school them in the art of home-seeking. Attending a liberal arts college may well push you to leave the place you grew up. It may well entail acculturating to a national professional mindset. But it does not entail a blind acceptance of the modern plight of homelessness—to the contrary, it teaches you to find this condition unsatisfying. National liberal arts colleges reinforce the aspiration to be at home, to live in place, while propelling you into a national culture. It is an unromantic aspiration, an aspiration grounded in the knowledge of what living in place has actually entailed.

Some three decades ago, Ernest Gellner wrote, "Time was when education was a cottage industry, when men [sic] could be made by a village or a clan. That time has now gone, and gone forever. In education, small can now be beautiful only if it is covertly parasitic on the big."[7] National liberal arts colleges demonstrate how the beauty of smallness can survive attachment to larger aspirations. Who is parasitic on whom seems a more open question.

The place of faculty in these national liberal arts colleges remains oddly ambiguous, to return to the question of what exactly it is we do in these places. Faculty are no longer—and this is both for better and for worse—part of the liberal arts college community in the way they once were, in the way that emeritus faculty describe their experiences in the liberal arts college of yore. Instead of this, as noted previously and I am sure not coincidentally, faculty at national liberal arts colleges are coming to accept and practice the standards of their professional disciplinary subcultures on campus.

Yet we would do well to consider carefully what it means for faculty to embrace national professionalism, especially in the classroom. Teaching our students to work within the confines of our own national disciplinary standards necessarily entails a narrowing of scope in what we teach. With such narrowing, the specificity of the classroom can come to resemble the specificity of modern academic research: a classroom in which the Socratic arts are increasingly confined to the narrowest of topics—and the adoption of discipline-specific forms of argument are privileged. At the extreme, this entails not the narrowing of a liberal arts education but its replacement: the classroom becomes a place of vocational training.

In an ironic and telling twist of fate, vocational training is precisely what most of the institutions that *U.S. News* calls "regional colleges" excel at: engineering, business, communication, nursing, pre-medicine, pre-law, pharmaceutical and medical technology, computer programming, ministry. To be a regional college, for *U.S. News*, is usually to be an excellent vocational school. The irony abounds.

How far we have come from the meaning of regionalism! Liberal arts colleges—before they were "national" liberal arts colleges—used to be agents of professionalism for the regions (the places) where they were located. Access to these colleges was more limited decades ago, so it might even be fair to say that they were the institutions through which the regional professional class trained its sons (and eventually daughters) to join its ranks. As regionalism has faded, and the national economy has been created, what liberal arts colleges do has changed. This is, in part, the point of this essay. Yet the larger point is that in a national economy and culture, this new role of national liberal arts colleges is critical.

Nationalism has enormous risks for liberal arts colleges. It forces them to navigate between the Scylla of vocationalism and the Charybdis of placelessness. One misguided tack and they easily become excellent centers of technical training or miniaturized universities, losing what is special to them in the process. What is the place of faculty who find their colleges in this precarious position? At our best, we say nevertheless, we harness the tension that is still at the heart of the national liberal arts college, and in the process we share with our students the possibility of simultaneously inhabiting and subverting their newfound national condition.

Wendell Berry and Wes Jackson have suggested that "our system of education until now has had only one major: Upward Mobility. Now, [they say], a second major needs to be added, and the name of this major will be Homecoming."[8] I have enormous respect for these two authors, and their argument is correct, as far as it goes. Yet it underestimates what is special and important at national liberal arts colleges. It is true that these colleges are exceptionally good at preparing their students in upward mobility, at preparing them to join our national professional culture. But they temper that preparation with a minor in homecoming, a minor that is still inherent within them. Thank goodness.

Notes

1. Author calculations based on college catalogs from a handful of prominent liberal arts colleges.

2. An admittedly imperfect way of thinking about this.

3. Compare http://colleges.usnews.rankingsandreviews.com/best-colleges/rankings/national-liberal-arts-colleges with http://colleges.usnews.rankingsandreviews.com/best-colleges/rankings/regional-colleges (accessed August 5, 2013).

4. A quick search of websites turned this up—it does vary by college.

5. Note that if we instead believe that we are actually training our students to think like political scientists, like chemists, or like historians, we have already moved beyond the liberal arts into vocationalism. On which see my comments in the second half of this essay.

6. More likely for the Berkeley alums than for the Bates—but this only serves to reinforce the point!

7. Ernest Gellner, *Nations and Nationalism* (Ithaca: Cornell University Press, 2009 [1981]), 38.

8. Wendell Berry, *What Matters? Economics for a New Commonwealth* (Berkeley: Counterpoint Press, 2010), 31–36.

The Liberal Arts and the Pursuit of Wisdom

Timothy Baker Shutt

Timothy Baker Shutt earned a BA in English at Yale (1972) and an MA and PhD in medieval literature from the University of Virginia (1978 and 1984). In between he taught English and history and coached swimming at St. Mark's School of Texas in Dallas. After a postdoctoral stint with the Mellon Foundation, he has been teaching at Kenyon College, where he serves as Professor of Humanities and Director of the Integrated Program of Humane Studies, for twenty-nine years. He has, long since, been awarded the College's Trustee Teaching Award, has three times been selected by the graduating class at Kenyon as baccalaureate speaker, and has on five separate occasions been awarded the Senior Cup, presented annually to that member of the Kenyon faculty or staff who "in the judgment of the graduating class has contributed most to the College and the Community." He has likewise published more than twenty recorded courses, most with accompanying short books, for Recorded Books and, for some, Barnes and Noble as well.

First of all, the liberal arts are old, with a pedigree stretching back into classical times, to Rome, if not, indeed, in some substantial sense, back to

Plato. And they rose to their first full exfoliation with the rise of universities during the Middle Ages—Paris, Oxford, Bologna, and the rest—with the crystallization of the traditional sevenfold path, the *trivium* and the *quadrivium*, the "threefold way" and the "fourfold way," grammar, rhetoric, and dialectic in the first case, arithmetic, geometry, music, and astronomy (which included, of course, a good deal of what we would term astrology) in the second. The specifics have changed in the meantime, as well they might over the course of eight-hundred-odd years and more. But the underlying set of skills has changed far less, however differently conceived and packaged: read with clear comprehension, write crisply and effectively, and speak crisply and effectively—*especially* speak crisply and effectively, for then, without question, and, I suspect, more than we are entirely happy acknowledging even still, persuasive speaking was the high road to wealth, influence, and power, to the extent that these were to be gained in any other way than by inheritance. And, beyond that, think, and, if necessary, argue clearly and effectively, and, to the extent possible, as a secondary but still highly important skill, become master of mathematics. Then and now. To that degree, the same story.

But why, one must ask. What made these skills and studies important? And here too, things haven't changed all that much. Again, and from the very outset—and, indeed, to greater or lesser degree ever since—the liberal arts have been by design a mode of education for an elite, even, at times, for *the* elite. Think of the "playing fields of Eton." The very phrase reveals as much, dating back, regrettably enough in that regard, to the slave-owning world of classical times and through the Middle Ages, when most physical work was the purview of serfs and artisans or, at best, yeoman or hired labor. The liberal arts, by contrast, were the arts of someone who was *liber*, or "free"—free not only in the sense of being free from slavery or servitude, but likewise free in the by no means unrelated sense of being free from the necessity of manual labor.

There is, of course, to our own ears and ethos something profoundly distasteful about these antecedents. We are in theory and by inclination—and to some nontrivial degree in fact—an egalitarian society, certainly in comparison to the societies of antiquity and the Middle Ages and, indeed, to the societies, or many of them, of more recent times and places. And on that account, even the notion of *having* an elite, let alone that of *training* people effectively to form a part of an elite, rather sticks in our craw. All positions are open to everybody, and all people are created equal is very much more our habitual line.

And yet, despite our conviction, there is, at least to my jaundiced eye, something at least a bit meretricious about all this. We don't quite play the game we talk. Not so much that our protestations are insincere, perhaps, as that they are more or less tacitly qualified. For, in fact, we do have an elite—all societies have an elite—and most of us, all things considered, would like to be part of it, may well, indeed, *be* part of it, and would like our children to be part of it as well. And, in truth, or so I would argue, we are not so much bothered as we might be by this state of affairs. What matters with regard to the society as a whole is not so much that an elite exists as what the elite is like. Warlords, priests, bureaucrats, convinced party leaders, merchant princes, machine politicians, charismatic strongmen, entrepreneurs, the cunning masters of drug cartels, and philosopher kings tend to make rather different sorts of leaders, and the societies they lead tend to differ accordingly. The trick, then, is to train or to generate the *best* elite, the most beneficent and effective leaders possible.

And that is where the liberal arts come in. For from the very outset, they have been a regimen designed to produce a beneficent elite, to produce not only leaders but good ones. And in that pursuit they have proved, if not entirely successful, at least as successful as any other means of fulfilling such goals.

I don't want to overstate the case. Clearly, there are many roads to leadership, to wisdom, to benignity, even to success. And clearly, the effectiveness of any mode of training depends in very large measure upon the receptivity and aptitudes of those whom the training seeks to benefit. You can't teach a cat calculus (although, as one of my students once pointed out to me, cats do surprisingly well computing parabolas as a practical matter, especially when confronted by, say, flying paper wads, weak though they may be in theory). All that conceded, though, over the course of the centuries, even millennia, the liberal arts have proved their value. They really do, as often as not, succeed in fulfilling their goals, at least to some valuable extent.

But—and here lies the rub—at the heart of that success lies a paradox. The liberal arts succeed in training leaders—and magnanimous, clear-thinking, balanced, and effective people, to the extent that they do so—not, or not so much, by seeking to do so directly, but rather by seeking something different, by seeking to pursue knowledge and wisdom, and virtue, not, or not so much (and this is something easily fudged), for their usefulness in attaining success and getting to the top, but for their own sake, as overriding, indeed, transcendent, values in their own right. And the effectiveness of the training, in both practical and transcendental terms, depends very largely upon the spirit in which that training is undertaken. In the end, faking it doesn't fly, however capable the faker. History and the world around us alike are littered with examples. The liberal arts only work—at anything close to their full beneficent power—with and for those who are genuinely committed to knowledge, wisdom, and virtue. The liberal arts are designed to train leaders. They are designed to train an elite. But they have their

full effect only upon those who embrace their goals. They do indeed teach
how to lead—how to read, how to think, how to understand, how to speak
and to convince, and how to write. How to learn and how to learn how
to learn. But more importantly and more deeply, they teach—or, or more
properly, prepare a *groundwork* from which one may perceive, encounter,
and indeed embrace—what one should *lead to*—knowledge, wisdom, and
virtue, of course, a firm and clear-sighted magnanimity of spirit, benignity
and justice, and courage in service of kindness and benevolence.

Once again, though, these glorious goals—and I do believe they are
glorious goals—must be pursued for their own sake, not as valuable attain-
ments in pursuit of other ends but as ends in their own right. And then,
to a very large degree, if perhaps only then, the other benefits fall in their
train. To put the matter in theological terms, "Seek ye first the kingdom of
God," and everything "shall be added unto you" (Matt. 6.33).

But why does this detachment, this disinterestedness matter? What
difference does it make? The short answer is that it discourages self-interest,
self-aggrandizement, or self simply as a primary goal. And that, in turn,
makes it much easier to learn by encouraging focus on the topic at hand
rather than on what it can do *for me*. Needless to say, such an attitude is
highly desirable in a leader.

Let me propose what may well be an unfair and inaccurate example—
and if so, I apologize—from personal experience. I spent my undergraduate
years at Yale, from 1968 to 1972, the height of the celebrated "sixties,"
which by and large I very much disliked. I by no means covered myself with
distinction, and Yale never has and never will count me among its most
distinguished alums. Among other problems, I had the wrong mindset. But
if Yale was disappointed in me, having squandered a precious admissions slot
upon me, I was disappointed too by Yale, and it took me years to understand
why. Only decades later, after close encounters with a good many more
graduates of Yale and comparably elite institutions, some my own immediate
professional superiors, did I figure out, to my own satisfaction at least, what
the problem was. And it was this: whatever the goals of the administration,
the faculty, and Yale's graduate students, about which I am in no position to
testify, the goals of the large majority of my fellow undergraduates were, so
far as I could tell, both then and now, quite emphatically *not* those of the
liberal arts—knowledge, wisdom, and virtue. Their goal was much simpler
and more straightforward. In a word, it was success. As a bond trader, a Wall
Street lawyer, a radiologist, a neurosurgeon, a chief executive, or whatever.
Or a politician. Many politicians. For all of which routes to wealth and
power a Yale diploma offered a gold-plated, "open sesame" entrée. And it
was that certification that counted.

Which, I gather, was why Yale, at least of my day and much to my surprise, was rife with cheating—and, as it happened, shoplifting and other modes of more or less petty dishonesty—to a degree vastly exceeding what I have seen at any other educational institution I have known. If you get away with it, what's the problem? One step closer to the goal.

And indeed, Yale of my day seemed to me often profoundly illiberal for another quite different and seemingly antithetical reason. I was there, to my regret, as the sixties crystallized, very self-consciously indeed and with immense self-congratulation, not as a "tune in, turn on, drop out" event, which bore at least a putative, and at times an actual, affinity with disciplines designed to encourage growth and enlightenment, but instead as a movement devoted to confrontation, to "activism," and, in many instances, to more or less explicitly Marxian revolution. In that guise, the sixties, to put the matter gently, showed little interest in inquiry and discussion and a great deal in ideological commitment and ideological purity. "Up against the wall," as the saying went. This too, and quite deliberately and explicitly, discouraged the pursuit of knowledge and wisdom. When you "take it to the streets," the discussion is over, and, indeed, "taking it to the streets" is designed, among other things, quite precisely to end discussion.

So part of the paradoxical virtue of the liberal arts is their detachment, their focus on knowledge and truth without immediate regard for personal—or even social—advancement. Which is why the self-interested scorn them, and why ideologues hate them and seek to replace them with indoctrination—both tendencies still much in evidence in the academic world of today.

But both groups—the ideologues, the self-seekers (and, heaven help us, the self-seeking ideologues)—are finally wrong. For the paradox is indeed a paradox, and despite their detachment and seeming indirection, the liberal arts are the best and most effective training for a leader—and even for an elite—in substantial part *because* they discourage self-interest and ideological ferocity and rigidity.

We don't want our leaders to be self-interested and focused on the main chance, and we do want them to be clear-sighted and clear-souled, and committed to careful thinking and the careful assessment of evidence. And we want them, to the degree that such a thing is possible, to be creatures of calmness, kindness, and goodwill. That is what is best for society. And that, as Socrates and Plato—or, more properly, as Socrates *according to* Plato—argued so long ago, is what is best for the individual as well, leader and member of an elite or otherwise. What's good for you is good for society, and what's good for society is what's good for you. *The Republic*'s "blissful Thrasymachus" (and many a postmodernist neo-Nietzschean) to the contrary, justice is *not* "the advantage of the stronger," and the happiest and most blessed among us are not the most rapacious, self-absorbed, and "unjust."

But let us step back for a moment and consider a bit more precisely how it is that the liberal arts assist in accomplishing these fine goals for leaders and lesser lights alike—if, indeed, and to the extent that they do.

It is not, certainly not primarily, in developing mastery of basic skills—literacy, numeracy, more or less competent speaking skills, and more or less competent writing skills—that the liberal arts work their distinctive magic. Such skills are, of course, in a sense prerequisite and indispensable for higher and even most forms of secondary education alike, but they are not skills over which the liberal arts can claim anything like exclusive ownership. Nor is it—or is it primarily—in learning how to perform a specific task or function, how to excel at a specific job, if you will, as a dental hygienist, a physical therapist, a paralegal, or a marketing specialist. Worthy tasks, each one—and many, many another—and deservedly popular fields of collegiate study, each one. But not, as generally conceived, fields forming part of a liberal arts curriculum.

A caveat here. Pretty much all of us have to do *something*. We cannot all and should not all devote ourselves to study and contemplation as a career and way of life. Society would stop in its tracks, and practical, directly career-focused studies have far more than "their place." They are indispensable. I repeat. Indispensable. They do—and *should*—dominate education, from elementary schools to law, business, and medical schools (medical research facilities perhaps aside), and engineering schools as well.

But the liberal arts still have their place, and it is a very important place. For in their indirection and detachment, in their insistence that students immerse themselves in a wide variety of subjects and modes of knowing, they encourage flexibility and facility in general. By encouraging students to think within the norms and conventions of a variety of disciplines, they encourage thinking *beyond* and *across* those boundaries—and about the inevitability or arbitrariness of those boundaries, as the case may be. They encourage—to make use for a moment of a bit of academic jargon—a sort of "meta-thinking," thinking not just about subjects, but about how we come to apprehend subjects. Thinking, in short, about the process of thinking. Which is where philosophy begins, both in a historical sense and in practice. This too is a mode of detachment, and a highly significant mode of detachment, from our usual modes of thought. It is, in a potentially most fruitful sense, highly destabilizing. It can open the door to obsession, hobby-horse-hood, and folly. But it can also open the door to insight and original thought, and, in the long run, to a communal advance in knowledge.

To make use of an athletic metaphor, the liberal arts are "cross-training" exercises, with corresponding benefits in strength and flexibility. Or, to make use of a pair of Darwinian metaphors—which may be not so much metaphors as simply statements of fact—the liberal arts represent a sort of cross-breeding and a source of the "random variation" that gives evolution its purchase. Total stability is death.

In this sense, the liberal arts seek not so much to teach this or that specific subject, but how to master *any* subject, how to "learn how to learn." This is, I take it, a substantial part of what folks mean in claiming, as champions of the liberal arts so often do, that the liberal arts encourage "critical thinking" or "critical reasoning skills." In any case, so far as I can see, such training represents the best available preparation for what Darwinians term the "uncertain futures problem." One reason why, to the enduring consternation of generations of no doubt well-meaning humanitarians, capitalist economies have so often outperformed "planned" economies is the annoying fact that, whatever your level of expertise, you can only plan for what you can foresee. And, in the absence of prophecy, our foresight is imperfect. Even if we're certified experts. If you've got lots of plans out there, though—and would-be capitalists always do, given the chance to devise and implement them—then the likelihood is that one might be right, or, failing that, but almost certainly, some are likely to be better than the others. One plan, one chance. Lots of plans, lots of chances. And the detachment and instability, the openness and flexibility, if you will, generated by the liberal arts generate in their turn lots of plans, in comparison to the more or less fixed templates encouraged by more rigidly career-focused instruction.

And that, in its turn, is why liberal arts graduates have disproportionately made good and effective leaders. They are *used to* dealing with new, unfamiliar situations and new, unfamiliar data—which the world generously provides in unceasing abundance—and they are good, by training, as the saying goes, at "thinking outside of the box." At their best, at least, they were never fully "in the box" in the first place.

But there is more, and I have saved what seems to me most important—and on the basis of centuries, even millennia, of testimony, as well as personal experience, almost unsayable—for the last. And yet, it is the heart of the program, that which gives light and life to the whole. And, unsayable as it is, it is what I have spent my life in the classroom, forty years now, trying above all to see and to say. For the liberal arts are, above all, a pursuit, indeed, a love, of wisdom.

But what does that mean? "Wisdom" is an odd term. We have pitched its value so high that the term, in practice, has become, in one guise at least, all but useless. People do not call themselves "wise," or, if they do, without self-directed irony, they run a very grave risk of being heard to say that they are sanctimonious, self-satisfied fools. And, at a lower pitch, by "wisdom" we generally mean something like canny, practical know-how.

The liberal arts, though, are in the last analysis a pursuit of wisdom in neither sense. And here is where things get more or less unsayable indeed, which is why wisdom teachers, like Socrates, Kierkegaard, Hasidic tsaddikim, and Zen masters, so often resort to irony, refusing to say what cannot be said in hopes that the novice, student, seeker, reader, disciple, interlocutor, or whatever, thus nudged, will accordingly *see*. It is, too, why poets, like Dante in the *Paradiso*, make such use of the so-called "inexpressibility trope," telling us how and, to some degree, why they cannot say what most needs saying in hopes of *evoking* it, of letting it, so to speak, take hold of you and sweep you away.

I am myself a Catholic and, in my own small and decidedly amateur way, a Dante specialist, so I have fewer qualms than most about saying what "it" is. But "God" is not the only name people use, and they make their approach in a variety of ways.

For Plato, it is the Form (or "shape") of the Good, which, "when seen," must "be reckoned the cause of everything upright and beautiful in all, begetting in the visible world light and the Lord of Light, itself the Lord giver of truth and intelligence, and in the intelligible world, that which a man must see to act rationally for himself or his community" (*Rep.* 517C). In the *Bhagavad Gita*, we are told that the "one who knows me . . . / . . . is freed from all forms of harm," and gains insight, "wisdom, / freedom from confusion, / patience, truth, and self-control" (10: 3, 4).

In all such cases, though, or in all such cases known to me, the presupposition is that whatever it is that we thus "see"—to the extent that we "see" it, and doubtless none of us "sees" it fully—that whatever it is that we thus "see" is the source of being and goodness alike, and to "see" it is to love it and so to be transformed and guided by it, to the depth that our apprehension—or blessedness—reaches.

A humbler name for all this is "truth," and I have heard it claimed that to believe in truth in pretty much any strong sense is *de facto*, if not necessarily *de voluntate*, to believe in god, or God, however impeccable otherwise one's atheist or secularist credentials—and that in that sense, if (as may well be) in no other, the vast majority of scientists are theists, who believe that we find ourselves implicated in a state of affairs that we did *not* make in accordance with our wills, that has its own determinate structure, and about which propositions can be formed, some of them true, the best of them testable, and others not. Others, indeed, demonstrably falsifiable.

And that belief, even from my own unabashedly theist and, doubtless, profoundly flawed, perspective is enough. As the theological formulation goes, "And ye shall know the truth, and the truth shall make you free (John 8:32). That is, in the end, what the liberal arts are about. But the truth in question need not be only theological. I don't myself quite believe, in fact, that it can't be theological *at all*, but likely enough I am wrong about that, and for our present purpose it hardly matters. For if you pursue that end, if you pursue truth—so the tradition argues—then you'll know what to do and how to it, you'll benefit your fellows in the process, and you'll live, so much ancient testimony and much more recent experience suggests, the best possible human life. May it be so.

About the Editors

SUSAN McWILLIAMS is Associate Professor of Politics at Pomona College, where she has twice received the Wig Distinguished Teaching Award. McWilliams received her BA in Russian and political science from Amherst College and her MA and PhD in politics from Princeton University. While at Princeton, she won the University Teaching Award from the Association of Princeton Graduate Alumni. She has also taught at Haverford College and was a longtime faculty member at the New Jersey Governor's School for Public Issues. McWilliams is the author of *Traveling Back: Toward a Global Political Theory* (2014) and the co-editor of three other books. Her writing has appeared in *American Review of Politics, Boston Review, Bust, The City, Commonweal, Front Porch Republic, Perspectives on Political Science, Political Science Quarterly, PS: Political Science and Politics, The Review of Politics, Southern California Quarterly*, and elsewhere. In 2014 McWilliams won both the Graves Award in the Humanities and a National Endowment for the Humanities Fellowship. She lives in Claremont, California, with her husband and two children.

JOHN E. SEERY is the George Irving Thompson Memorial Professor of Government and Professor of Politics at Pomona College, where he teaches political theory. He was graduated *summa cum laude* from Amherst College and was named a Danforth Fellow. He received his MA and PhD degrees in political science from the University of California at Berkeley and went on to teach at Stanford University, University of California at Santa Cruz, and Tufts University before landing at Pomona College. Twice he has received

Pomona College's Wig Distinguished Teaching Award. In 2009 he was the recipient of the Phi Beta Kappa Society's Sidney Hook Memorial Award. In 2010–2011 he served as the Laurance S. Rockefeller Visiting Professor for Distinguished Teaching at Princeton University. In 2013 he received the American Political Science Association's discipline-wide Distinguished Teaching Award. He is author of several books: *Political Returns: Irony in Politics and Theory from Plato to the Antinuclear Movement* (1990); *Political Theory for Mortals: Shades of Justice, Images of Death* (1996); *America Goes to College: Political Theory for the Liberal Arts* (2002); *Too Young to Run? A Proposal for an AGE Amendment to the U.S. Constitution* (2011); with Daniel W. Conway, is co-editor of *The Politics of Irony: Essays in Self-Betrayal* (1992); and is the editor of *The Political Companion to Walt Whitman* (2011) and *George Kateb: Dignity, Morality, Individuality* (2014). He teaches courses in the history of political thought as well as thematic courses, such as Political Freedom, The Idea of America, The Politics of Comedy, Hannah Arendt, and The Idea of Money. He lives in Claremont, California, with his wife and two children.

Index